BS
605.2
.K48
1992
v.1

KERYGMA
the BIBLE in DEPTH

Resource Book

REVISED EDITION

the **KERYGMA**
program

FOUNDATIONAL COURSE

KERYGMA
the BIBLE in DEPTH

Revised Edition

RESOURCE BOOK
by James A. Walther

BS
605.2
.K48
1992
v.1

© 1992, 1984 by James A. Walther. All rights reserved. No portion of this publication may be reproduced, stored in an electronic system, or transmitted in any form or by any means, electronic, photocopy, recording or otherwise, without the prior written permission of the copyright owner. Brief quotations may be used in literary reviews.

Kerygma Program Study Resources are published and distributed by The Kerygma Program, 300 Mt. Lebanon Boulevard, Pittsburgh, PA 15234. Phone 800/537-9462. Fax 412/344-1823.

Chronology of the Bible and the maps are from Today's English Version Bible text. Copyright © American Bible Society 1966, 1971, 1976. Used by permission.

The Scripture quotations contained herein are from the New Revised Standard Version of the Bible, copyrighted, 1989 by the Division of Christian Education of the National Council of the Churches of Christ in the United States of America, and are used by permission. All rights reserved. ISBN 1-882236-09-2

300 Mt. Lebanon Blvd. Pittsburgh, Pennsylvania 15234

This edition of

Kerygma: The Bible in Depth

is dedicated to the memory of

Barbara J. Minges

a faithful disciple of her LORD,

a careful student of Scripture,

a dedicated Christian educator,

and a gifted, gracious colleague.

CONTENTS

Foreword ....Page v

Preface ....Page vi

Introduction   The Bible as a Whole ....Page 1
    Part One   What Is the Bible?
    Part Two   How Did We Get the Bible?
    Part Three   How Shall We Study the Bible?

Theme One   God Saves a People ....Page 25
    Part One   The Exodus: Pattern of God's Saving Acts
    Part Two   Deliverance after the Exodus
    Part Three   God's Saving Act in Jesus Christ
    Part Four   Deliverance of the Church

Theme Two   People Find God Is Faithful ....Page 53
    Part One   Promise and Covenant in the Hebrew Scriptures
    Part Two   Promise and Covenant in the New Testament

Theme Three   People Reflect about God ....Page 67
    Part One   Thinking about Who God Is
    Part Two   Asking How God Can Be Both Just and Loving
    Part Three   Knowing the Unknowable God

Theme Four   People Live in God's World ....Page 87
    Part One   Views of the World in the Hebrew Scriptures
    Part Two   Good News in All the World

Theme Five   God's People Have Leaders .... Page 103
    Part One   Early Leaders in the Rise of the Nation
    Part Two   Prophets and Later Leaders
    Part Three   The Baptist, Jesus, and Apostles

Theme Six		**God's People Have Rulers but One Sovereign**	............Page 127
Part One		Yahweh, Kings, and a United Kingdom	
Part Two		Rulers and the Divided Kingdom	
Part Three		Jesus and the Kingdom of God	

Theme Seven — **God Demands a Righteous People** ....Page 145
- Part One — The Law of God
- Part Two — Prophets' Call for Righteousness
- Part Three — Jesus and the Law
- Part Four — Righteousness in the Church

Theme Eight — **God's People Learn Wisdom** ....Page 175
- Part One — Wisdom in the Jewish Scriptures
- Part Two — Wisdom in the New Testament

Theme Nine — **God's People Worship** ....Page 191
- Part One — Early Backgrounds and National Rites
- Part Two — Devotional Life, Public and Personal
- Part Three — Worship in the New Testament Setting

Theme Ten — **God's People Have Hope** ....Page 213
- Part One — Israel's Hope
- Part Two — Apocalyptic Hope
- Part Three — New Hope in Christ
- Part Four — The Book of Revelation

Conclusion — **Last Things** ....Page 243

Appendix ....Page 249

Books of the Bible

Chronology of the Bible

Maps

The Twelve Disciples

Foreword

Many persons have contributed to the success of earlier editions of *Kerygma: The Bible in Depth*, and these must be acknowledged in this present revised edition. So that all may be thanked without risking priorities, the following are listed in alphabetical order (without academic and ecclesiastical preferments): Frank C. Bates; Gordon J. Freer; Donald L. Griggs; John E. Mehl; David Merritt; Dale K. Milligan; Barbara J. Minges; William Squier; James A. Walther, Jr.

The present revision is in partial response to many persons who have communicated concerns about inclusive language and other questions arising from the 1983 edition. Special appreciation for invaluable work in the process of revision is due the General Editor, D. Campbell Wyckoff, John Mehl, Theological Consultant, and Donald Griggs, Educational Consultant. The office staff of The Kerygma Program has also performed indispensable services.

Finally, thanks to the many Kerygma leaders and study groups who have shared their ideas, achievements, and enthusiasms. Especially important was the original group, whose boundless interest pressed the horizons of the program from its beginnings.

An appropriate word of Paul has long been a favorite of mine: *What do you have that you did not receive?* (1 Corinthians 4:7b), which I like to paraphrase, "None of us is as smart as all of us."

March, 1992   James Arthur Walther, Sr.

Preface

You are undertaking an in-depth program of Bible study that offers big challenges and unique rewards. You are joining thousands of persons who have devoted the requisite effort and have received the substantial benefits.

History

Kerygma: The Bible in Depth began in a congregational setting. The Rev. Dale K. Milligan asked James Arthur Walther, a professor at Pittsburgh Theological Seminary, to develop a comprehensive Bible study program for adults. Pilot classes were formed, and the initial course ran for forty-five weeks in 1970-71.

The first publication and church-wide use was made by the United Church of Canada beginning in 1977. For this edition a Leader's Guide was added. Dr. Gordon Freer and a dedicated group of associates were responsible for its success. It was this edition that was used in the United States from 1977 to 1983. The course was adopted by the Joint Board of Christian Education of Australia and New Zealand, which produced an edition of this book in 1979.

In 1983 a revised edition was produced in the United States. It has become apparent in the intervening years that a further revision is desirable. Those who have used the 1983 edition will quickly note some changes. The statement of half of the themes has been reworded to reflect inclusive language. Theme 9 has been moved to become Theme 4, and a concluding session, LAST THINGS, has been added. The text material in every theme has been carefully revised. The overall form and content, however, remain substantially as originally conceived.

We are pleased with this latest revision. The layout and design should enhance its appeal to participants. The text improves on previous editions, provides greater clarity and is easier to use. However, the primary text has always been the Bible. The success of this study is found in the manner in which it guides participants through the scriptures.

The Kerygma Program does not have a denominational bias. It has been used by over twenty denominations, and a Catholic adaptation has been published under the title *Harper's New American Bible Study Program*.[1]

---

1 San Francisco: Harper & Row, 1990.

The Biblical Foundation of *Kerygma: The Bible in Depth*

There are at least three particular ways in which this program focuses on the biblical material. One has to do with the method by which we organize our study. A second involves the learning goals we set. A third is how we find lasting significance in what we have studied and learned.

1. *Kerygma: The Bible in Depth* uses a *thematic* approach to the Bible. This is one of its distinctive features. Its special value is that it presents a "Bible whole" grasp of material that is too often studied piecemeal. Practically all Christian churches affirm that the Bible is one sacred book. Thus it is appropriate to approach it whole in order to learn a framework by which one can organize and keep together further intensive study of its parts. The themes in this program are directed toward this end.

The themes come from the biblical material rather than from creeds, literary analyses, or historical frameworks. Each theme title states something about God and people, for interaction between God and people is everywhere in the literature that makes up the Bible. One could begin a study by reading the whole Bible and then derive a way of systematizing its contents for further study and use. Experienced Bible scholars have developed the ten themes used here to organize and simplify your study from the start. Hundreds of persons who have studied the Kerygma way have testified that this method produces an effective grasp of the Bible whole.

The value of this program will become increasingly apparent if you are patient. A building rises piece by piece, and the foundation gives only a rough indication of the nature of the finished structure. So do not push the program to teach you everything in the first few sessions. Gradually, as you work through the Bible in the different themes, you will broaden and deepen your grasp of the material part by part and as a whole. To change the figure, think of the themes as more or less parallel tracks. One day you will realize that the Bible has become new and exciting for you. You will have a fresh understanding of what "inspiration" means, for it will not be a teaching you have been expected to accept but an experience that has come alive through your Bible study.

2. While we are ranging through the Bible again and again, we shall not neglect learning particular portions and outlines of parts. The thematic approach helps this happen but not always in the way you may expect. We shall emphasize some parts of the Bible more than others. There is precedent for this in the Bible itself. For example, New Testament authors use five books of the Old Testament far more than all the other books. Again you will need patience. Only when you can move easily among the biblical books will the practicality of such emphases become evident to you.

This suggests hard study. Although some persons may receive benefit from this Kerygma Program with minimal effort, the full value comes to those who are willing to study hard. Before we are through, we shall have an organized picture of the contents of much of the Bible. You will be challenged to learn, even to memorize some passages by rote. "Biblical literacy" (a term we sometimes hear) is scarcely possible without mastery of a fairly extensive collection of details. This Resource Book sets large tasks before you.

3. Unless *Kerygma: The Bible in Depth* is to be little more than an intellectual exercise, there must be a further focus. Inevitably we must ask what significance this study has for believing and living today. This is territory beyond the biblical material itself, of course, and the answers to such questions will be influenced by varying confessional backgrounds. The name chosen for the program implies that the study-task is not finished until contemporary meaning is addressed. *Kerygma* is a word from the Greek New Testament. A *keryx* is a herald, one who proclaims news; *kerygma* refers to the message that is proclaimed. Our program of study points to the message(s) proclaimed in the Bible, and proclamation that has not been received and responded to becomes practically useless.

Our aim, therefore, is not just to master a quantity of biblical details. Although intriguing data abound in the Bible, the book was never intended to be used as an almanac or encyclopedia. It is a book with purpose. Biblical interpreters always have the difficult task of trying to identify the purpose. The Gospel of John states a clear purpose of that book: ... *these [signs] are written so that you may come to believe that Jesus is the Messiah, the Son of God, and that through believing you may have life in his name* (20:31). We shall try to determine what such purpose, for example, meant for the writer, for the original hearers, and finally for us.

Biblical interpreters and theologians often distinguish between what a text meant and what it means. Our first task is to become so familiar with the biblical texts that we can learn what they meant in their original settings. Unless we do that, what we think the text means today may be only a projection of our own ideas. To take the Bible seriously requires that it be studied with the best available resources and the most diligent application. Thus we can deal responsibly with this third focus only if we have made the first two foci sharp and clear.

Some Suggestions about the Resource Book Material

At the beginning of each part of each theme there is a **Summary** of what is in that part. Then follows a list of the **Basic Bible References** that will be treated. This list is the minimum that you should read in preparing the part. The references occur again at the appropriate places in the text. There is also a list of **Words** with which you should become familiar. You may be startled and then overwhelmed by the total amount of Scriptural material presented.[2] Bible references pile up quickly. For some this is not an insuperable problem; for others the practical limitations of time available make it next to impossible to study all the references as they are given. In any case, the text of the Resource Book itself should be read through early in the time one allots to the study, for this helps to tie together the Scripture passages.

As a partial aid for those who must trim their study to fit a time limitation, there are further, built-in aids to help in setting a schedule. Here is an approximate evaluation of terms, symbols, and signs used with the Scripture references:

* **Boldface Type**. These references are basic and are printed in **boldface** so you cannot miss them. Ordinarily they are also the ones listed at the beginning of each part.

* "Read." These references are also very important. Of course, if you find the passage is already familiar, you may go through it very quickly.

* "See." These references are evidence for or explanation of statements in the Resource Book text. Probably you can follow the ideas presented without reading these passages, but they are backup support for the subject. You may skip these references if you trust the author!

* Footnotes. These add explanatory material that could break the thread of thought if included in the text. Their content is therefore optional for study. (The footnote on this page is an example.)

* *Italics*. Quotations of exact words from the biblical text are printed in *italics*. Unless otherwise noted, these quotations are from the New Revised Standard Version.

Some references are given as integral parts of the Resource Book text. No simple guideline can be offered regarding the relative importance of these passages. With experience in studying the material will come skill in sorting the levels of value. For example, in Theme 5, Part 4, complete references for Paul's mission travels are given, but the Resource Book focuses on selected incidents.

---

[2] Readers familiar with the 1983 edition may note that an effort has been made to reduce the number and extent of references in this edition. Since some students enjoy the challenge of the more extensive readings, however, the reduction has been modest and care has been taken to preserve full coverage of each biblical subject presented.

You should not be satisfied with studying only the minimum of material. The more of the Bible passages you read, the better you will grasp the Bible as a whole. Then you will somehow find time to read more of the references. In any case, you can go back later and check passages you did not read.

Do not infer from this analysis of references that some dogmatic down-grading of parts of Scripture is at work. It should be obvious that we cannot read all the words of every biblical book. We believe that all of the Bible is inspired, but inspiration does not mean that every verse is equally inspiring. We confidently trust that the Bible validates its own inspiration, not by proof texts, but precisely as it shows that it is God's book for God's people.

Throughout the text of the Resource Book you will come upon questions about what you are reading. In the first sessions there may be a space for you to compose a brief answer. This will then become a part of your personal resources. Often you may want to write a longer response in a separate notebook.

At the end of each part there are items **For Further Study and Reflection**. First come texts to be memorized or fixed as to location, content, or context. They are the **Memory Bank**. Biblical literacy involves absorbing as much of this material as possible. Then there are "second-mile" subjects, labeled **Research**. These will enrich one's understanding of the theme but are not essential to it. Last there is **Reflection**, which offers leads to help one find contemporary meaning and application.

Four reservations should be observed about how you utilize the study material in group time. [1] Prime time should be reserved for consideration of the principal theme material. [2] The leader's judgment should usually have priority in distributing group time. [3] The individual rights of each group member must be respected (see 1 Corinthians 14:29-33). [4] It is not fair to take group time to make up for study time one has not managed to find.

Anticipating the Introduction

Before we start our study of the contents of the Bible, we shall consider **the Book** as **a book** made up of many **books**. This is an important and serious introduction. Treat it as you would an introduction to a person you very much want to know better. This involves not only absorbing as much as you can about your new acquaintance but also being as conscientiously open and friendly as you can manage!

Since there is much to master in *Kerygma: The Bible in Depth*, make an auspicious start by preparing the first part well. Some group time will be spent, of course, in organization and arrangements. It is vitally important, however, that you grasp at the outset the details that are offered as basic tools for further progress. Consider carefully your personal response to questions that are raised in the material. Analyze what you think and know at the outset so you can gauge your growth in understanding as you progress through *Kerygma: The Bible in Depth*.

You are challenged to expand your **Memory Bank** if you do not already know the suggested material. Make a bright beginning by accepting the challenge. Those who have done the work before have judged that the elementary tasks presented here are not what is sometimes called "Mickey Mouse stuff." Be an achiever from the start! God's unique book deserves the best efforts you can apply, and God will surely bless your efforts in this study of the Bible.

THE BIBLE AS A WHOLE

What Is the Bible?

PART 1

SUMMARY

It is important at the beginning of this study to consider what we think about the Bible and to recognize why it should be studied whole. To facilitate this study we should learn the names of the books of the Bible in order, for they provide a kind of table of contents. It is also important to know how and why these particular books comprise the Bible. This is known as the development of the "canon."

BASIC BIBLE REFERENCES
Matthew 5:17; 7:12
Luke 16:29, 31; 24:44
John 1:45
Acts 28:23
Romans 3:21

WORD LIST
Apocalypse
Apocrypha
Canon
Catholic Epistles
Deuterocanonical
Former Prophets
Latter Prophets
Septuagint
Torah
Writings

What Is the Bible?

Put this question to any group of people, and there will be almost as many different answers as there are people. This is not surprising, for the Bible is many things. One definition that children sometimes learn goes like this: "The Bible is a library of books inspired by God." In what respects do you agree with this definition? If you do not agree with it, how would you change it? What reservations might some people have about it?

In the space below write your own answer to the question about the Bible. *What is the Bible?*

Later in the program you will be asked to compare your answer now with your growing understanding of the Bible. The better you know the Bible, the more you will appreciate how difficult it is to describe it adequately in a brief statement. If you are willing to grow in your understanding of the Bible, you will discover that your answer to the question will change as you learn.

Whatever else the Bible is, it presents a vast amount to be read. That is one reason some people never read it at all, and it certainly adds to the difficulty of understanding it. The division of the Bible into many parts—"books"—some of them with difficult names, adds to the complication.

There are important differences among various groups of people about what books to include in the Bible. The number of books in the New Testament is generally agreed to be twenty-seven. There are different counts for what is usually called the Old Testament.[1] Most Protestants list thirty-nine books. The New American Bible, the most widely used Catholic version, lists forty-six books, but this includes material that expands several of the thirty-nine books.[2] For Jews, sacred Scripture consists of the thirty-nine books but in an order different from that used in Christian Bibles. In our study we shall use the sixty-six books common to all editions of Christian Bibles, but we shall also give some attention to several of the additional books.

Learning the Contents

Our first task is to become familiar with the names of all of the sixty-six books. If they are not familiar to you, think of it as learning the alphabet in order to use a dictionary or other library resources—or as a beginning golfer who has to learn the designation and intended use of each club in the bag. To learn what is in the Bible we must be able to find our way around in it efficiently.[3]

It is helpful and appropriate to learn the books in groups. Sunday School materials sometimes picture the Bible as groups of books in sections on a bookshelf. This is a useful idea. In the Appendix of this Resource Book there is a summary of several different groupings of the books. Refer to this now, for it will be useful later.[4] In what follows we shall use the order of the sixty-six books that is common to most editions of the Bible, but we shall note the differences in other groupings.

Books of the Old Testament

In the Old Testament the first five books are called *Torah* by Jews. This Hebrew word means "instruction." Legal rules and regulations are prominent in these books, so they came to be

---

[1] Some writers refer to this collection as "The Hebrew Scriptures" because they feel that "Old" suggests that it is out-of-date or has been replaced. They refer, then, to the "New" Testament as "Christian Scriptures." But this distinction is not accurate, for Christians consider the Old Testament to be a part of their Holy Scriptures. We shall call it the "Old Testament" because most literature on the Bible does so, meaning that it comes from a period earlier than the New Testament.

[2] There is further information on this subject on page 3 and in Theme 1, Part 2.

[3] To demonstrate this need, open the Bible at random and note what book is named at the top of the page. Then decide whether you know what book precedes it and which comes after it. Try this exercise a few times, and you will know how much effort you need to expend on this assignment.

[4] More information about these books will be given later. In the column "The Greek Bible" you see names of books in addition to the common list of thirty-nine.

referred to as "the law." Although there is much more in Torah than "law," the New Testament usually refers to these books as *the law*. The names of the books are:

Genesis, Exodus, Leviticus, Numbers, Deuteronomy.

The next books in the common order are:

Joshua, Judges, Ruth, First and Second Samuel, First and Second Kings.

Excluding Ruth, the Jewish Scriptures call this group the *Former Prophets* because of an ancient belief that the books were written by or at the direction of early prophets. The group was treated as four books. "First" and "Second" are carry-overs from the days when Scripture was handwritten on scrolls, and Samuel and Kings were each divided onto two scrolls.

We are combining the Hebrew order with our common order because it will help us understand how the Old Testament was first put together. In the Hebrew Scriptures, Ruth is a part of the third and most diverse group of books, called *Writings*[5]. This group also includes:

First and Second Chronicles, Ezra, Nehemiah, Esther.

In addition, we add to this group five books that are sometimes referred to as the "Books of Poetry":

Job, Psalms, Proverbs, Ecclesiastes, Song of Solomon.

The next books in the order we are following are:

Isaiah, Jeremiah, Lamentations, Ezekiel, Daniel.

In the Hebrew Scriptures Lamentations and Daniel are classified as *Writings*. Isaiah, Jeremiah and Ezekiel, along with "The Twelve," are called the *Latter Prophets*. The names of the Twelve are:

Hosea, Joel, Amos, Obadiah, Jonah, Micah, Nahum, Habakkuk, Zephaniah, Haggai, Zechariah, Malachi.

---

[5] Remember that the order of books in the Hebrew Scriptures is somewhat different from that of most Christian Bibles; see the list in the Appendix.

These are sometimes referred to as "Minor Prophets," but this may be misleading. "Minor" refers only to the length of the individual books. The Hebrew Scriptures put them together because they could be copied on one scroll. The four books of the *Former Prophets* and the four of the *Latter Prophets* form the second part of the Hebrew Scriptures, *Prophets*. Keep in mind this threefold division, Torah, Prophets, and Writings.

Books of the New Testament

In the New Testament the four Gospels come first:

Matthew, Mark, Luke, John.

These are followed by a book about people and events in the early church from the coming of the Holy Spirit on Pentecost to the end of the career of Paul:

Acts.

Then follow letters traditionally attributed to Paul:

Romans, First and Second Corinthians, Galatians, Ephesians, Philippians, Colossians, First and Second Thessalonians, First and Second Timothy, Titus, Philemon.

Here "First" and "Second" actually refer to different books or letters.

Following this collection there is a sizable book that is part letter, part sermon or tract:

Hebrews.

This book is sometimes included with the next group, variously called "general" or "catholic" epistles, meaning that they were intended for the whole church ("catholic" means "according to the whole"):

James, First and Second Peter, First, Second, and Third John, Jude.

Finally there is the book entitled:

Revelation.

Be careful not to refer to this book as *"Revelations"*; read what the writer calls the book in the first verse. It is also referred to as the "Apocalypse," from the Greek word for Revelation.

The groupings summarized above show that these books are related to two particular religious traditions. The persons, events, and ideas dealt with in these books have exceptional significance for those traditions. The Old Testament has a thread of continuity in that it deals with the story of a particular people who had a very strong sense that they were uniquely a people of God. The New Testament deals with another people who regarded themselves as uniquely a new people of God but, together with Jews, inheritors of the Old Testament tradition.

Why These Books?

These lists and groups comprise the collection of sixty-six books. It is reasonable to ask why the collection contains precisely these books. During both the period covered by the Old Testament and the first century of the Christian era, other writings that are not included among the sixty-six books were produced in Jewish and Christian communities. A few of these are included in all Catholic Bibles, and many editions of other versions include them. We shall note several such books. There are many more, however, that are not included in any modern Scripture collection. Some of these provide details that supplement Bible study. One example is Enoch, which is quoted twice in Jude 14, 15.

The process by which Judaism and the Christian church finally decided what books should belong among their authoritative Scriptures is referred to as selecting and closing "the canon."[6] The canon is the list of books officially accepted as uniquely sacred Scripture. These final results were reached by processes of development.

The Old Testament Canon

In Jesus' day the sacred Jewish Scriptures consisted of the Torah[7], the Prophets, plus the Psalms and most of the other Writings. Note how this is reflected in these New Testament passages: **Matthew 5:17; 7:12; Luke 16:29, 31; 24:44; John 1:45; Acts 28:23; Romans 3:21**. How does each of these passages refer to canonical Scripture?

Sometimes the word scripture(s) is mentioned in the New Testament without specifically naming a book or group of books. These are references to what we may call the Bible of

---

6 "Canon" is from a Greek word that meant "measuring stick," hence, "standard" or "model."
7 Sometimes these five books are referred to simply as "Moses" because he is the principal figure in them.

the first Christian century.[8] There was no authoritative and final list of books (canon) until early in the Christian era. A "Palestinian Canon" consisting of twenty-four books (thirty-nine as we divide them today) was generally accepted after A.D. 90. It was written originally in Hebrew.[9]

A somewhat different list of books became the Scriptures accepted by the large colony of exiled Jews who lived in Alexandria, Egypt. Since that was a Greek-speaking city, it was inevitable that Hebrew Scriptures would be translated there. This process began in the third century B.C.[10] This collection eventually included some writings that were never accepted into the canon that was authoritative in Palestine.[11] This Greek Bible became known as the *Septuagint*. The name comes from the Greek word for "seventy," since an early legend attributed the translation to seventy men. The additional books that it included have traditionally been called the *Apocrypha* (from a Greek word meaning "hidden," referring to their secondary authority), but more recently they are known as "deuterocanonical" (a term indicating a second canon). We shall consider in the next part the influence of the Septuagint.

The New Testament Canon

The first collection of Christian books was probably a group of Paul's letters. 2 Peter 3:15b, 16 implies that some of these letters were widely known at a very early period. The process by which books written in the early church came to be accepted as uniquely authoritative was affected by several factors. Connection with an apostle was important. After the last apostles died, the church was spurred to sort and judge its growing literature. The spread of the church beyond Palestine brought a need for authoritative, written guidance for new congregations. As more and more writings—various gospels, "acts" (of church leaders), epistles (letters), apocalypses (visions, special revelations)—were produced and some of them possibly included false teaching, decisions had to be made.

The earliest lists of Christian Scriptures usually contained at least two-thirds of the books that finally became canonical. It was not until late in the fourth century, however, that a canon consisting of precisely the twenty-seven books we now recognize was approved by an authoritative church assembly.

---

8 See Matthew 22:29; Mark 14:49; Acts 17:2; Romans 4:3; 15:4; James 2:8. Also note Luke 24:27.

9 A few short passages are in Aramaic, a language closely related to Hebrew. Aramaic was the native tongue of Jesus and was widely used in eastern Mediterranean areas in his time. The books of the New Testament, however, were all written in Greek.

10 Some writers on biblical subjects now use BCE ="Before the Common Era" rather than B.C. ="Before Christ" and CE ="The Common Era" rather than A.D. ="Anno Domini" ("year of the Lord").

11 A principal reason for rejecting some of these books in Palestine was that they were written in Greek. The Greek language was used widely in Palestine at this time, but Jews held firmly to Hebrew as the language of their religion.

...ata that affect an answer to this question. In Part 2 we shall ...ions reached our day. Then for the rest of *Kerygma: The* ...ning all we can about the contents of the books in the col- ...can derive from the whole book.

...rmeates Western culture and is significantly present in much ...s reason enough to study the contents and message of the ...further motivated by what the Bible contributes to our life

...s of the Bible occurred during a period of about a thousand ...literature has been faithfully preserved for some two thou- ...arkable history has taken place not merely because gifted ..., nor because books were rare and precious before modern ...erished because it records the continuing experiences and ...ugh which they came to know who God is and to gain some ...d purpose in the world.

...ook that has been revered by two great traditions. It claims ...od guided the persons and events that carried the great story ...itual experiences. This continuity running through the Bible ...to become new generations of the people of God. Thus God's ...r in the unity of the Bible and in its influence through the ...anding the Bible whole.

AND REFLECTION

...is recognized in education today. This section will usually ...ture just covered and urge that they be learned. They will ...and a basic resource for understanding and interpreting the

...e sixty-six books of the Bible in order, and by groups.

Research

1. Review your answer to the question, "What is the Bible?" Look for statements from well-known persons that address this question. Compare these statements with your answer.

2. Ask several friends whose judgment you respect to give you their answers to the question, and note how their responses are similar or different from one another.

Reflection

1. What difference does it make what you think of the Bible? How may your answer to this question affect your study of the Bible?

2. Do you think the canon should ever be opened to add books to the Bible? What are your reasons?

THE BIBLE AS A WHOLE

INTRO

How Did We Get the Bible?

PART 2

SUMMARY
The history of the Bible from its canonization to the present is remarkable. The ancestry of the New Revised Standard Version through over four and a half centuries is an example. Other important threads of the story reach back from Luther through the Middle Ages, and the earliest translations are also noteworthy. These facts and careful study of the available options should influence our choice and use of contemporary versions.

BASIC BIBLE REFERENCES
(See Research 3)
Genesis 1:1-8
Psalm 23
Matthew 5:1-12
1 Corinthians 13

WORD LIST
Edition
Paraphrase
Revision
Translation
Vernacular
Version

A Unique History

No book can match the record of the Bible for publication and distribution. When the American Bible Society issued *Good News for Modern Man, The New Testament in Today's English Version*, in 1966, it was received with such enthusiasm that in less than ten years it sold ten million copies! And this is not just a modern phenomenon. Wherever Judaism and especially Christianity have spread, the Bible has been the most widely circulated book. We probably think of this expansion in terms of printed pages, but it was also true before printing from movable type was invented in the 1450's. It was pointed out in Part 1 that the translation process began even before there was a New Testament. Today the Bible or part of it may be read in nearly 2,000 languages or dialects.

In English a number of different translations, versions, and paraphrases are readily available. It is important to know how this came about so we may make intelligent choices among them. Since there is a gap of nineteen hundred years between us and the writing of the latest books of the New Testament, knowing what happened during that long time helps us to appreciate our Bible in English more fully.

Several terms are commonly used in referring to various parts of this process. "Translation" calls attention to the procedure of moving from one language to another, for example, from Latin into Spanish. "Version" usually refers to a Bible that has resulted from translation, for example, the American Standard

Version. All versions depend upon translation, but the terms are occasionally used interchangeably. A "revision" is based upon an already existing version, and an "edition" refers to the way a publisher presents a version.

Although all translation involves some interpretation (since no two languages are exactly alike) "paraphrase" implies a conscious measure of interpretation that tries to remove from the text any ambiguity or uncertainty of meaning. Thus "love of God" is an accurate translation of a New Testament Greek phrase, but it may be paraphrased either "the love God has for us" or "the love we have for God."

An English Tradition

The New Revised Standard Version (NRSV) is the result of the longest continuous stretch of history of the Bible in English. "New" means it is a revision of the Revised Standard Version (RSV). The RSV New Testament appeared first in 1946, the complete Bible in 1952. A new edition with minor changes was issued in 1972. Significant changes in contemporary English usage and some new knowledge of the earliest Hebrew and Greek texts dictated the need for further revision, and the NRSV appeared in 1990. Responsible revision requires (1) that the translation be thoroughly reviewed and (2) that the language of the new readers of the text (the "revised version") be carefully considered.

The "Revised" in RSV is evidence that this version is based on an earlier work, the American Standard Version (ASV) of 1901. The ASV in turn was a revised edition of the English Revised Version (ERV), which was published in Great Britain in 1885. By the middle of the nineteenth century, knowledge of the Hebrew and Greek texts had moved much closer to the originals, and this moved biblical scholars to produce the ERV.[1] Thus we have already worked our way back a century toward the beginning of this tradition.

The ERV was a revision of the King James Version (KJV) of 1611.[2] This seventeenth century book is doubtless the noblest monument of the English language. It was produced by an assembly of forty-seven men appointed by James I, and most of the ablest biblical scholars in England served. Because of important changes in English a "modernized" edition of the KJV was produced at Oxford in 1769, and later editions of the KJV stem from this revision.

---

1 No original manuscript of a book of the Bible is known to exist today. Texts now in use, however, are nearer to the originals than any generation has known since the early Christian centuries, and our present texts are thoroughly reliable. Indeed, in 1968 a Greek New Testament text was published, which for the first time ever has been approved by the major Bible Societies of the western world and the Roman Catholic Pontifical Biblical Institute.

2 In Great Britain this is known as the Authorized Version. This title recognizes the royal authorization by King James I, while "KJV" places the book in its historical setting.

The KJV was actually a revision of the Bishops' Bible, which had been produced in 1568. It in turn was a revision of the Great Bible of 1539. This version, named because of its large size, was produced under the auspices of King Henry VIII for particular use by the Church of England.

The Bishops' Bible was an official response to the popularity of a Bible version that had been produced in Geneva in 1560 by refugees from the tyranny of Queen Mary. The Genevan Version was widely accepted, partly because of its convenient size and its inclusion (for the first time) of verse numbers. It rivaled the KJV until the middle of the seventeenth century. It was used by Shakespeare and Bunyan and was the Bible taken to the New World by the Pilgrims in 1620. Although it relied heavily on the earlier English versions, it was not in the direct line of the KJV ancestry.

The Great Bible was dependent (through several intervening versions) upon the first printed English Bible, which was published by Myles Coverdale in 1535. The New Testament of Coverdale's Bible was dependent upon the first printed English New Testament, published in Germany by William Tyndale in 1526. He was opposed by religious authorities in England and died a martyr in 1536—ironically the year after his work had been used by Coverdale without official opposition.

Thus the NRSV, while utilizing the best texts now available and written in English of the late twentieth century, is heir to 465 years of translation history. Its predecessor, the RSV, was approved by Protestant, Roman Catholic, and Eastern Orthodox Christians. This is only one of the many modern versions available, of course, but its background is unique. The NRSV is the version used in *Kerygma: The Bible in Depth*.

Back Through the Middle Ages

At about the same time that Tyndale and Coverdale were working, Martin Luther was translating the Bible into German (1522-1534). Just before this, the great Dutch scholar Erasmus had published a Greek New Testament in 1516. Meanwhile, the invention of the printing press was having a profound effect upon the world. The first complete printed book was a Latin Bible (done by Johann Gutenberg in 1456). Before this, at the end of the fourteenth century, an Oxford clergyman, John Wycliffe, had translated the Latin Bible into English (1384-1395), and many handwritten ("manuscript") copies were produced. These events were signs that the Bible had moved out of the shadow of the Middle Ages.

It is remarkable how the Bible was preserved and thrived during the thousand years before Wycliffe. Remember that every word had to be copied by hand during that period. Still the Bible spread all over the Middle East, North Africa, and Europe. Thousands of Bible manuscripts from those years have survived. They form a firm base for the work of translators and Bible scholars today.

Among the earliest translations from the original Hebrew and Greek, the most influential one was the Latin, for that was the official language of the Roman Empire and then of the Western Christian church. In 384-404 a conscientious scholar named Jerome produced what became the official Latin version, which prevailed until the twentieth century. It replaced a number of earlier Latin versions and was known as the "Vulgate," from the Latin word meaning "for the common people."

The Earliest Times

In discussing the Old Testament canon, the Septuagint version was mentioned.[3] From the earliest years in the history of Judeo-Christian Scriptures there was translation into different languages. The Jews of Alexandria felt that their sacred Scriptures were such an important, living force that it was necessary for those Scriptures to be available in the language they spoke in their daily life.

This conviction carried over into the later experiences of God's people. Although Jesus spoke Aramaic as his native language, Greek was the principal language of the world in which he lived.[4] It was natural, therefore, that the books of the New Testament should be written in the Greek common in the western Mediterranean world of that day. Moreover, when Paul quoted the Old Testament, he usually followed the Greek version.

Which Versions Today?

This survey of the history of the Bible as a book establishes some precedents for the use of the Bible today. We have noted the importance of the original Hebrew and Greek forms of the biblical texts. We have also seen evidence that, wherever the faith that comes through the Bible has gone, the book has been translated into the languages of the peoples. This heritage places significant responsibility upon the church today to continue this vital tradition.

In light of all this, consider the following recommendations concerning the choice of Bibles for serious Bible study:

- The position of the NRSV as the current bearer of 465 years of unbroken tradition commends it for special acceptance. It is also a living witness that

---

3 Part 1, page 6.
4 Jesus probably could also speak Greek. His conversations with Pilate would almost certainly have been in Greek or possibly even in Latin, for Pilate would hardly have used Aramaic.

centuries-old versions are not adequate for contemporary Bible study. The Bible is not anchored in any past time, even those ages in which its books were produced.

- There are other valuable versions that have been translated directly from the original languages into contemporary, literary English. *The Revised English Bible* (REB, 1989) is a revision of *The New English Bible* (1961-1970). *The New Jerusalem Bible* (NJB, 1985) is a revision of *The Jerusalem Bible* (1966). Both of these are fine versions.

- Many people want a Bible with language as simplified as may be consistent with accuracy of translation. *The Good News Bible: Today's English Version* (TEV or GNB, 1976) is intended particularly for persons who want a reliable translation into everyday speech. The expertness and experience of the American Bible Society translators commends this as the best vernacular (that is, common speech) version.[5]

- Paraphrases contain a greater element of interpretation than is employed in more literal translations. For this reason they have limited usefulness in serious Bible study. *The Living Bible* (1971) is an example. It was prepared principally from English translations rather than from the original texts, and it has been widely criticized for many elements of interpretation that do not accurately represent the original texts. The paraphrase of J. B. Phillips, *The New Testament in Modern English* (1973), on the other hand, has been warmly recommended by many Bible scholars. Some interpretation is inevitable in any transition from one language to another, but it is very important to distinguish this work of faithful translation from the imposition of bias. One may find devotional help in an old version or a modern paraphrase, but great care should be exercised in separating this from the process of serious Bible study.

This part would be incomplete without further mention of the vitality of Bible translation and study in the Roman Catholic Church today. The success of a French translation by Dominican friars at the École Biblique in Jerusalem led to the NJB referred to above. The English version was made from the original languages, with the study notes making use of those of the French version. Another stream of Catholic biblical tradition produced the New American Bible (NAB, 1970; New Testament revised, 1988). This version is used in much American Catholic liturgy and study today.

---

5 As this Kerygma program is being revised, the American Bible Society is preparing a new *Contemporary English Version*. The New Testament has already appeared (1991), and the whole Bible is planned for the near future. Since it is suitable for children, it is called *The Bible for Today's Family*. It is a commendable vernacular version.

In some ways it would be helpful—and comfortable—to have only one generally used version from this time on. That cannot be, for reasons that should be apparent from the material covered in this part. We should therefore take advantage of the legitimate values of diversity, some of which are:

- The best of the contemporary versions represent the finest biblical scholarship available today.

- These versions offer an opportunity for all Bible readers to enrich their understanding by comparing versions.

- The wide variety of available versions should enable each person to find at least one version particularly attractive.

- Here is evidence that the Bible is still a vital, contemporary book!

FOR FURTHER STUDY AND REFLECTION

Memory Bank

1. Identify in one or two sentences:

Jerome	KJV
Vulgate	NRSV
Tyndale	TEV
Coverdale	NAB

Research

1. For more background on the need for modern versions, read the excellent statement in the Preface to the NRSV ("To the Reader"), which is included in most editions.

2. To understand the difficulty of manuscript writing in the days before printing, copy by hand (preferably with pen and ink) the first chapter of the Gospel of John. Then have someone else copy your copy. Compare the copies with the original. (To match conditions in the Middle Ages you should not wear eyeglasses or use electric light!)

3. Secure several different versions of the Bible (including especially some of those mentioned in this section), and compare the following well-known passages:

> Genesis 1:1-8
> Psalm 23
> Matthew 5:1-12
> 1 Corinthians 13

Make note of some differences that are particularly striking. These may be discussed in group time.

Reflection

1. What are some advantages and some problems in using modern translations or versions?

2. How has the study of this part affected your appreciation and understanding of the Bible?

THE BIBLE AS A WHOLE

INTRO

How Shall We Study the Bible?

PART 3

SUMMARY
Varying reasons for studying the Bible lead to varying ways of study. Our purpose is to understand the Bible whole. To accomplish this we shall follow themes drawn from the Bible itself. These deal at all points with God and people. The settings are in particular times and places. Helpful tools are readily available, especially study Bibles, concordances, and Bible dictionaries.

BASIC BIBLE REFERENCES
Jeremiah 31:31-34
Mark 6:30-44

WORD LIST
Concordance
Judeo-Christian
Themes

Ways and Means

People have many reasons for studying the Bible. There are also many ways of studying the Bible, and particular ways of study especially suit particular reasons for study. Most Christians believe that the Bible is of supreme importance as a guide for faith and life. In practice, however, they are likely to focus on parts of the Bible that seem to relate most comfortably to their life situation. As a result they become familiar with a narrow range of biblical material. Thus the guidance of the Bible is inevitably restricted and may become a kind of rubber stamp upon notions already held.

Recall your own experiences in Bible study. What courses have you taken? How many books of the Bible have you read? How many have you studied? With which ones are you really familiar? Can you relate them to the Bible as a whole? Make some notes so you can arrive at an overall picture of your Bible knowledge.

Sooner or later we must give detailed attention to particular parts of Scripture. But acquaintance with some books of the Bible (even knowing the names of all of them!) is no substitute for a grasp of the Bible as a whole book. Our desire to understand the Bible, then, should bring us to study it whole. That is what we propose to do in *Kerygma: The Bible in Depth.*

IN:3

One Book

It is noted on page vii that most Christians affirm the oneness of the Bible. How do the standards of your church state this? We may find that some passage of the Bible is particularly and immediately applicable to our life situation. But if we isolate that part from the whole, we shall be in peril of missing its real meaning. In Paul's letter to the Romans Martin Luther found the key that led him to reform his theology, but he later wrote commentaries on most of the biblical books. His translation of the Bible into German became one of the principal foundations of the movement he began.

A broad knowledge of the Bible as a whole is needed for understanding its particular parts properly. This is even true of the portions we think we know best. The New Testament, for example, is packed with references to and quotations from Old Testament Scripture. Jesus' ministry was lived out against a background of Old Testament tradition, and New Testament writers regularly found in the Old Testament vital clues for understanding the mission and message of Jesus. We may also say that the New Testament provides an extension and outcome of many Old Testament themes and a fulfillment of many Old Testament hopes.

Two Common Ways of Study

A common procedure for studying the whole Bible is to begin with Genesis and work through book by book to the end of Revelation. This method is sometimes undertaken by an individual in private study using no reference aids. It requires a great deal of perseverance, and many well-meaning persons with good intentions have bogged down in such an attempt. There are enough stories in Genesis to carry one through the book, but the difficult details of Exodus, Leviticus, and Numbers are discouraging, to say the least. Similarly, the beginning of Matthew may be baffling. In this method the main track of the materials is in peril of being lost.

The whole Bible may also be covered without following the books in order if one has a careful curriculum laid out. The International Uniform Lesson Series offers such a plan. It has been in use for about a century, and has been the staple of many Sunday School classes. It is designed to cover the Bible in a six-year cycle. It has two drawbacks. First, it takes too long to get the whole picture with too many chances to lose continuity. Second, its emphasis inevitably falls upon the parts, and the oneness of the Bible, while taken for granted, becomes difficult to keep in view.

A Thematic Approach

Kerygma: The Bible in Depth follows a thematic approach. Church statements about the Bible assume that something holds the many books of the canon together. That unity is found in themes that run throughout the whole Bible. By following ten themes through the Bible we can be introduced to the Bible whole. These themes will be the main highways, crossing and recrossing the biblical landscape, and they will foster familiarity with the historical landmarks and the related scenes.

This approach involves several fundamental presuppositions:

1. That the themes give practical, usable clues to the oneness of the Bible, and that their recurrence throughout both Testaments provides ties among the various parts.

2. That the Judeo-Christian heritage is rooted in history, which constantly relates God and people.

3. That the Christian church's confession of Jesus as the Messiah inescapably links Christian and Hebrew experience, history, and literature.

The Bible is an experience-centered book. Therefore, its roots in history are important. Abstract thought and theoretical precept are not common in the Bible, and those parts that do not describe the experience of the people are nevertheless closely connected to what is happening or has happened to the people. This helps identify themes that develop directly from the biblical texts.

What Themes?

A list of themes could be derived by first studying every part of the Bible as intensively and objectively as possible and then working out themes from the results of that study. Such a procedure, of course, would be slow, cumbersome, and far too complicated to perform in most study groups. This work, however, has already been done, and the themes that are identified will prove to be truly biblical as they appear throughout the sacred Scriptures.

The experiences that gathered and consolidated a people of God were first of all events of deliverance, so our first theme is **God Saves a People**. In the Old Testament the critical moment is the exodus from Egypt, which is memorialized in the Passover celebration. This becomes a focal point for the continuing relationship between God and the Hebrew people. In the New Testament the mission of Jesus culminating in his death and resurrection is identified as the crucial experience that establishes a new relationship between God and a new people of God, the Christian church.

The exodus provided evidence that God keeps promises, for long before that event God made a covenant with the Hebrew ancestor Abraham. God's people from time to time fail to be faithful, but they discover that always **People Find God Is Faithful** (Theme 2). This is profoundly demonstrated in the New Covenant established through Jesus.

The Bible rarely presents theoretical discussion about God. Rather, **People Reflect about God** (Theme 3) as a consequence of deliverance and faithfulness. They declare God's creative power. They wrestle with good and evil, with God's justice and love. Ultimately they claim to know God best through the revelation in Jesus Christ.

The land where the Hebrews settled was an ancient, international crossroad, so they could not escape experiencing that **God's People Live in God's World** (Theme 4). Their relationship to that world was often ambiguous as they tried unsuccessfully to avoid involvements outside their limited land. The Christian church, however, early moved into the surrounding world with a profound sense of mission while nevertheless trying to maintain a distinctive separation from that world.

All through the Bible **God's People Have Leaders** (Theme 5). Most of the sustained narratives are carried along by the life and experiences of these persons, who are appointed by God for their tasks. There are patriarchs, judges, prophets, priests, kings, seers, apostles, and other more ordinary people who do extraordinary things.

Kings are a special kind of leader. They are anointed to rule as God's particular representatives, for the Hebrews thought of God as their supreme ruler. A time came when there was no longer a Hebrew king. Later Jesus reemphasized the kingship of God, and the Christian church saw Jesus as the fulfillment of expectations of an anointed savior-ruler. Thus there is the double truth that **God's People Have Rulers but One Sovereign** (Theme 6).

From their earliest perceptions God's people understood that the divine rule imposes requirements. The Bible regularly presents these as law, and the counterpart is always righteous living. Put simply, **God Demands a Righteous People** (Theme 7). The new revelation in Jesus Christ brings new perceptions of this double emphasis, especially as a law of love.

There are areas of knowledge and understanding that God's people share with wise and moral people around them. The Bible includes portions, even books, of this, for **God's People Learn Wisdom** (Theme 8). Hebrew wisdom, however, has a special quality rooted in its special relation to God. The New Testament has some portions of wisdom like the Old, but the church's confrontation with Western thought brings new dimensions. Jesus Christ becomes the focus of wisdom.

The relationship between God and people takes on special qualities as **God's People Worship** (Theme 9). The Bible offers rich resources for expressing and celebrating this worship: ritual, psalms, hymns, prayer, and sacrament. Continuity between the Testaments broadens and deepens this theme.

From earliest times God's people believed in a divine guarantee of their future. When exile brought despair, they found new courage in new kinds of expectation. Jesus' death dashed his disciples' faith for the future, but his resurrection became a new guarantee of ultimate victory. The Revelation provides a final proclamation that **God's People Have Hope** (Theme 10).

Some Observations

The Bible everywhere presupposes God and people, and in all the themes these are constants. God is rarely the object of discussion in the sacred Scriptures. People in a special relationship with God are always in view, and no people are beyond God's concern.

The Judeo-Christian emphasis on history is important. Some attention to dates is instructive. For example, the last days of the Judean monarchy were roughly contemporary with the rise of Greece in the eastern Mediterranean, and Confucius was teaching in China when Nehemiah was rebuilding Jerusalem after the Babylonian exile. The Bible is an entry to those times and places long ago. Occasionally other literature from antiquity and the results of archeological research throw light on the biblical texts. It is important to realize that this was a real world, these were real people. What they knew about God and life may become valid and applicable for us precisely as we recover their experiences and thoughts.

The ten themes presented here do not exhaust the thematic possibilities of the Bible. Careful study of these ten, however, will give us a grasp of the whole and so prepare us for further productive study.

Some Tools To Use in Study

There are several tools for Bible study that are of prime worth, and so we introduce them at the outset of *Kerygma: The Bible in Depth*. Learn how to use them. It will be helpful to have your own copies.

Almost every edition of the Bible has some helps. There are editions called **Study Bibles**, which contain extensive helps. One of the best-known is *The New Oxford Annotated Bible*. Such editions usually provide running outlines that are very helpful in following the contents of books and parts of books. The cross references in the margins or footnotes of many other editions of the Bible are basic aids for identifying relationships between verses and are particularly useful for moving back and forth between the Testaments. Other notes may provide information necessary for further understanding the text.

Look at several examples. A note at 2 Samuel 22:1-51 should call attention to the fact that the poem there is repeated in Psalm 18. You may also learn that 2 Samuel 23:8-39 is repeated in 1 Chronicles 11:11-47. **Jeremiah 31:31-34** should have a note helping you to find out more about the idea of "covenant" and indicating that this entire passage is quoted in the New Testament in Hebrews 8:8-12 and in part at Hebrews 10:16, 17.

Mark 9:42-48 shows a number of footnotes in the NRSV; note the variety.[1] **Mark 6:30-44** is the story of the feeding of the five thousand. The story is told in parallel passages in the other three Gospels: Matthew 14:13-21, Luke 9:10-17, and John 6:1-13. A study Bible identifies these parallels and may indicate how they fit into the context in each Gospel.

A **concordance** has several important uses. It lists occurrences of Bible words by books, chapters, and verses and gives enough of each particular verse to identify the usage. An "exhaustive" concordance lists every occurrence of every word. There are also abridged versions. Each concordance is based on a particular version, although some give limited reference to several versions.[2] With a concordance you can locate any verse in the Bible if you remember one word. You can also trace the use of a given word in various books of the Bible, which is helpful when you are following themes or other ideas in scripture.[3]

Again check some examples. You could have found the relationship between Jeremiah and Hebrews by looking at the entries for the word "covenant." You would also have located

---

[1] The number will vary with the edition. It is not necessary at this point to understand all of these notes. Some of them may be discussed in group time. It is one of the objects of this study program to help you learn about such matters, but many of the details will be considered more conveniently at a later time.

[2] Of course you should use a concordance that matches the Bible version you are studying. If a concordance for another version is available, it may prompt you to use that version to supplement your study.

[3] If you use a computer, programs are now available that will rapidly perform search and show functions. These programs are a tremendous help in Bible study.

the four stories of the feeding of the five thousand if you had been hunting for one of them under the words "thousand" or "loaves" or "baskets." You might also have found that Mark 8:1-10 and Matthew 15:32-39 give another narrative in which four thousand are fed.

A Bible Dictionary lists the most important word-subjects in the Bible and provides more or less extensive articles explaining the subjects. (Some Bible dictionaries are more complete than others. One is in five large volumes!). These articles often include the language background of the word; a survey of its use and importance throughout the Bible; historical, geographical, and archeological data where appropriate; and even notes on the significance of the word in times and circumstances outside the Bible.

Each of these aids supplements the others. For example, you might be studying the Passover. You would probably begin at Exodus 12. There a study Bible will give you an introductory note. A Bible Dictionary will expand upon this and will refer you to other Passovers mentioned in the Bible. A concordance will enable you to pursue the study another way by checking all of the references to "Passover" in the whole Bible.

Some study Bibles have abridged concordances and dictionaries. These are useful for quick reference and for learning to use these tools. They will probably whet your appetite for more complete editions. Here at the outset of this study it is important to learn to utilize every aid available. Remember that your group leader is also an important resource and will help you become familiar with your learning tools.

FOR FURTHER STUDY AND REFLECTION

Memory Bank

Review the ten themes (in boldface above) until you can restate them in order.

Research

1. What are the areas of the Bible about which you know the least? What do you think are the main reasons why these are unfamiliar? In which themes do you think these areas will fall?

2. On a list of the books of the Bible note which themes you think will relate to the respective books. File this for checking later.

3. Study the chart in the Appendix that presents a time comparison of biblical and secular events. What other data would you like to see added to the chart? What resources would you consult to secure this information?

Reflection

1. Are some parts of the Bible more important than others? Think of reasons for answering both yes and no. How can you account for the fact that the New Testament uses some Old Testament books far more than it does others?

2. How important is history? How does it relate to religious faith? What difference does it make whether events described in the Bible really happened?

GOD SAVES A PEOPLE

THEME 1

The Exodus: Pattern of God's Saving Acts

PART 1

SUMMARY

In dealing with the Bible thematically we start with a theme that is crucial throughout the Old and New Testaments: the proclamation of God as one who saves a people. Our study begins with the story of the exodus, the deliverance of the Hebrew people from slavery in Egypt. Although this is not from the first book of the Bible, the event is a real beginning; for it shaped the Old Testament belief in a saving God.

Primary information about the exodus is found in the book that takes its name from the event. We survey the role of Moses and learn about the inauguration of the Passover. There are many other references to the exodus and Passover in other parts of the Old Testament.

NOTE: There is a great deal of study-work in this part. Its importance in relation to understanding the Bible whole justifies extra effort now. Organize your study time. The Resource Book selects key parts of the much more extensive Bible text; so emphasize the Bible reading. Use the Resource Book to help relate the various texts to each other.

BASIC BIBLE REFERENCES
Exodus 1-4; 12; 14; 15:1-21; 20:2
Deuteronomy 6:20-23
Psalm 78:12-16

WORD LIST
Manna
Pentateuch
Passover
Sea of Reeds
Yahweh

Background of the Exodus

Our study begins with the people of Israel, whose experiences and relationship to God are the principal concern of most of the Old Testament. Their formative experience is referred to as the "exodus".[1] In that experience a particular people became aware that they were a special people with a special relationship to God. Earlier stories in the book of Genesis tell about their ancestors and give strong hints of divine destiny, but that book is really a sort of introduction to the story of God's people. Their continuous story begins in the book of Exodus.

The story of the people of the exodus is dominated by a great leader named Moses. According to tradition, Moses receives major credit for assembling, editing, and handing down much of the material in the first five books of the Bible.[2] In Introduction, Part 1, we noted a reflection of this tradition in the phrase, *the law of Moses* (Luke 24:44). Ancestors of the Israelite people, particularly Abraham, are honored in various ways and degrees, but it is clear that Moses is the pivotal figure in the formation of the nation and its primary traditions.

When the Hebrew people[3] began their national development, they did not have a clearly organized religious faith. Their particular relationship with God begins in the exodus-deliverance from Egypt. Moses becomes the interpreter of the event. From

---

1 The word comes from two Greek roots meaning "the way out."
2 These five books are often referred to as the Pentateuch, a word that means "five books."
3 "Hebrew" and "Israelite" may be used interchangeably at this stage in our study. The background of these and other national names will become clearer as we progress.

a unique revelation Moses gains a new understanding of God. Moses then leads the Israelite people in the name of God, and they begin to recognize their special position with God. The formative experience in the Pentateuch begins with recognizing that GOD SAVES A PEOPLE. We must look at the texts about this experience with considerable care.

Moses' Early Years

At this point read **Exodus, Chapters 1 through 4**. Some parts of this narrative may be somewhat familiar to you, and certain parts are more important to remember than other parts, but begin by reading it all.

Now work on answers to the following questions. If you are uncertain about your answers, read the relevant passages again.

- What brings on the crisis for the Israelites in Egypt?

- How does Moses' background particularly fit him for leadership?

- Why is Moses in the wilderness territory of Midian?

- When God confronts Moses, what is Moses' response?

- How does God validate Moses' commission?

- Who is Aaron, and what is his function "on the team"?

The God Moses Met

Among peoples of the ancient Near East the *name* of an individual was of great significance. It regularly signified something about the person, and to know the name established a special relationship with the person. This usually meant having some power with the person. In Exodus 3 Moses is told the *particular* name of God. "God" may be used as a general term in our language, usually with a small *g*. This is also true in the Hebrew language, and the general term "gods" frequently occurs. One god, that is, a particular god, was usually known by a particular name.

Scholars do not agree as to the precise translation of the name of God-who-spoke-to-Moses. Check various Bible versions, and note how they render Exodus 3:14. The Hebrew language-form of this name has four consonants: Y H W H. Scholars do agree that the English form of this name should be spelled and pronounced "Yahweh." The NJB uses this form in the Old Testament. All the other versions recommended in *Kerygma: The Bible in Depth* render the name as "the Lord" (with CAPS and SMALL CAPS), the form used in the KJV.[4]

Preparation for the Exodus: the Passover

Now skim Exodus 5-11. Some details may be interesting, but they are not very important for the main point of the narrative. The fact that "magic tricks" did not change Pharaoh's mind suggests that they are not the principal reason that Moses became the leader of God's people. His real power was *possession of the name of God*. Pharaoh's persistent refusal to release the Hebrews increases the dramatic tension and leads up to the Passover and flight from Egypt.

Read **Exodus 12**. The Passover became the central symbol of deliverance for Israel, and modern Judaism still recalls it in an elaborate festival. The background of the latter remembrance is in Exodus 13:1-16. The book of Deuteronomy contains theological reflections upon these early events. **Deuteronomy 6:20-23** retells the significance of Passover.

The Exodus Event

Now comes the second act of the drama in which GOD SAVES A PEOPLE. The narrative is sketchy. The purpose is not to preserve precise details for a historical record but to declare God's saving action by which God's people begin their long trek to nationhood. Read the story in **Exodus 14**.

---

4 Extreme sensitivity to the holiness and power of the name of God led Jews in reading to substitute the word "Lord" for YHWH, and the old Greek translation usually followed this substitution. The term "Jehovah" came from combining the vowels of the Hebrew word for "Lord" with the consonants YHWH.

The place of this deliverance has been associated traditionally with the Red Sea (locate it on a map), but the background of the Hebrew name for the place and geographical hints in the text suggest that the crossing was north of what we now call the Red Sea in an area more appropriately called the Sea of Reeds.[5] The exact details of what took place and how it happened are not really the main concern of the text; the result and its lasting meaning for Israel are what is most important. The deliverance by Yahweh is the kernel of the passage.[6]

From a relatively early time Israel celebrated the story of her salvation in religious rites. **Exodus 15:1-21** recalls such a celebration. Two lines from this song, verses 20, 21, are considered by scholars to be one of the earliest memories from Israel's literary tradition. Note that this piece is attributed to Moses' sister Miriam.

From the Exodus Onward

From Exodus 15:22 through Chapter 18 there are stories of what took place on the journey to Mount Sinai. Scan these quickly. Several incidents are recalled in the New Testament. There you will read about manna and about water from the rock. Remember these details for future reference. They are among God's saving acts on behalf of the Hebrew people.

Our study continues to be selective, for it is not possible to cover every detail in the Bible literature even though we are undertaking study-in-depth. Several criteria determine the choice of which texts we shall study. (1) The text should clarify or illustrate the theme being studied. (2) We should become familiar with Old Testament passages that have been used pointedly or creatively in the New Testament. (3) Details that contribute to a useful knowledge of the Bible whole are important. This last category includes well-known stories and frequently quoted passages that contribute to what we have referred to as biblical literacy.

Some of the narratives about Sinai and the further wanderings in the wilderness will be examined under other themes. Here we bring together references to the Passover and exodus that are found in other books of the Old Testament. For this survey we shall mention a large number of references from Bible books that are to be studied later. This is to highlight the importance of the subject. Read as much as you can find time for.

---

5 See the footnotes in NRSV. On the map of Egypt and Sinai in the Appendix, this area is in the region marked as "Bitter Lakes."

6 The nature of what we call "miracle" is interesting and no doubt important, but to explore it at this point would surely involve us in theological and perhaps scientific discussion. This would lead us away from our principal purpose in this study, which is to learn about the Bible on its own terms. The Exodus text accepts this event as an act of Yahweh without further explanation, and later texts are concerned with its meaning and not clarification of how it happened.

Passover and Exodus Elsewhere in the Old Testament

The Passover is mentioned in the rest of the Pentateuch among various regulations for the religious and civil life of Israel. Leviticus 23:4-8 and Deuteronomy 16:1-8 contain directives concerning the recurring observance of Passover. Numbers 9:1-14 tells about the second anniversary observance of the deliverance from Egypt. Then rules follow for handling problems that may arise regarding irregularities in observances. A resident alien may join in the festival.

Much later a particularly impressive Passover was celebrated in Jerusalem under King Josiah, a successor of King David. 2 Kings 23:21-23 records the story; 2 Chronicles 35:11-19 has a more elaborate account.

The Old Testament frequently refers to God as the one who delivered Israel from Egypt. The preface to the Ten Commandments[7] reads, *I am the LORD your God, who brought you out of the land of Egypt, out of the house of slavery* (**Exodus 20:2**). In Deuteronomy 5:15 (from a passage where the Ten Commandments are repeated with some small differences) the reason for keeping the Sabbath Day is tied to recollection of Israel's slavery in Egypt. For other references, see Deuteronomy 6:12; Judges 6:8, 9; 1 Samuel 10:18; 12:6; and Psalm 81:10.

When the Israelite people were at the threshold of the Promised Land, they took an oath of allegiance to Yahweh, and they based it on the deliverance from Egypt (Joshua 24:16, 17). When the prophet Jeremiah wanted to mark the beginning of Yahweh's authoritative dealing with Israel, he pointed to that same deliverance (Jeremiah 7:22, 23; 11:7; 34:13). The reference is also common in the Psalms. **Psalm 78:12-16** mentions several events we have noted. Psalm 114 weaves some of the same details in with other material we shall study later. Psalm 135:8, 9 contains more allusions, and 136:10-16 uses the story in a responsive setting.

The prophet Hosea appeals to the people on the basis of God's acts in Egypt (Hosea 11:1; 12:13; 13:4-6). Isaiah offers encouragement of a similar sort (Isaiah 11:16). In the midst of national troubles, other prophets offer assurance of God's deliverance because of the deliverance from Egypt (Ezekiel 45:21; Haggai 2:4, 5; Zechariah 10:10-12). When the Jews returned to their homeland after exile in Babylon, they kept the Passover (Ezra 6:19).

God's people came to understand that it was characteristic for God who had delivered them from Egypt to save them again and again. It is a central insight (=theme) around which their

---

7 The Ten Commandments are examined closely in Theme 7.

understanding of their existence and destiny is set. In the next part of this theme we shall study other experiences of Hebrew national deliverance, and in those stories the exodus is often recalled.[8]

FOR FURTHER STUDY AND REFLECTION

Memory Bank

1. Memorize Deuteronomy 6:20-23. Introduction, Part 2, suggests that you use NRSV, but REB, TEV, NJB, and NAB are good alternatives. Since you have these options, memorization need not be word perfect as long as you learn the sense of the text accurately.

2. It will be helpful to keep a notebook with a record of passages learned and a list of Basic Bible References, plus a few words to remind you of the content of these passages. Many of these passages will be referred to later. Experiment to find what helps your memory most. If you are really serious about understanding the Bible, prepare each part of this program as though you were going to have a written examination on it!

Research

1. Look up the word "Jehovah" in a Bible Dictionary. (The reference may lead you to one or more other articles.) What can you learn about the use of the term today?

2. Ask a Jewish rabbi or another knowledgeable Jewish person how the Passover is celebrated today. What does it mean to modern Jews? What can you learn about its importance for you? (If you cannot make a personal contact with a Jew, read about Passover in a Bible Dictionary or an encyclopedia.)

Reflection

1. If the very ancient stories in this part raise problems for your Christian faith, share these problems in the group session. We have barely begun our study. Be patient. Many things will become clearer as we learn more of the Bible.

2. How do you think God is involved in the troubles of people in the world today? What are some modern parallels to the exodus experience?

3. In your own journey of faith how have you been freed from some kind of slavery? In what ways have you been led into a new life? How was the liberating power of God revealed to you?

---

[8] This line of thought will also be reflected in Theme 2, People Find God Is Faithful.

GOD SAVES A PEOPLE

THEME 1

Deliverance after the Exodus

PART 2

SUMMARY

The experiences of the exodus provided a pattern for interpreting the saving relationship between Yahweh and people. In the years following the exodus Israel was delivered repeatedly from desperate situations in ways that the people understood to be God's acts.

Under the rule of kings, Yahweh was still the power who produced the notable events in which Israel was saved. The prophets became the chief interpreters of this point of view. When the Hebrew nation eventually went into exile, a new exodus became their hope. Still later, after that exodus took place, the Hebrews were again under repressive foreign domination, and God helped them again to achieve political freedom.

BASIC BIBLE REFERENCES

Numbers 20:1-13; 21:4-9
Deuteronomy 1:1-8
Joshua 4
Judges 6, 7
1 Kings 18:17-39
2 Kings 5:1-16
Ezekiel 37:1-14
1 Maccabees 1:1-2:48

WORD LIST

Ark of the Covenant
Baal
Ebenezer
Exile and Restoration
Intertestamental Period
Israel and Judah
Judge
Messiah

From Sinai to the Promised Land

Experiences in the wilderness following the exodus from Egypt were extremely difficult for the unorganized host of people led by Moses and his brother Aaron. Exodus and Leviticus recount various stories and the divine instructions given at Mount Sinai. Some structure for the would-be nation is provided, but the people were still far from being settled in a definite land. There are too many details for us to note them all, so we shall develop just enough outline to give continuity to the stories of deliverance, which are our focus in this part.[1]

The departure from Sinai is described in Numbers 10:11-36. The people were led by a *pillar of cloud by day* and a *pillar of fire by night* (Exodus 13:22). These were evidence of Yahweh's directing presence. The people survived fearful experiences in the wilderness and were saved repeatedly by divine action.[2] Several instances are especially noteworthy because they are recalled later.

Exodus 17:2-7 tells how Yahweh supplied the people's need for water by having Moses strike a rock. **Numbers 20:1-13** recounts a similar story, but in this instance Moses and Aaron displease Yahweh because they take credit for the action. In **Numbers 21:4-9** Yahweh sends *poisonous serpents* because the people are *impatient* and speak *against God and against*

---

1 We shall return to these books in other themes. It is part of our way of study to reinforce familiarity by repeated exposure to many parts of Scripture.

2 On the map of Egypt and Sinai in the Appendix you can trace the route of the journey of the Israelites.

Moses. When Moses prays for deliverance, Yahweh tells him to make a bronze model of the serpents and *set it on a pole*. People who are bitten are saved from death by looking at this figure. Later, Israel meets and defeats in battle Sihon, king of the Amorites, and Og, king of Bashan (see Numbers 21:21-35). These events are remembered later as examples of Yahweh's deliverance (for example, Joshua 9:10).

Finally Israel reaches the east bank of the Jordan River, the threshold of the Promised Land, approximately opposite the city of Jericho (see Numbers 22). There the king of Moab enlists the help of Balaam, who has a reputation for putting effective curses on people. At the end of a long section (through chapter 24) Balaam (influenced by Yahweh) gives Israel a blessing rather than the expected curse. The event is referred to in seven other biblical books. Perhaps the most curious detail in the story is the donkey who talks (Numbers 22:21-35)–a feature that can make one miss the focus of the passage.

Deuteronomy 1:1-8 gives the literary setting for the whole book. Most of Deuteronomy is in the literary form of an oral recital of Israel's history up to the threshold of the Promised Land. The book is attributed to Moses and offers theological interpretation of events. Verse 5 indicates that the book has been edited later. We shall return to Deuteronomy in another theme.

Invasion and Settlement in Canaan

After Moses' death Joshua assumes leadership, and the people of Israel cross the Jordan (Joshua 3:7-17). At a location called Gilgal they erect a memorial monument of twelve stones brought from the east side of the Jordan. Read **Joshua 4**. Notice especially verses 21-24, and recall the role played by the Passover in Israel's remembrance of God's deliverance. Joshua 5:10-12 tells how the first Passover in the Promised Land was observed. From that time on, the *manna*, which had fed them in the wilderness, was no longer provided. Most of the rest of the narrative about the settlement of the new land recounts military offensives. More details will follow later.

After Joshua's death, the settlement led the people to adopt some of the life style of pagan neighbors; and matters began to go badly for Israel. Judges 2:16 says that Yahweh *raised up judges* to deliver the people. In most of these stories the focus is on the human leader. We shall return to them in Theme 5. For now, read the story of Gideon, **Judges 6, 7**, where the part played by Yahweh is prominent.

Deliverance in Samuel's Time

Samuel is sometimes referred to as the last of the judges and the first of the prophets. His career marks a transition in the national life of the Israelites. Their enemies in this period are the Philistines, who inhabited the southwestern part of what we know as Palestine.[3] Samuel is God's designated leader for Israel at this time. At one point the Philistines capture Israel's sacred *ark of the covenant*[4], but it brings them such bad fortune that they return it. Samuel gathers Israel for national penitence and renewal (1 Samuel 7). The Philistines make a military move against them, but Yahweh delivers them. Samuel celebrates the occasion by setting up a memorial stone, which he named *Ebenezer*. (What does the name mean? See the footnote for 1 Samuel 7:12.)

A local hero named Saul rose to be king of Israel (See 1 Samuel 9, 10). We shall study the kings in Theme 6, but here notice Samuel's words in 10:1, *You shall reign over the people of the LORD and you will save them from the hand of their enemies all around*. The narratives about subsequent deliverances make it clear that Yahweh is the deliverer, who saves the people through the kings. After a victory over the Ammonites, Saul declares, *today the LORD has brought deliverance to Israel* (1 Samuel 11:13).

The same theme persists when David becomes king after Saul. For example, 2 Samuel 22 contains *a song on the day when the LORD delivered David from the hand of all his enemies*. Psalm 18, which is attributed to David, is almost identical with this song.[5]

Elijah and Elisha

Deliverance of the people is not always from an outside threat. Under a later king named Ahab, worship of the pagan god Baal threatened Israel's faith. Ahab's queen was Jezebel, from the Phoenician city of Sidon. She worshiped Baal and influenced Ahab to promote that worship. The prophet Elijah confronted the prophets of Baal on Mount Carmel in the presence of a great assembly. Read the story in **1 Kings 18:17-39**. It was a great victory for Yahweh.

Other stories about Elijah's conflict with Ahab and Jezebel illustrate that God saves individuals as well as a people. God's care, however, always is shown in a community connection. In 1 Kings 17 Elijah is on the run from Ahab, and God saves the prophet in the wilderness by sending *ravens* to feed him. Then he is directed to stay with a widow in the

---

3　These people had immigrated earlier from the Aegean basin, and their culture was quite different from Israel's. It is ironic that the name "Palestine" is derived from a Greek form of "Philistia."

4　The making of this ark is recounted in Exodus 25:10-22. We shall study this further in Theme 3, Part 1.

5　For general reference, the time of David's reign is about 1000 B.C. See the chronology chart in the Appendix.

village Zarephath, near the Mediterranean seacoast in Phoenician territory. It is a time of famine, but Yahweh extends the widow's supply of oil and meal to save her and Elijah. After the victory on Mount Carmel, Elijah runs again; but Yahweh sustains him and gives him new orders (See 1 Kings 19).

Dramatic stories of Yahweh's power to save continue with Elisha, Elijah's successor. Read **2 Kings 5:1-16**. Note that Naaman, like the widow of Zarephath, was not an Israelite. Another startling story is in 2 Kings 6:8-23, where God's protection of the prophet is vividly illustrated.

Into Another Slavery

The period of the kings is examined in Theme 6. You may already know that the nation became divided into two kingdoms, north and south, usually referred to as Israel and Judah respectively. The final fall of the Northern Kingdom, Israel, and its suppression by the power of Assyria is related in 2 Kings 17:1-6.[6] Notice the interpretation by the narrator in verses 7, 8 and the striking reference to the deliverance from Egypt. The story continues in 2 Kings 18:9-12.

The Southern Kingdom, Judah, survived for more than another century. During the intervening years God's control and action are emphasized. When the king and the people rely upon God, they are saved from danger. A notable deliverance took place under King Hezekiah. The story is recorded three times: 2 Kings 18:1-19:37; 2 Chronicles 32:1-23; Isaiah 36:1-37:38. Freedom, however, was short-lived.[7] The beginning of Judah's exile to Babylon is related in 2 Kings 24 and 2 Chronicles 36.[8]

The prophet Isaiah was active in Judah, particularly in the reign of Hezekiah. Jeremiah comes along somewhat later. He got into serious trouble for prophesying doom (Jeremiah 37, 38), but his warning soon became reality. Chapters 39 and 52 give particulars.

When God's people encounter trouble, they cry out for deliverance. This ancient cycle is repeated during Judah's exile. Psalm 137 is set in Babylon and illustrates the lament. The despair and hope fill this time and are expressed by the biblical writers from the period.

The prophet Ezekiel gave strong warnings before the exile; but when it came, he turned to hope and visions of restoration for the exiles. **Ezekiel 37:1-14** presents a memorable vision

---

[6] The date for this is 722/721 B.C.

[7] The fall of Jerusalem came in 587 or 586 B.C.

[8] The relationship of Samuel-Kings and Chronicles is somewhat complicated and need not concern us here. Chronicles seems to reflect the viewpoint of Judah and to contain more theological reflection than Samuel-Kings.

of a valley full of dry bones. God promises that the people will surely have new life in their homeland.[9]

Hosea, perhaps more than any other Old Testament prophet, expresses assurance that God will save the people, even in the face of deepest despair. See Hosea 11:1-11; 13:4, 5. Another striking prophetic passage is Joel 2:12-32.

The New Exodus from Exile

The deliverance of God's people from the Babylonian exile offers many parallels to the exodus from Egypt. The two events form a kind of bracket for the story-line of the Old Testament.[10] There is also a geographical bracket, for Egypt was to the west, and Babylon was to the east.[11]

Details of this new exodus are not easily recovered, for the historical references in the biblical records are sketchy. The release became possible after Persia under King Cyrus conquered Babylon. In Isaiah 45:1 Cyrus is called Yahweh's *anointed*; the Hebrew word gives us the term "messiah." The title may seem extravagant, but it shows how strong was the hope for deliverance and the faith that the divine purpose for God's people moves history.

Cyrus decreed amnesty for the Jews and set in motion their restoration to their homeland. Ezra 1 and the book of Nehemiah are both concerned with these events, but the exact relationship between the two is not clear. Although details are sketchy, the rebuilding of the Jerusalem wall and temple is manifestly very important. The book of Haggai and part of Zechariah also deal with the new temple.

Two Later Resources

The narrative half of the book of Daniel (Chapters 1-6) is set in the exile years, but most Bible scholars think that the writing itself is from the second century B.C.[12] This makes it the latest literary record of God's deliverance of God's people in the Old Testament. It tells how God saved Daniel and his friends from the adversities of exile, and it encourages God's people to the same kind of faithfulness that brought deliverance to those men. Two stories are especially well known: deliverance from the *furnace of blazing fire* (Chapter 3) and from *the den of lions* (Chapter 6).

---

9 "Promise" is examined in Theme 2.
10 Check the chronology chart in the Appendix. This second exodus is dated in 538 B.C.
11 The ancient world of the Old Testament is studied in Theme 4.
12 Recall that in Introduction, Part 1 we learned that the Hebrew canon considered the book of Daniel a "Writing," that is, a part of the latest additions to the Old Testament.

Events and religious developments after the Old Testament but before New Testament times are seldom discussed in Bible study courses. One sequence of events, however, is important as background to the political, social, and religious environment of Jesus' life and teaching. After the conquests of Alexander the Great in the middle east (334-323 B.C.), the Jews were confronted by the Greek world and its culture. This new kind of paganism threatened those who were trying to be faithful to the Torah and the Jewish way of life.

A successor of Alexander, Antiochus IV, was king of Syria, which then included Palestine. He called himself "Epiphanes," which means "the glorious." He tried to force Greek culture upon the Jews and to restrict their religious observances. A pious Jew named Mattathias launched a sort of holy war using guerrilla tactics. Under his son Judas, who was given the nickname Maccabeus ("the hammer") the resistance was successful. Read the story in **1 Maccabees 1:1-2:48**. In 1 Maccabees 4:24, 25 the army of Judas gives glory *to Heaven*. This is their way of crediting God with victory. The temple was purified from pagan defilement, and for about a hundred years the Jews had a semblance of self-rule. This period extended from 166 to 63 B.C., when the Roman general Pompey conquered Jerusalem. The fleeting glory of the Maccabean deliverance was surely not forgotten when Jesus' contemporaries were appraising his mission.

FOR FURTHER STUDY AND REFLECTION

Memory Bank

1. Retell in your own words the story of

      a) Gideon
      b) Elijah at Mount Carmel
      c) Ezekiel's vision of the dry bones
      d) Judas Maccabeus

Research

1. Consult a Bible atlas or other resources for information about the wilderness between Egypt and Palestine; between Babylon and Palestine.

2. From a Bible Dictionary gather information about "manna."

3. Investigate the history and culture of the Philistines.

4. Try to find New Testament references to

      a) water from the rock
      b) the serpent on the pole
      c) Elijah and the widow
      d) Elisha and Naaman
      e) Balaam

5. Make a simple outline of events covered in this part. It will be valuable for reference later.

Reflection

1. What connection, if any, do you see between the material in this part and the establishment of the modern state of Israel?

2. What kinds of deliverance may a nation today expect from God? Under what circumstances?

1:2

GOD SAVES A PEOPLE

THEME 1

God's Saving Act in Jesus Christ

PART 3

SUMMARY

The New Testament builds upon a unique event of deliverance, the resurrection of Jesus Christ. This event gave radical significance to Jesus' death by crucifixion. His followers interpreted the crucifixion-resurrection in various ways, both in continuity and in discontinuity with Old Testament traditions, particularly the exodus. A new perception of the people of God emerged. Spiritual identity rather than land and nation became the focus, and this fostered a mission to the world. The focus throughout is Jesus Christ as the source of salvation.

BASIC BIBLE REFERENCES
Matthew 28:18-20
Mark 15
Luke 4:16-30; 24
Acts 1:8; 2:14-42
Romans 6:1-11

WORD LIST
Crucifixion
Day of Preparation
Sabbath
Samaritan
Transfiguration

How the Good News Started

The New Testament, like the Old Testament, has two beginnings, one as literature and another as life experience. The literary beginning is a genealogical table in Matthew 1. The life experience is a stupendous act of deliverance that marked a new era in the relationship between God and people. In a sense, a new exodus took place, but this time the dramatic event had a new range.

The first exodus impressively ushered a people into new freedom, marked by their physical experience under a great leader, Moses. The freedom was concrete. It produced a people whose new status was national, geographical, and religious, all at the same time. In somewhat lesser degree the exodus from Babylonian exile was similar.

The New Testament exodus was not immediately so obvious. There was no physical deliverance of a group of people in a society. No politically independent nation was formed. No geographical land was promised. The new company of people was convinced that in one momentous event God had delivered them decisively from a slavery that was marked by evil, sin, and death. The people of God were suddenly newly defined. Their continuity and discontinuity with the people who came from the old exodus experiences are the subject of much of the New Testament.

The Crucifixion. The revolutionary sequence of events began in a most unlikely manner. Read **Mark 15**. The story of Jesus' crucifixion and death hardly needs elaboration. All four Gospels recount the ordeal, each contributing some unique details. The political overtones are evident in the Roman use of the term *King of the Jews*, which the Gospel of John says offended the Jews (John 19:15, 19-22). The cross, which was such a horrible sign of Roman cruelty, political degradation, and human suffering became a revered symbol in the Christian church. Christians believe that Jesus was God present as a human being. That God should thus join with people and then go to the cross on their behalf is almost beyond human thought. But God crowned the love shown on the cross by the victory secured through the resurrection.

The Resurrection. Read **Luke 24**. What do verses 8, 32, and 45 suggest to you about the significance of the resurrection and postresurrection appearances of Jesus? For further insight read Acts 1:1-14.[1] To understand how important Paul thought these appearances were, read 1 Corinthians 15:1-11. Now read **Acts 2:14-42**. The Jewish festival of Pentecost came seven weeks after the resurrection. God's Spirit filled Jesus' followers,[2] and Peter became the spokesman-interpreter of the occasion. In his sermon Peter quotes Joel 2:28-32. What significance can you find in this? In Acts 2:22-36 Peter summarizes the Jesus-events. What point do you see in this?

Continuity with the Old Testament

Luke 9:28-36 recounts the transfiguration[3] of Jesus. In verses 30, 31 Luke writes that *Moses and Elijah...were speaking [to Jesus] of his departure*. The Greek word translated *departure* is *exodus*. It is noteworthy that the exodus idea here refers to the end of Jesus' ministry. A reader steeped in traditions of the Old Testament should immediately make the connection between the climax of Jesus' life work and God's pattern of deliverance.

The Gospels indicate that this interpretation originated with Jesus himself. The association with Moses here and elsewhere is one sign. In the wilderness stories we noted the serpent on a pole. John places a specific reference to this story in the narrative of Jesus' interview with Nicodemus (John 3:14, 15).

Perhaps the most important connection is the deliberate choice of Passover season for the Jerusalem trip that led to Jesus' death. Mark tells three times that Jesus foresaw that he

---

[1] Acts is Volume 2 of Luke's writings (see also Luke 1:1-4). The story takes up where Luke 24 leaves off. Why do you think these two books were separated in the final form of the New Testament?

[2] God's Spirit is discussed in Theme 3.

[3] This word means "change of appearance." It is regularly used in referring to the experience described in this passage. The story occurs also in Matthew 17:1-8 and Mark 9:2-8, but the word exodus is used only by Luke.

would suffer and die (8:31; 9:30-32; 10:32-34). All four Gospels specifically set the events of Jesus' last week at Passover time (Matthew 26:1, 2, 17-19; Mark 14:1, 2, 12-16; Luke 22:1, 7-13; John 13:1, 19:14). Jewish traditions both then and now associate Elijah with the coming of the messiah. On the basis of Malachi 4:5, Elijah is expected *before the...day of the LORD comes*, and this is memorialized in the Passover celebration. Recall also **Mark 15:36.**

The cry in **Mark 15:34** has often presented difficulty for interpreters, for indeed God had not *forsaken* Jesus. The words are from Psalm 22:1, and a careful reading of the rest of the psalm—which Jesus surely knew well—moves from despair to reassurance. Note verses 4, 5. There is description of terrible suffering, but in verse 24 God's response is affirmed. The final verse declares *future generations will...proclaim...deliverance*. Continuity with the Old Testament helps us understand the gospel.

Discontinuity with the Old Testament

At the same time, what was specifically new about God's saving act in Jesus Christ is best seen in how it differs from the Old Testament traditions. The crucifixion-resurrection was almost immediately interpreted as deliverance from a slavery, not of the body, but of the mind and spirit. The deliverance produced freedom from *sin*. Look again at **Acts 2:37-40**. *Repent and be baptized*, Peter proclaims. These are the steps to be taken in response to the sacrifice and lordship of Jesus Christ. The outcome of this is divine forgiveness of sins.

Paul develops and emphasizes this interpretation. Read **Romans 6:1-11**. Paul declares that deliverance from slavery to sin is directly connected to the death and resurrection of Jesus and its effect on those who accept Jesus' lordship. Much of the letter to the Romans deals with this theme. In 3:9-18 there is a collection of quotations from the Old Testament (mostly from Psalms) that indicate that slavery to sin is a universal problem. Jesus uses the same idea in John 8:34-36.

While we are emphasizing one thread of thought, it is necessary to add that GOD'S SAVING ACT IN JESUS CHRIST is described and interpreted by New Testament writers in other ways. What Jesus accomplished was so overwhelming that the early church explained the experience in a variety of ways. Remember, therefore, that when the text speaks in one way about the message, the whole message is assumed. The resurrection was, we might say, the trigger that set the church in motion and mission; but the first Christians understood clearly that Jesus' life and teaching, the cross, and the resurrection were totally bound together.

Since they believed that the true God selected a special people in the exodus, it is natural that the New Testament frequently picks up this thread of history. The early church was convinced that it was in continuous relationship with that history. Exactly what this relationship involved became a complicated matter for New Testament writers. Paul is particularly concerned with this question. He deals with it pointedly in Romans 9-11, which we shall look at again below. For now note 11:1, 2. The rapid spread of the Christian church in the Mediterranean world showed that God was doing something new with a delivered people.

It was a complex problem to relate the old and the new events. The Gospel writers found many interesting connections in addition to the extensive use Jesus made of the Old Testament. An example is Matthew's story about the flight of the holy family to Egypt (Matthew 2:13-15). It is connected with Hosea 11:1 to indicate that Jesus made a symbolic exodus from Egypt. We may understand that he is a new representative of God's people, one who later will lead them symbolically out of the universal captivity to sin. In Matthew 4:2 Jesus' temptation in the wilderness is preceded by *forty days and forty nights*,[4] which may remind us of Moses' stay on Mount Sinai (Exodus 24:18) or the wilderness journey of the Israelites for *forty years* (Joshua 5:6). In Acts 7:17-38, 52 Stephen, an early church leader, retells the exodus story to show connections with Jesus (6:13, 14).

Jesus' New Message

The Israelites of the first exodus were quite exclusive. Their relationship with Yahweh set them apart, and it was probably important in the early years of their nationhood that they should emphasize this difference from their neighbors. Their early laws stressed kindness to *resident aliens* (as in Exodus 22:21 and Leviticus 19:33, 34). Jews at the time of Jesus, however, had become quite narrow in their feelings against both non-Jews in their midst and neighboring peoples.

Jesus' teaching and his dealing with persons quite clearly show that he believed God to be concerned about all people. Very early in his public ministry Jesus spoke in the synagogue of his home town Nazareth. Read **Luke 4:16-30**. The reading from the prophets that day was to be from the book of Isaiah.[5] Jesus selected Isaiah 61:1, 2, a message of deliverance for oppressed people. From our perspective, we can see that this was a program for Jesus' ministry. His further comments, however—we might call them illustrations in a sermon—turned his hearers against him, and they ran him out of the village. The Old Testament passages he used told of deliverance for non-Jews. (Can you imagine a similar story about a Syrian being told in an Israeli synagogue today?)

---

[4] Notes in a study Bible usually show parallel passages in the first three Gospels. Here, for example, the parallels are Mark 1:13 and Luke 4:1, 2.

[5] Synagogue worship included a passage from the Law (Pentateuch) and a passage from the Prophets. This is true today in synagogue services.

Jesus' message was for all who would listen. Several incidents from his ministry deal kindly with Samaritans, a neighboring people despised and shunned by the Jews. There is a lengthy account in John 4 about Jesus' conversation with a Samaritan woman at a well in Samaria. Also, one of his best-known stories is usually called "The Parable of the Good Samaritan" (Luke 10:30-37). Jesus' open-minded attitude led his critics on one occasion to label him a *Samaritan*, which they meant as an insult (John 8:48). Perhaps the best-known summary of GOD'S SAVING ACT IN JESUS CHRIST is John 3:16, where *everyone* is the key word.

Paul and God's New Salvation

For Paul this open offer became crucial, and it affected his whole life and thought. The story of how he changed from a narrow, hate-filled rabbi into the apostle to the Gentiles is treated in Theme 5. More than any other early church leader Paul saw how far-reaching was the new deliverance brought about by Jesus. The most extended discussion of the matter is in Romans 9-11, an important but difficult passage. There Paul carefully explores the relationship between Jews and Gentiles as people of God. To the surprise of God's people in Israel (Jews), a host of people outside Israel (Gentiles, non-Jews) is flocking to accept God's saving offer. At 9:25, 26 Paul refers to Hosea 2:23, and 1:10, when he says Yahweh declares, *Those who were not my people, I will call "my people...."*[6] This direct relationship between the prophet's words and the apostle's application is a good illustration of what "fulfillment" means. In Romans 11:26 Paul declares that *all Israel will be saved*, and this comes almost at the end of the long consideration of how both Jews and Gentiles are people of God.

The new people saved by God in Jesus Christ are a body united by God's Spirit; they are not a national nor an ethnic group. It is therefore natural that they should recall the saving event in terms of what Jesus Christ did. Instead of *God, who brought you out of the land of Egypt, out of the house of slavery*,[7] Paul writes of *God...who raised [Jesus Christ] from the dead*.[8] This act has the power to bring new life to everyone who is willing to receive it from God (1 Corinthians 6:14; 2 Corinthians 4:14), and so it is good news.[9] See how Paul uses these words together with *salvation* (the noun that means the act of saving; deliverance) in Romans 1:16. Compare this with John 3:16, 17.

Salvation and Mission

The New Testament makes it clear that this salvation is meant for all humanity, so inevitably God's people have to understand that they have a mission to take this good news to all the

---

6   Hosea 2:23 is quoted also in 1 Peter 2:10 in a passage that emphasizes the new relationship of God and Christian people.
7   Exodus 20:2.
8   Galatians 1:1; 1 Thessalonians 1:10.
9   "Good news" is a synonym for "gospel."

world. A concise statement of this is the "great commission," **Matthew 28:18-20**. Another summary, **Acts 1:8**, serves as a practical outline of that book. Paul had a unique sense of mission, to which he refers repeatedly in his letters; among many examples, see 1 Thessalonians 2:1, 2.

FOR FURTHER STUDY AND REFLECTION

Memory Bank

1. Among the many references that should be remembered from this part, several levels may be distinguished:

    - some verses should be *memorized* word-for-word;

    - the content of some verses may be *recalled* without word-for-word precision;

    - some references are to be *identified* (chapter and verse numbers as appropriate).

Matthew 28:18-20	The "great commission"—memorize
Mark 15	The crucifixion—identify
Luke 4	Jesus' sermon in Nazareth—identify
Luke 24	Emmaus road encounter—identify/recall
John 3:16	Best-known verse—memorize
Acts 1:8	Outline of Acts—recall
Acts 2	Peter's Pentecost sermon—identify
Romans 6:1-11	Application of resurrection—recall
Romans 9—11	Jews and Gentiles—identify

Research

1. Why did the apostolic band feel they had to elect a successor to Judas (Acts 1:15-26)? What criteria did they use in making their choice?

2. In a Bible Dictionary read the information on the Samaritans. With this in mind, review John 4 and Luke 10:30-37 to see what new meanings emerge.

3. Check the word "gospel" in a concordance. Note references that you think shed light on this theme.

4. Compare the list of resurrection appearances in 1 Corinthians 15:5-8 with those recorded in the Gospels and Acts. (Look for the emphases, not for differences.)

Reflection

1. Explain in your own words why Christian creeds confess the Old Testament to be an essential part of the Bible.

2. There is a sense in which the Gospels came into being backwards. Explain. What are some reasons for beginning this part with Luke 24?

3. What are some ways GOD'S SAVING ACT IN JESUS CHRIST affects people now? How can you apply this to yourself?

GOD SAVES A PEOPLE

THEME 1

Deliverance of the Church

PART 4

SUMMARY

As Israel was delivered many times after the exodus, so Christians of the early church were delivered again and again after the great saving act in Jesus Christ. The book of Acts gives many instances, and Paul's career is full of examples. The scope of God's deliverance thus spreads to take in individuals, groups, and communities. Ultimately, the world is the goal. Confrontation with imperial political power leads to victory as the exalted Christ is seen in the visions of the book of Revelation.

BASIC BIBLE REFERENCES
Mark 2:1-12; 13:1-13
Acts 4:1-22; 12:1-19
1 Peter 4:12-19
Revelation 1; 3:20, 21; 5

WORD LIST
Apocalyptic writing
Doxology

A Deliverance Model in Jesus' Ministry

We noted in Part 3 how the New Testament moves away from an emphasis on deliverance of nation and land. This does not mean that now all things happen in the realm of the spirit. There are dramatic, physical-life experiences. Salvation brings people into the church, which exists in nations and lands but is not tied to them.

The link between physical and spiritual deliverance is already marked in the ministry of Jesus. **Mark 2:1-12** tells about a paralyzed man brought to Jesus for healing. Jesus' first words to the infirm man declare that his sins are forgiven! Unfriendly critics in the crowd challenge Jesus' right to say such a thing. What is the logic of Jesus' response? At this stage in his public career, it appears that Jesus is regarded mostly as a teacher and charismatic healer, or even a popular prophet.

In associating physical and spiritual deliverance Jesus reflects the Hebrew view that human life is one: body and spirit are not to be treated separately from one another. For further examples in the Gospels, see Matthew 8:16; Luke 8:1, 2; John 5:14.

First Years of the Church

Read **Acts 4:1-22**. Try to sense the excitement in the church at that time. Note how it is heightened by confidence that God will deliver these new Christians out of any and all adversity. At first, trouble comes mainly from local Jewish leaders who think that a heretical movement is mushrooming under their noses. They oppose it, sometimes violently.

Consider some details in this episode. What caused the first clash (4:1, 2)? What would be the particular concern of the Sadducees in this matter (compare Mark 12:18)? Note the cross-and-victory theme (4:10). The Old Testament quotation in Acts 4:11 is from Psalm 118:22; it appears also in the synoptic Gospels and 1 Peter 2:7. Acts 4:12 is a succinct statement of the good news about Jesus' saving power.

The story of Ananias[1] and Sapphira, Acts 5:1-11, is startling and difficult. The consequence of their dishonesty is very severe. The impact of their discovered guilt may have contributed to their deaths. The incident must have been seen as a deliverance of the church from danger arising within its own community. (Stories of a similar nature occur in the early history of Israel.)

The rest of Acts 5 tells how the apostles were arrested for their public preaching. They were delivered from prison by an angel and continued their witness. A wise Pharisee named Gamaliel[2] makes a prophetic judgment in 5:33-39, and the apostles are freed to continue their ministry.

Acts 12:1-19 recounts how Peter is delivered from prison on another occasion. Observe several details. The first record of the martyrdom of an apostle is in 12:2. Verses 5 and 12 show an effective solidarity between Peter and the local church people. Verse 11 declares that Peter's freedom has come from the LORD. There is no further importance attached to the remarkable circumstances of the deliverance. The humorous incident in 12:13-16 shows how vividly the church remembered the event.

Acts 16:16-40 tells about still another release from prison. Paul and his companion Silas are engaged in a mission trip that takes them to the Macedonian city of Philippi. There they are jailed, but an earthquake opens the prison. Since the jailer was held personally responsible for his prisoners, it is a moment of intense drama. The jailer asks Paul and Silas, *Sirs, what must I do to be saved?* (verse 30). Consider the various implications of the question. The answer leads the jailer to *become a believer in God* (verse 34).

The most ironic drama of all is that the church has been, in a way, saved from Paul himself. The story is first related in Acts 8:1-3; 9:1-22.[3] He had begun his public career as a Jewish leader by violently opposing the church. After a confrontation with Jesus in a vision

---

1 Two other men are named Ananias in Acts; this one is mentioned only here.
2 He was Paul's teacher. See Acts 22:3.
3 This event is so important in Acts that it is retold in two other passages, Acts 22:3-16 and 26:9-19. Paul also refers to it in several of his letters.

on the way from Jerusalem to Damascus, Paul becomes the most ardent advocate of the mission of the church.

Paul as Interpreter of Salvation in Christ

GOD'S SAVING ACT IN JESUS CHRIST is prominent in Paul's letters. The death of a holy man might seem to be a strange way to bring about deliverance, so the apostle repeatedly explains how this has become true precisely in the case of Jesus. Sometimes his discussion relates closely to this theme; sometimes the connection is indirect.

The term "messiah" is applied to Jesus sparingly outside of Pauline writings. "Messiah" comes from a Hebrew word meaning "anointed one." The term "Christ" comes from a Greek word with the same meaning; so the terms are practically equivalent. A suffering, dying messiah was next to impossible for Jewish traditions to accept. Jesus' victory over death, however, made it possible to apply Messiah/Christ to him. In the New Testament it is Paul who makes this name prominent.[4] It was the transition from the Jewish environment to the Greek-speaking world that brought "Christ" into common use. Here, then, is a strong link with the Old Testament hope of a deliverer. Note Acts 5:42 in NRSV.

We have already proposed that the truth about salvation is greater than any one attempt to define it. Indeed, it is greater than the sum of all descriptions. Paul addresses this matter in 1 Corinthians 1:17-25. Note especially verse 18. A major part of this letter is directed toward problems in the local church. The Corinthians need to be saved from themselves! In chapter 5 he deals with a particularly difficult situation. The treatment he prescribes is set in Passover language; see 5:7, 8.

Salvation, the Church, and the World

The deliverance of both individuals and communities is always in view in the New Testament, for the saved individual is always set in a Christian community. 1 Timothy 1:15, for instance, concerns the saving of particular persons. Ephesians 5:25 specifically speaks of the church. Sometimes a text is not entirely clear in the English version, for "you" may be singular or plural; for example, in Ephesians 2:8 the Greek original has a plural pronoun.

The full scope of the deliverance brought about by Jesus Christ was not immediately clear. The first followers were closely bound both ethnically and geographically. As they spread, however, all limits were broken. Soon the Gentile world in the eastern Mediterranean—modern Lebanon, Turkey, and Greece—was included. Peter had a dramatic experience in

---

4 About 72 percent of the occurrences of "Christ" are in the Pauline letters.

preaching to a Roman centurion, Cornelius (Acts 10, 11), and Paul's labors and travels were particularly effective in spreading the good news.

Paul did not foresee a time in which the church or its individual members would be in a life-and-death struggle with political world powers. In Romans 13 Paul expresses support for the Roman government. He took advantage of the privileges of his Roman citizenship. Examples are in Acts 16:37, 38 and 22:25-29; see also 1 Timothy 2:1, 2.

1 Peter 4:12-19 implies a different situation, where it appears that God's people may risk punishment by the state simply because of professing their faith. **Mark 13:1-13** warns of just such a danger. Note carefully the setting of Jesus' discourse in this passage from Mark: Jesus is discussing the future of the Jerusalem temple—which was in fact destroyed by a Roman army in A.D. 70.

The Book of Revelation

The last book of the Bible[5] foreshadows complete disruption of the life of the church. Read **Revelation 1:1-11**. Here some details that can be readily understood are mixed with material that surely requires explanation. Most of the language you find strange is in a literary form known as "apocalyptic," a word that refers to "revelation" of hidden matters[6]. The book is often called "the Apocalypse," for this word and "Revelation" mean the same thing. "Apocalypse" comes from a Greek root and "Revelation" from the Latin equivalent.

Apocalyptic writing is by nature somewhat obscure, for it deals with visions and with the future. We therefore need more help to understand this book than we do with much of the rest of the New Testament. We introduce it here because its message deals with the victory of Jesus Christ and the deliverance of the church. The doxology—an ascription of *glory* (1:5, 6)—declares that Jesus Christ *freed us from our sins by his blood.*

John, the seer who wrote the Revelation,[7] was in exile because of his Christian witness (1:9). The message of the book is directed to seven churches in a kind of circuit of which Ephesus was the anchor-city. Locate them on a map. The entire book is to be read and heard in a congregational setting: note 1:3, *the one who reads aloud...those who hear.*

Revelation 1:12-20 assures the seven churches that their future is guaranteed by their divine LORD. Verse 18 makes it clear that the *one like the Son of Man* is the exalted Jesus Christ.

---

5 That is, the last book in our canon of scripture. Part 4 of Theme 10 is devoted entirely to this book.
6 You can study the term "apocalyptic" in a reference book such as an encyclopedia or a Bible Dictionary, but for now you do not need detailed information.
7 His identity is uncertain. We shall take up the question in Theme 10, Part 4.

His death and resurrection give assurance that he has control over the destiny of the churches. The *mystery* in verse 20 reveals that he is actually among them and holds their safety in his *right hand*. This assurance is essential to the interpretation of all the rest of the book.

Chapters 2 and 3 contain messages to each of the seven churches. Each little letter concludes with a promise of a gift for *everyone who conquers*. In **Revelation 3:20, 21** the Christ declares that the promises are good because *I myself conquered*.

In Chapter 4 the scene changes to heaven. John attempts to describe in words the strange details of heavenly scenery. He has had a vision of what, in the very nature of the case, is finally indescribable. After all, how can one declare in words the greatness of the Creator God?

Read **Revelation 5**. First, *a Lion* is introduced, described by two Old Testament allusions. Then in a startling switch at 5:6 there is no Lion but *a Lamb*. The Lamb alone can open the seven-sealed scroll, which will reveal the future that John so desperately wants to know. The Lamb is *standing as if it had been slaughtered*.[8] The description would fit the Passover lamb. John the Baptist calls Jesus *the Lamb of God* (John 1:29, 36), and Paul calls Christ *our paschal lamb* in 1 Corinthians 5:7. The death of the Lamb has brought about the deliverance and victory of God's people, and therefore the Lamb can reveal the destiny of all creation (that is, *open the scroll*; Revelation 5:2, 9, 10). Revelation 4 praises God the Creator; Chapter 5 proclaims God the Redeemer.

It requires a separate course to study the book of Revelation in detail.[9] Here we may note briefly several more illustrations that show how the book is a fitting climax to this theme. In Chapter 7 two great throngs of people are saved. First there is an elaborate, symbolic counting of people saved on earth. Then there is *a great multitude that no one could count*, who appear before the heavenly throne. They are *robed in white, with palm branches in their hands*, both symbolic of victory (7:9). There are three hymns, the first of which begins, *Salvation belongs to our God...and to the Lamb* (7:10). They *have come out of the great ordeal* (7:14), which is described in the next eleven chapters.

In Revelation 15:3 a throng of victors *sing the song of Moses...and the song of the Lamb* (see Exodus 15:1). The whole book of Revelation is filled with Old Testament phrases and ideas; there are literally hundreds of such references.

---

8   Check this verse in REB and NJB.
9   The Kerygma Program offers such a course, *Revelation: Visions for the Church in Crisis*.

Revelation 19:10 declares that *the testimony of Jesus is the spirit of prophecy*. Everything in the experience and future of God's new people is bound up with the proclamation about Jesus. All that Christians hope for is already secured by the victory of Jesus Christ. The final chapters of the book contain visions of how it will all turn out. God says, *See, I am making all things new* (21:5).

FOR FURTHER STUDY AND REFLECTION

Memory Bank and Research

1. Theme 1 in some ways offers the essence of *Kerygma: The Bible in Depth*. It is important that you have a good grasp of the theme. This is a good time, therefore, to review all four parts, both Resource Book text and Bible texts.

2. How has the study of this theme helped you to understand the Preface and the Introduction better?

Reflection

1. Where and how do the biblical insights in this theme affect the life of God's people today? Make notes, which you may share with others in your study group.

PEOPLE FIND GOD IS FAITHFUL

Promise and Covenant in the Hebrew Scriptures

THEME 2

PART 1

SUMMARY
Behind the exodus event were traditions that told how God had established a relationship with a particular people, namely Abraham and his descendants. At Sinai this relationship was formalized in a covenant, and the responsibilities of the people were set forth. Later God promised David that his descendants would always sit on the throne of Israel. The prophets became the interpreters of Israel's covenant obligations, and they denounced unfaithfulness in leaders and people. Beyond such unfaithfulness and the exile that resulted, some prophets looked to the time of a new covenant.

BASIC BIBLE REFERENCES
Genesis 12:1-7; 15; 17:1-22; 28:10-22
Exodus 6:2-8; 24:3-8
Numbers 14:18, 19
Deuteronomy 26:5-9
2 Samuel 7:1-17
Isaiah 55:1-5
Jeremiah 31:31-34
Hosea 11
Amos 3:1-3
Micah 4:1-8

WORD LIST
Canaan
Circumcision
Covenant
Cubit
Patriarchs

Long Before the Exodus

Theme 1 looks at the Bible from a particular perspective: the experiences and memories of a people who believed that God delivered them from slavery, danger, and despair. The Hebrews remembered the Passover-exodus experience as the foundation of their national identity and destiny, and they continued to celebrate it.

The exodus experience, however, was not the first time these people became aware of God. It is clear that they already possessed stories and traditions that were later recorded in their sacred literature. This background was surely a factor that helped Moses to convince the Hebrews that his call and leadership were God's will for him and them.

Several of these ancient stories told how God had acted on their behalf, and they added assurance that their future was bound up with God's faithfulness. The well-known story of Noah and the ark is recounted in Genesis 6-9.[1] Several particular details should be noted here. In 8:21, 22 God promises *never again* to *curse the ground* nor to *destroy every living creature* as had occurred in the great flood. In 9:8, 9 God declares, *I am establishing my covenant with you and your descendants*. The rainbow is designated as a guarantee of this covenant. God tells Noah, *This is the sign of the covenant that I have established between me and all flesh that is on the earth* (9:17).

---
1 Genesis 1-11 is studied in Theme 3.

God's simple declaration is taken as a guarantee of the future. The word *covenant* is often used to refer to such promises of God. It is a key term in this theme, and we shall develop our understanding of it as we progress through this study.

Abraham and Family

The story of Abraham is told in Genesis, Chapters 12-25. Stories about his immediate descendants are recounted in Chapters 26-50. At this point we shall study only a few of these stories, but we shall return to more of them later. **Genesis 12:1-7** recounts the beginning of the special relationship between God and Abraham's clan.

Genesis 15 tells the strange story of the establishment of the covenant between God and Abram (as he was called at first). The important detail here is the initiative on God's part: God makes a covenant to be faithful. In **Genesis 17:1-22** the covenant is extended to include a demand for faithfulness on the part of Abraham and his descendants. Circumcision becomes a sign or symbol of this covenant relationship, and it has survived until today as a distinctive mark of Jewish religion.

In Genesis 17:5 Abraham's original name is changed. See the NRSV footnotes for the significance of the two names. His wife's name is also changed, for (you should remember) names were very important personal identifications among the Hebrews. A story is also told of how their son Isaac got his name (again, see the footnote in the NRSV). Ishmael was the son of Abraham and Sarah's slave Hagar and thus was a "second-class" descendant. We note Ishmael because later traditions make him the ancestor of Arab tribes that became enemies of Israel.

The covenant promise is renewed to Isaac (Genesis 26:1-5) and to his son Jacob. Read **Genesis 28:10-22**. Here is the story of Jacob's vision at Bethel (again, see the footnote for the appropriate meaning of the name). Later, God renews the promise and gives Jacob a new name, Israel, which becomes the family and national name (Genesis 35:9-15).

The story of Jacob's family revolves around the career of his son Joseph. The story is told in Genesis 37-50. Joseph became a slave in Egypt but, in a remarkable series of events, rose to be a very high-ranking official there.[2] During a famine Jacob and his family traveled to Egypt to join Joseph, and this accounts for the fact that *the descendants of Israel* were eventually enslaved there (for details see Exodus 1). God, however, promised that they would become great and eventually leave Egypt (Genesis 46:1-4).

---

2 There is another look at his story in Theme 5.

The promise to Abraham and the covenant that certified it provided the basis of assurance for the exodus. At the burning bush in Midian, Yahweh was identified as *the God of your ancestors, the God of Abraham, the God of Isaac, and the God of Jacob* (Exodus 3:15). The promise of a land (3:17) is elaborated in **Exodus 6:2-8**, where the covenant with the patriarchs[3] is repeated. In Exodus 13:5 the promise is made even more emphatic, for it is said that Yahweh *swore* to give the land to the people. Oath-taking, often calling on God as the guarantor, was common in the biblical world. Thus God's own oath is the ultimate certainty.

The Covenant Obligation of the People

A covenant usually implies two consenting parties. So far we have considered Yahweh's part. It must occur to you that the people have some obligation in the covenant relationship. Read **Exodus 24:3-8**. When Israel camps at Mount Sinai, Yahweh gives Moses *words* that are to regulate Israel's life, and these are referred to as *the book of the covenant*. As in Genesis 15, the covenant is ratified by a blood offering. This material is studied in more detail in Theme 7.

Unfortunately, the people were not always faithful to their part of the covenant. Moses meets with Yahweh again on the mountain. While he is gone, the people make a gold *image of a calf*, to which they offer worship. The story is in Exodus 32. Yahweh is angry and threatens to destroy the people. Moses pleads with Yahweh and reminds Yahweh of the covenant oath made to the patriarchs. *And the LORD changed his mind about the disaster that he planned to bring on his people.*[4]

This narrative reflects the primitive view that God has human-like emotions and may be argued with. On the other hand, it clearly affirms that GOD IS FAITHFUL, even in the face of the people's unfaithfulness. Although there are covenant requirements for the people to fulfill, God keeps the covenant promises whether or not mutual obligations are met.

In Numbers 13, 14 another story illustrates the same truth. Some time after Sinai is left behind, spies are sent into the Promised Land, Canaan, to see whether it would be safe to move in. After forty days the spies bring back a very *unfavorable report*—except for the optimistic, minority opinion of Joshua and Caleb. The people then raise *a loud cry* and wish they could *go back to Egypt*. Again Yahweh threatens to punish the people, but Moses quotes

---

3 "Patriarchs" is often used to refer to Abraham, Isaac, and Jacob. Sometimes Joseph and his brothers are included.

4 Exodus 32:34, NRSV. Several modern versions make a conscious effort to eliminate "masculine-oriented language related to people, so far as this can be done without distorting passages that reflect the historical situation of ancient patriarchal culture" (Bruce M. Metzger, chair of the NRSV committee). It is clear in Scripture that God is not a masculine being (see Genesis 1:27). English, however, lacks a third-person pronoun that includes both masculine and feminine, so it is practically impossible to avoid the use of one or the other. NRSV, REB, NJB, and TEV all elect to follow the original texts, which use masculine pronouns. Bear this note in mind where you read such texts.

Yahweh's promise (from Exodus 34:5-8). Read **Numbers 14:18, 19**. Yahweh declares, then, that Israel will get to the Promised Land; but the generation that *gathered together against me* will die in the wilderness.

Deuteronomy contains a review of Israel's experiences in the wilderness and restates the people's obligations to Yahweh. **Deuteronomy 26:5-9** is sometimes called a "little creed" because it expresses so neatly Israel's understanding of who they were. Chapters 26-28 order rituals, and these are constant reminders of Yahweh's promises. The people's response includes sacrificial offerings. (Note Deuteronomy 29:1.)

After the people enter the Promised Land, the promises and obligations are repeatedly renewed. Just before his death, Joshua, Moses' successor as leader, recounts the covenant promises and challenges the people to serve Yahweh. He bases his appeal upon Yahweh's past faithfulness, and the covenant relationship is renewed. (See Joshua 24.)

Note that so far God's covenant promise principally concerns children/family and land/nation. The Hebrew people thought mostly in concrete terms. Thus circumcision, the covenant sign given to Abraham, was physical. Only later shall we observe abstract or "spiritual" promises.

The Covenant with David

In Themes 5 and 6 we shall study Israelite national life under their kings. Here it is important to look at a special covenant promise made to King David. Read **2 Samuel 7:1-17**. Notice that *house* is used to refer both to a temple and to David's dynasty. Yahweh assures David that his royal line will continue forever. In a little psalm called *the last words of David*, the king says, *God...has made with me an everlasting covenant, ordered in all things and secure* (2 Samuel 23:5).

When David's son Solomon becomes king, he builds a great temple and moves Israel's sacred symbols into it. In his public address at the temple dedication he repeatedly refers to Yahweh's faithfulness to promise and covenant (see 1 Kings 8:14-26). Yahweh responds by renewing the covenant promise but adds a warning that the king and the people must keep the commandments and statutes (1 Kings 9:1-9).

Several Psalms reflect this relationship between Yahweh and the king. They are often called "royal psalms." Psalm 2 is a notable example. Other illustrations are Psalms 18:49, 50; 72:1-19; 89:19-37; 132; 144:9-15.

The Prophets and Human Failure

A covenant is an agreement of relationship between parties. PEOPLE FIND GOD IS FAITHFUL, but the people must keep their side of the agreement. Yahweh's faithfulness does not give the people a license to ignore their covenant obligations. We have already observed how unfaithfulness and rebellion—often called simply *sin*—led Israel to oppression and suffering. The working out of divine promises may be hindered by human failure. This cycle of sin over against promise and deliverance is a very serious concern for the prophets, who speak for God. At many points in their writings, covenant-promise, sin, and deliverance intersect.

The prophet Amos is notable for his denunciation of Israel's sins. His book begins by denouncing the sins of neighboring peoples, which would undoubtedly be very popular with his hearers. At Amos 2:6, however, he makes a dramatic switch and accuses Israel of awful sin. His charges become graphic and vehement. Read **Amos 3:1-3**, where the prophet declares that it is precisely because of the intimate relationship between Yahweh and Israel that punishment is coming. In Amos 9:11-15 a note of hope is sounded.

The prophet Micah also denounces the wickedness of God's people and predicts punishment. He foresees, however, a time when Jerusalem will become the center of the world's longing for peace. Read **Micah 4:1-8**. Christians have noted that in 5:2-4 Micah looks for a future deliverer of God's people to come from Bethlehem. The prophet's expectation was probably based on the promise to David, for Bethlehem was David's home town.[5] Micah's book concludes with a hymn on the faithfulness of God (7:18-20).

The Prophets and God's Faithfulness

The book of Hosea focuses intensely upon Yahweh's faithfulness to Israel. Even though Israel rejects Yahweh and deserves divine judgment, Yahweh is determined to show love for the wayward people. Hosea engages in symbolic actions that make his message startlingly clear. For example, at Yahweh's bidding Hosea marries a woman who had been a whore. They have three children, who are given symbolic names that illustrate the prophet's message (chapter 1). Hosea's domestic situation becomes a living illustration of Yahweh's loving faithfulness to unfaithful Israel.

The rest of the book contains dire prophecies interspersed with promises. Yahweh struggles to supplant judgment with forgiving, faithful love. When Hosea's wife is completely

---

5 1 Samuel 16:1, 4, 13.

unfaithful, he takes her back and declares that this is a sign of what divine mercy is like. Read **Hosea 11**. This was mentioned in Theme 1, but it should now have added meaning.

When the Hebrew kingdoms face disaster and exile, the prophets emphasize Yahweh's covenant faithfulness and hold out hope for renewal. Micah charges the people with terrible failure to keep their covenant obligations, but at the end he speaks of God's pardon and *faithfulness* (Micah 7:18-20). Ezekiel twice declares that Yahweh will make *a covenant of peace* with the people, and the royal line of David will be restored (Ezekiel 34:25; 37:24-26).

Jeremiah 31:31-34 is a very important covenant passage. Yahweh will make a *new covenant*, and it will bring a new time when all will *know the LORD*. This passage is quoted in its entirety in the New Testament, and we shall note it in Part 2. In 33:14-16 Jeremiah associates the fulfillment of Yahweh's promise with a reestablishment of David's kingly line.

Isaiah 55:1-5 is another notable passage. The prophet writes of *an everlasting covenant* between God and people, based on divine love for David. In a brilliant burst of vision, the prophet sees Yahweh's people mediating between *nations* and *the Holy One of Israel*.

FOR FURTHER STUDY AND REFLECTION

Memory Bank

1. Here is a summary list of references that you should remember from this part.

Exodus 6:2-8	Covenant with Israel through Moses
Deuteronomy 26:5-9	Israel's "little creed"
Isaiah 55:1-5	An everlasting covenant for all
Jeremiah 31:31-34	A new covenant
Hosea 11:1-4	Yahweh's faithful love

Research

1. We have noted how important the Hebrew people considered names to be. List the name changes in this part and include the meanings.

2. Study the names of Hosea's children. What is their significance?

3. The number 40 appears often in the Bible. Start a list of references where you have seen it and watch for its recurrence.

4. In a Bible Dictionary or other reference book read about covenants in the ancient Near East and how they may be connected with treaties. What is your evaluation of this connection?

5. Circumcision is still a sacred rite in Judaism today. How is it understood now?

Reflection

1. Is there any rite in Christianity that compares with circumcision? How is such a symbol meaningful in the life of the church?

2. What modern equivalents of covenants can you think of? How may they be related to biblical covenants?

3. How, and to what extent, is the covenant idea important in the life of Christian communities today?

4. What do God's promises mean to you? In what ways is God's relationship to you dependent upon your "keeping your end of the bargain"?

PEOPLE FIND GOD IS FAITHFUL

THEME 2

PART 2

Promise and Covenant in the New Testament

SUMMARY
The career of Jesus dramatically reversed the disappointment that God's people experienced again and again in the centuries after the exile. Jesus believed that he was fulfilling Old Testament promises in a special way, and the early church elaborated this belief. The Epistle to the Hebrews especially focuses on the covenant idea. Paul also deals with it in several epistles, and there are important references in other books.

BASIC BIBLE REFERENCES
Mark 14:24
1 Corinthians 11:23-26
Galatians 3:15-29
2 Timothy 2:11-13
Hebrews 1:1, 2; 8; 10:11-18; 13:20, 21

WORD LIST
Allegory
Mediator
Pentecost
Testament/Will

A Bridge from Old to New

People who confidently expected that covenant promises would all be fulfilled after the exile were disappointed. Jerusalem was partially restored and the temple was rebuilt, but the glory of the golden years of Solomon never returned. Freedom was limited, always in peril, and then it was lost again. The Maccabean revolution ended oppression from outsiders, but the precarious independence lasted scarcely a century. The Romans came with their garrisons and taxes. Popular feeling for God's covenant faithfulness was surely at low ebb when John the Baptist and then Jesus stirred up wide anticipation that fulfillment of promises was at hand.

Jesus and Fulfillment

The Gospels record only one instance where Jesus makes explicit reference to God's promise. At the meeting in Jerusalem where the two disciples from Emmaus report how the risen Jesus revealed himself to them, Jesus appears and declares that *what my Father promised* will happen (Luke 24:44-49). Shortly thereafter, at Pentecost, God's Spirit comes with new force and fullness upon the people, and this becomes the fulfillment of which Jesus spoke.

Peter's sermon at Pentecost is the first recorded challenge to the public from Jesus' followers after the resurrection. Peter concludes the message by urging the hearers to respond, and then he declares that God's *promise* is now offered to all (Acts 2:14-42; note verses 38 and especially 39).

In a broader sense, however, Jesus considers his total mission to be a fulfillment of God's covenant promise. He implies this when he often invites people to a renewal of faith. In his sermon at Nazareth (Luke 4:16-30) he says explicitly, *Today this scripture has been fulfilled in your hearing*. He has just read the announcement of *good news* from Isaiah 61:1, 2. The Gospel of John quotes Jesus many times as connecting his coming with God's purposes (for example, John 5:43; 10:10; 17:8, 18, 21).

Jesus' words at the Last Supper make a clear covenant connection. Read **Mark 14:24; 1 Corinthians 11:23-26**; and see also Matthew 26:28; Luke 22:20. In sharing *the cup* his disciples share in *the new covenant*. The covenant is made *in my blood*—that is, the cross ratifies the covenant. The church has always understood that, in some way, the sacrifices and ceremonies that marked Old Testament covenants are superseded by Jesus, *the Lamb of God, who takes away the sin of the world*! (John 1:29.)[1]

The Epistle to the Hebrews

God's faithfulness viewed as a covenant relationship became so important in the thinking of the Christian church that its new Scriptures were known as "The New Testament," which is another way of saying "New Covenant." The Hebrew Scriptures, which Christians also held sacred, they then began to call "The Old Testament" or "Old Covenant." Remember that Christian teaching has always kept both Testaments together as "the Word of God."

The double meaning of "covenant/testament" is worked out in Hebrews 9:1, 15-22. NRSV uses the word *will* in place of "testament,"[2] and the footnote indicates that it is equivalent to "covenant." REB begins Hebrews 9:1, *That is why the new covenant or testament of which he is the mediator....* At this point simply observe this word shift; we are not concerned with the difficult meaning of the rest of the passage.

Read **Hebrews 1:1, 2**. The author immediately states the old/new contrast. God's past communication was varied but incomplete; now God *has spoken to us by a Son*, that is Jesus (first named in 2:9). The epistle spells out how the Son is better than the former channels of God's communication. God's "new" is better than the "old."

---

1 Various sections of the church have explained this new understanding in different ways and celebrated it with different liturgies, but they all affirm the underlying truth.

2 Lawyers speak of one's "last will and testament."

Hebrews 8 declares that Jesus has become a heavenly *high priest*, and he works with *a better covenant* based on *better promises*. In Part 1 we studied Jeremiah 31:31-34. Here that passage is quoted in full and is a highlight of the epistle. For those who accept the new covenant, the old is becoming *obsolete*. The transition is not by chance. As if to emphasize this, Jeremiah 31:33, 34 is quoted again in **Hebrews 10:11-18** in relation to Christ's sacrifice for sin. Probably Jesus took from Jeremiah the expression *new covenant*, which occurs in the words at the Last Supper. Notice also Hebrews 10:23, *he who has promised is faithful*.

Hebrews 13:20, 21 is often used as a liturgical benediction. It begins with the resurrection and then speaks of *the blood of the eternal covenant*. This ties Themes 1 and 2 closely together.

Paul and God's Covenant Faithfulness

In Hebrews, Jesus is *the mediator of a new covenant* (Hebrews 12:24). "Mediator" and "covenant" are also associated in Paul's letters, although his lines of thought are quite different. Read **Galatians 3:15-29**. Paul argues that God's people live, not by the old law, but by God's promises, which are older. Again the multiple meaning "covenant/will" is used. The covenant promises were given through Abraham long before the covenant law was given through Moses, so the earlier form of God's "will/covenant" is not annulled by the latter.[3] Paul also argues (verses 19, 20) that because the law came by a mediator, it is less final than the promises God gave directly to Abraham. Paul's arguments may seem extremely complicated, but we can appreciate and accept his emphasis on the faithfulness of God's promises.

Theme 1, Part 3, introduces Romans 9-11, where Paul discusses the relationship of Jews and Gentiles. In 9:4 he says that, among other things, *the covenants* and *the promises* belong to Jews. He goes on to claim that the Jews of his time have rejected God's plan and that God has accepted the Gentiles. At 11:26, 27, however, he asserts that *all Israel will be saved*, and his supporting Scripture recalls Jeremiah 31:33.

In 2 Corinthians 1:18-22 Paul insists that his message is always positive—not *"Yes and No"* but *always "Yes."* This is because in Jesus Christ *every one of God's promises is a "Yes."* This is yet another way of saying that Jesus has become the new expression of God's faithfulness. Paul goes on to say that God's *Spirit* is a *first installment* of what this means for our future.

---

[3] Do not get sidetracked by how wills function today. Paul was a first-century rabbi, not a twentieth-century attorney. In any case, he might argue that the law does not explicitly annul the covenant promises, so the law must serve some function other than to establish the relationship between God and people.

Other New Testament Resources

Stephen's speech in his own defense (which we have already mentioned; see Acts 7) stresses God's covenant-promise. In Acts 7:5 he recalls God's promise of land and descendants to Abraham, and in 7:8 he recalls *the covenant of circumcision*.[4] In 7:17 the deliverance from Egypt is referred to as *the time...for the fulfillment of the promise*.

2 Timothy 2:11-13 is a useful summary of what this theme is about. *The saying* must have been current in the church after the middle of the first century. Note that if you were to read it through and keep the parallels, you would expect the fourth line to read, "If we are faithless, he also will be faithless." But there is the surprising reversal, which is then identified as showing something specific and unique about God. It implies that God can't be other than God...and PEOPLE FIND GOD IS FAITHFUL. This *saying* comes in a context of resurrection, *gospel*, and *salvation*, and is followed with a challenge to faithful living.

The message of the book of Revelation emphasizes the victory of deliverance (recall Theme 1, Part 4). The word "promise" does not occur in the book, and "covenant" is mentioned only in connection with the ark in heaven (Revelation 11:19), but God's people repeatedly receive assurance that their future is secure with God. See, for example, 3:20, 21. God's faithfulness and the victory of Christ are celebrated throughout the book (note 1:4-6 and 21:5-7).

FOR FURTHER STUDY AND REFLECTION

Memory Bank

1. Identify and *memorize:

Acts 2:39	Promise to God's people
Acts 7	Stephen's defense
Romans 9-11	Jews, Gentiles, and covenants
*1 Corinthians 11:23-26	The Last Supper
Galatians 3	Paul on the new covenant
2 Timothy 2:11-13	God's surprising faithfulness
Hebrews 8	The new and better covenant
*Hebrews 13:20, 21	A benediction

---

4 Here the sons of Jacob are called *the twelve patriarchs*. This extension of the term is because they became the ancestors of the twelve tribes of Israel.

Research

1. Luke 1:67-79 contains a hymn attributed to Zechariah, father of John the Baptist. Study this passage to see how it speaks of deliverance and covenant-promise.

2. How may Acts 2:39 be related to Peter's quotation from Joel earlier in the same sermon?

3. Galatians 4:21-31 contains what Paul calls *an allegory*. He says it concerns *two covenants*. Look up "allegory" in an unabridged dictionary, and choose the definition that seems to fit this passage. Try to follow Paul's line of thought.

4. How is modern will-making different from the testament/will passages we have studied in this part? It may be helpful to discuss this with a lawyer.

Reflection

1. What does it mean to say that Old Testament promises are "fulfilled" in the New Testament? If you have an opportunity, discuss this with your group leader or someone else who has been thinking about it.

2. Outline a meditation on the subject "God Is Faithful," basing it on 2 Timothy 2:11-13 or Hebrews 1:1, 2.

PEOPLE REFLECT ABOUT GOD

Thinking about Who God Is — PART 1

SUMMARY
The people who learned that God saves and is faithful formed questions about who God is. How does God relate to all creation? The narratives of Genesis 1-11 are one way the Bible deals with such matters. These and other early traditions show how difficult it is to understand God when only human terms are available. "Where" is God? How does God "think"? Other issues include the uniqueness of God, the nature of other gods, and the various names by which God is known in the Old Testament.

BASIC BIBLE REFERENCES
Genesis 1-3; 8:20-22
9:11-17
Exodus 20:1-6; 25:10-22
Psalms 8; 139:1-18

WORD LIST
Anthropomorphism
Ark of the Covenant
El Elyon, El Shaddai
Prehistory
Tabernacle
Theology
Yahweh
Sabaoth

Transition to This Theme

This theme grows out of the previous ones—Theme 1, in which the saving deeds of God bring into being a particular people of God, and Theme 2, in which the people find that God is faithful. The Old Testament does not tell us how these experiences led PEOPLE to REFLECT ABOUT GOD. It is clear, however, that questions about God arose. Some of these questions are scattered through the Scriptures, and there are some attempts at providing answers. Such questions and answers are the subject of our study in this theme.

When we say that deliverance by God led a PEOPLE to REFLECT ABOUT GOD, we are drawing a general conclusion from the texts. The people thought and wrote mostly about their experiences, and logical reflection was unusual for them. The Hebrews were at home in history, not in philosophy. If someone had asked them what they thought about God, they would likely have replied by telling what God had done and how they had been involved in what happened. Even when they declared God's faithfulness or recalled God's promises, they did it by marshaling evidence from experience rather than by stating reasoned conclusions. (Recall Deuteronomy 6:20-23.) This means that a "doctrine" of God or a concept of "the nature of God" does not appear in most of the Old Testament. That is simply not how the people of the Old Testament thought.[1]

---

1 Part 3 indicates that this changed in parts of the New Testament because late in the Old Testament era Greek thought began to touch the Near East. Paul took Christian faith into the Greek world, and theological reflection came into the mainstream of biblical thought.

But throughout the Old Testament new experiences bring new perceptions about God. These are often identified as revelations from God. We might call them theological insights, but God inspires them. Such breakthroughs appear at crucial points of biblical history. Christians believe that reflection about God reaches its unique and definitive point in the New Testament and that human questions about God receive their decisive answer in Jesus Christ.

For the sake of organizing our study we consider this theme in three parts, but the division is really artificial. Part 1 looks for what is back of God's saving faithfulness, that is, what is God's true identity. Part 2 considers the problem posed by the apparent conflict between God's love and justice. Part 3 probes how God, who must be ultimately unknowable, has become known.

We are using broad, comprehensive themes to examine what the Bible says, but at the same time we are trying to master the component books. Some of the material is appropriate in more than one part of our study. Thus, the three subjects of this theme are not neatly separated but are woven throughout the passages. To consider how God can be both loving and just (Part 2), we must assume that God is somehow knowable (Part 3), and both these matters are part of understanding who God is (Part 1). Moreover, these matters reach behind and beyond deliverance and covenant faithfulness.

Back to Beginnings

Yahweh told Moses to tell the Israelites, *the God of your ancestors* has *given heed to you...*(Exodus 3:16). There is a direct connection between this news and the relationship of God to these people in the past. We infer that the traditions about God went very, very far back. Stories were carefully and faithfully handed down from generation to generation. And questions must have been asked. "Where did God come from?" "What did God have to do with the beginnings of the world and human life?"

This takes us to Genesis 1-11. If you read all of Genesis at one sitting, you realize that the principal story line of the book begins with Abram in Chapter 12. At that point narrative details begin to lengthen. In a sense what comes before is a kind of "prehistory," that is, a collection derived from ancient, tribal traditions that must have been preserved in oral form from the times long before the Hebrew people had a written language.

The Hebrews were not unique in having traditions about origins. Primitive peoples all over the world had their stories about creation. When we compare Genesis with nonbiblical traditions, we readily see that the biblical narratives are remarkable for their beauty and reserve. There is a simplicity about the creation story, for example, that is not found in other

Near Eastern literatures. This is due in large measure to the monotheism of the people who preserved and recorded the material.

Most scholars today agree that the material in the Pentateuch was collected and edited into its final form during and just after the Babylonian exile (roughly 597-538 B.C.). This further illustrates what the order of our first three themes suggests: that the historical interest of God's people developed backward from their national experiences through their patriarchal roots to their prehistory. This emphasizes how important God's people thought it was to connect their later history with the very beginning. It also helps us understand the nature of that prehistory.

Examination of Genesis Texts

Genesis 1 and 2 contain two accounts of God's creation of all things. The second begins at 2:4.[2] Read these accounts, noting the similarities and the differences. The most important point throughout is how God's creative power is linked with the origin of the world and the beginnings of humankind. Note that in 1:27 *the image of God* includes *male and female*.

Chapter 3 explains how humankind first became alienated from God their Creator. Verses 14-19 are in poetic form and summarize basic human woes. In verse 15 there is a symbolic assurance of deliverance. Genesis 4:1-16, the story of Cain and Abel, tells more about the origins of wickedness in the world. Genesis 4:20-22 notes primitive beginnings of certain skills and arts.

In these narratives God is portrayed in human terms. In 3:8 God takes an evening walk; in 3:21 God is a tailor; in 4:9 God asks Cain where his brother Abel is. Such usage is called "anthropomorphism." The word comes from two Greek words that mean "human form." It describes referring to God in physical, human terms. How did those who handed down the ancient stories think about God? Perhaps we should expect a people who thought mostly in concrete terms to use "anthropomorphic" language. Probably it is impossible to escape some use of such language.

Chapter 5 features a genealogical catalog. Such lists were valued by the Hebrews to provide an unbroken link with the remote past and to give them confidence as they faced the future.[3] Two of these ancient persons have become famous for peculiar reasons.

---

2 The name *Yahweh (=the LORD)* does not occur until this point. This is one indication that two traditions have been joined.
3 A long list in Nehemiah 7:5-69 serves a similar purpose. Matthew 1:1-17 and Luke 3:23-38 present genealogical lists to explain Jesus' ancestry.

Verses 21-24 imply that Enoch escaped the ordinary human experience of death. His son Methuselah is noted as the all-time record holder for birthdays!

Chapters 6-9 cover the complete story of Noah. The earth has become so wicked that Yahweh regrets having *made humankind* and determines to start over again by destroying all but one human family. How Noah escapes the destroying flood by building an ark is a familiar story. Afterward he builds an altar and offers *burnt offerings* to Yahweh. Read **Genesis 8:20-22**. The covenant theme is prominent. Read **9:11-17**.

Chapter 10 and most of 11 contain genealogical tables extending from Noah to Abram. 11:1-9 has a story about the origin of world languages. Note Yahweh's part in verses 5-8. In verse 7 Yahweh speaks in the first person plural: *Let **us** go down.* (We passed over a similar usage in 1:26.) The expression likely implies a heavenly council presided over by Yahweh.[4] These anthropomorphic passages need not confuse or upset us. It is not fair to expect people of that age to reflect about God in theological forms like those that develop much later.

God as Communicator

Our texts assume that God easily communicates with people. In Genesis 12:1 *the LORD said to Abram* and in 35:1 *God said to Jacob*. We are not told just how God spoke in such instances, and we do not know just how the earliest readers of these texts understood the way God spoke. The language is anthropomorphic. Perhaps people thought that a voice spoke from an invisible source.

Sometimes God communicates through messengers, and there are instances where these are treated as the very presence of God. In Genesis 18 *three men* visit Abraham, but without any note of a change Yahweh is speaking (verse 13). Then in 19:1 we read of *the two angels*, which seems to connect directly with the previous narrative. Later in the chapter they are again *men* and still later Yahweh takes over.

Sometimes God's communication employs unusual means. In Exodus 19:7-25 Yahweh makes a spectacular appearance at Sinai with nature-fireworks. A kind of taboo is attached to the mountain, and Yahweh reaches the people only through special persons. In Exodus 33:7-11 Moses meets Yahweh *face to face, as one speaks to a friend,* but in verses 17-23 Moses is permitted to see only Yahweh's *back*. In Deuteronomy 5:22 Yahweh *spoke with a loud voice to your whole assembly*. We must admit that it is difficult to relate these

---

[4] Such a picture occurs in 1 Kings 22:19-22; in Job 1:6-12; 2:1-6; and in Psalm 82:1.

stories to each other. The traditions seem to have been collected and edited without being completely homogenized.

Eventually the Hebrews became convinced that humans really could not see God. The Gospel of John declares, *No one has ever seen God* (John 1:18). We shall return to this matter in Part 3.

Can God Be Influenced?

Several passages in the Pentateuch imply that God's intention can be altered, in circumstantial detail if not in general purpose. Abraham's three visitors at Mamre (Genesis 18) tell him that Yahweh intends to destroy Sodom. Abraham undertakes to dissuade Yahweh, apparently because his nephew Lot lives at Sodom. Yahweh tolerates Abraham's argument, and before Sodom is destroyed, Lot is rescued (Genesis 19:15-25)[5]

Genesis 32:22-32 tells how Jacob wrestled with *a man* at the ford of the river Jabbok. Jacob takes this person to be God's direct representative, and he manages to gain a blessing from the divine figure.

In Theme 2, Part 1, we noted how Moses bargains with Yahweh when the people make and worship *a calf* of gold (Exodus 32). The story is sketchy. Yahweh intends to start over again with Moses (like Noah?), but after Moses pleads and *the LORD changed his mind*, Moses is commanded to get on with the journey to the Promised Land (Exodus 33).

In all of this and throughout the Bible, the unquestionable difference between God and humans is marked. This separation, however, never obscures the faith that people are unique in creation and are in everlasting relationship with the Creator. See **Psalms 8** and **139:1-18.**

Can God Be Located?

Browning's poem *Pippa Passes* has a familiar line: *God's in his heaven—All's right with the world*. In most of the Old Testament God is "at home" in heaven but meets the people at a special place, *the ark of the covenant*. Read about its construction in **Exodus 25:10-22**. The Ark becomes in effect God's throne, and later we shall study how God was thought of as king (Theme 6). During Israel's wilderness wandering the Ark was kept in *the tabernacle*, a kind of portable temple. Once the people are settled in Canaan, Jerusalem becomes the place where Yahweh dwells (as in Psalm 122:1, 2; Zechariah 8:3).

---

5 Sodom and its sister city Gomorrah have become bywords for civic wickedness. Lot's wife *looked back, and she became a pillar of salt* (Genesis 19:26). Jesus refers to both of these stories (Luke 17:28-32).

Sometimes Old Testament texts draw the conclusion that if Yahweh rules over one place, other gods may rule over other places. Read **Exodus 20:1-6**.[6] The first commandment implies the existence of *other gods*. These commandments indicate that, while there may be other gods, Israel is to worship the one and only true God. The thinking of the people among whom Israel lived may be seen in 1 Kings 20:22-25, where a neighboring king believes that Israel has *gods of the hills.*

In order to make clear the absolute difference between Yahweh and all other gods, the second commandment forbids all physical representation of God; that is, Israel must have no idols. Exodus 13:21 tells that Yahweh's presence during the wilderness wandering was revealed *in a pillar of cloud by day...and in a pillar of fire by night,* but this seems not to have satisfied the people. The story about the calf of gold points up the practical difficulty of following an invisible God. The second commandment is remarkable in view of the idolatry prevalent among Israel's neighbors.

Names of God

The Old Testament calls God by names other than *Yahweh,* but this name occurs well over twice as often as any other (about 6,800 times). Exodus 6:3 says that *God Almighty* was the divine name used in appearances to the patriarchs. NRSV explains in a footnote that this name is *El Shaddai* in Hebrew, and NJB uses this Hebrew form. *El* is perhaps as close to a "generic" term for "god" as the Old Testament provides. (Remember Jacob's dream of the ladder to heaven at Beth-El [="house of God"], Genesis 28:19.) *El* often occurs in the plural formation *elohim*. Technically, this is a "plural of majesty," as a king used to say "we" when he meant only "I, the king."

In Genesis 14 Abram meets Melchizedek, who is called *priest of God Most High.* This divine name is *El Elyon* in Hebrew. It occurs elsewhere in the Old Testament and in a Greek form in Mark 5:7 and other passages. God is also called *the LORD of hosts,* in Hebrew *Yahweh Sabaoth*. This name occurs frequently; familiar texts are Psalms 24:10; 46:7, 11; Isaiah 6:3. The name may come from Yahweh's leading the host of Israel or from Yahweh's ruling over the host of heaven (Psalm 148:2). Frequently *Yahweh* is combined with a form of *Elohe,* and in NRSV this becomes *the LORD God or the LORD, the God.*

Gradually, the separation between God and mortals became sharper. By the time after the exile, the Jews even considered the name *Yahweh* too sacred for humans to pronounce. When Scriptures were read aloud, a generic word for *lord* was substituted (in Hebrew,

---

6 The Ten Commandments are repeated in Deuteronomy 5:6-21.

adonai; so in Numbers 11:28 *My lord Moses*). This is still the practice in Jewish synagogues today.

In the Greek Old Testament and in the New Testament there is one word for lord/LORD, *kyrios*. Early copies of the Septuagint kept the four consonants of "Yahweh," *YHWH*, but read aloud *kyrios*, LORD. In the New Testament one must look at the context to decide whether "LORD," a divine title, is intended or "lord," a human title of respect. About the 16th century A.D. a Christian translator combined the consonants YHWH with the vowels of *adonai* and produced the hybrid "Jehovah," a word that never existed until that time.

FOR FURTHER STUDY AND REFLECTION

Memory Bank

1. Stories you should be able to retell:

>   Creation (Genesis 1, 2)
>   The flood (Genesis 6-8)
>   The tower of Babel (Genesis 11:1-9)
>   Abraham entertaining three strangers (Genesis 18:1-22)
>   Jacob wrestling at the Jabbok (Genesis 32:22-32)
>   The Golden calf (Exodus 32)

2. People you should be able to identify:

>   Cain and Abel (Genesis 4:1-16)
>   Methuselah (Genesis 5:25-27)
>   Noah (Genesis 6-8)
>   Lot (Genesis 13; 19:15-26)

3. Everyone should know the Ten Commandments. This part includes the first two, so learn Exodus 20:1-6.

Research

1. Genesis 9:25, 26 was quoted by persons who tried to justify black slavery in the 19th century. Try to trace how their argument could have gone. What is the significance of *Canaan* in the text?

2. In a dictionary or encyclopedia find the meanings of "henotheism" and "monotheism." How is Moses associated with the development of Hebrew monotheism?

3. Find out all you can about *the ark of the covenant*. What was its function in Hebrew belief and worship? If you have seen the movie, *Raiders of the Lost Ark*, compare the ideas about the Ark reflected there and in the biblical material.

Reflection

1. What is "theology"? Is it always related to the Bible? What theological insights can you find in this part?

2. How do Old Testament ideas about God clarify or complicate your own reflection about God?

3. How does God speak to us? How do we speak to God?

SUMMARY

Serious reflection about God raises a dilemma: revelation of the divine will shows that God is just; experience of the divine patience shows that God is loving. The difficulty of reconciling these two aspects of God appears in a number of Old Testament stories. The problem expands to ask why God tolerates evil in the world. Jonah and Job present two classic ways to get at the matter. The personification of evil is a problem unresolved until the end of the New Testament. Faith is the persistent biblical response to these broad questions.

BASIC BIBLE REFERENCES

Exodus 34:6, 7
Job 1; 2; 3; 38:1-11; 40:1-9; 42:1-6
Psalm 73
Jonah
Revelation 12:7-12

WORD LIST
Dualism
Theodicy

PEOPLE REFLECT ABOUT GOD

THEME 3

Asking How God Can Be Both Just and Loving

PART 2

Raising the Question

Because of the golden calf at Sinai, Moses in frustrated anger destroys the tablets with the Ten Commandments (Exodus 32:15-19). Later, however, he intercedes for the people (32:31-34), and Yahweh shows gracious compassion toward the people (33:12-19). Moses then prepares two new stone tablets, and Yahweh renews the covenant (34:1-28). **Exodus 34:6, 7** is a remarkable pronouncement of Yahweh's nature. Here the declaration of saving faithfulness is coupled with the caution of sure justice. *Love and faithfulness* extend to *the thousandth generation* while guilt and *iniquity* punish only *to the third and fourth generation*. The remainder of Chapter 34 spells out in detail some of God's commandments.

If these two aspects of Yahweh's character seem to be in conflict, be assured that Yahweh does not have a split personality. Most of the Old Testament simply accepts love and justice as fundamental characteristics of God and describes the appropriate effects. Stories of God's saving faithfulness tend to stress love, but God's justice never allows unfaithfulness of the people to pass without note. David receives a great covenant promise, but his sin is roundly condemned. God's justice is aimed at reclaiming the offending persons, but many biblical stories tell of fierce affliction for flagrant, persistent sin.

There are places in the Old Testament where some of God's people question this issue more deeply. Since God loves the people and keeps covenant promises in spite of their unfaithfulness and rebellion, why do they persist in such wicked ways? If God is indeed just and almighty, how can such opposition be tolerated? When, where, how, and why did human disobedience arise? In philosophical language this is the problem of evil. The Old Testament, however, is not a philosophical book, so we should not be surprised to find these questions dealt with in different ways. Here the questions and answers are usually presented in poetry, drama, and story.

Adam and Others

Stories in Genesis 3 and 4, which we noted in Part 1, touch the questions we are asking. It is fundamentally important to distinguish what these passages mean in their context and what Jewish and Christian theologians have made of them. For example, there is a real difference between the story of Adam and Eve's disobedience in Eden as it stands in Genesis and the doctrines of sin that theologians have derived from it.

Why didn't Yahweh God simply destroy Adam and Eve when they went astray? God punished them severely, but in one sense they got away with the rebellion. There are other passages where the apparent success of evildoers is faced frankly. In 1 Kings 19:1-10 Elijah is terribly upset because Yahweh has allowed Jezebel to chase him out of the country. Jeremiah wonders (12:1-4) *why does the way of the guilty prosper*?

Read **Psalm 73**. In verses 1-14 the psalmist describes vividly *the prosperity of the wicked*. In verses 15-28 he decides that God's way is finally best. This is really an affirmation of faith rather than a reasoned solution.

When God's people are oppressed by their enemies, another question is raised. Often it is a psalmist who insists that Yahweh ought to do something about their plight. Sometimes it takes the form of a hope that Yahweh will pay back the enemy (Psalm 137:7-9). Sometimes it is suggested that the people's predicament may be a reflection on Yahweh's power. *Is the enemy to revile your name forever?* (Psalm 74:10). *Why should the nations say, "Where is their God?"* (Psalm 79:10).

This may imply, of course, that God is neither just nor loving. But always God's people work through to a response of faith, as in Psalm 73. When King Hezekiah was distraught because of an Assyrian invasion, Isaiah counseled him, *Do not be afraid*; and it turned out that this faith was justified.[1] During the Babylonian exile the prophet assured the people that Yahweh would respond to their plight (see Isaiah 40:27-31; 43:1-7).

---

1 This story was mentioned in Theme 1, Part 2, page 34.

The Problem of the Prophet Jonah

Two Old Testament books deal at some length with our present question. Neither finds a simple answer. First, read **Jonah**. Observe what a very minor part the *large fish* plays in the story. The first two chapters tell how Jonah decides to run away from Yahweh's call to go to Nineveh. The fish is a part of Yahweh's strategy to get Jonah back on call. Jonah's psalm of thanksgiving is evidence that he recognizes Yahweh's goodness. *Deliverance belongs to the LORD!*

Jonah answers the second call to go to Nineveh. When the people of Nineveh turned *from their evil ways*, Jonah is miffed, and complains to Yahweh because the prophecy of calamity has been replaced by mercy. Jonah does not learn from the object lesson that follows, and Yahweh gently scolds Jonah.

Ask yourself what view of God is imbedded in this narrative? How does Jonah expect Yahweh's justice to be exercised, and what is Jonah's role? There is also the matter of how Israel, the hearer of the story, is involved. But that is a subject for Theme 4. Here we are concerned with the contrast between what Jonah expects and what Yahweh actually does.

Where have we read words like Jonah 4:2 before? Are the circumstances in any way similar? What sort of character does Jonah manifest? How do you think the reader is expected to react? Why do you think the story ends so abruptly?

The Problem of Job

Second, we consider the book of Job. It is long and in many ways difficult, but here we shall confine ourselves to how Job poses the problem we are studying.[2] The book may be read as a drama. Archibald MacLeish wrote a modern play J. B., inspired by the biblical book. Begin by reading **Job 1, 2**. Notice that Job 3:1-42:6 is in poetic form.

The dramatic intensity of the book is present already in the prose prologue, for Job, his family, and his friends do not have the information set forth in the heavenly scenes. It is precisely here that the problem of the book is posed: how can a just and loving God do this to Job? How can Job's awful misfortune and suffering be reconciled with a loving God? Job steadfastly denies that this treatment is just, but in Job 2:10 the author is careful to point out Job's integrity before God. Read **Job 3**. Job complains to God, but he carefully avoids an accusing confrontation.

---

[2] We shall meet Job again, particularly in Theme 8.

In Job 4-28 three friends try to convince Job by somewhat conventional arguments that God is just. They have an oversimplified view of God's justice: the wicked are punished and the innocent are spared. Job's suffering must come from wickedness, they argue; and his only hope is to throw himself upon God's mercy. Job responds to each in turn, and he sums up his case in Chapters 29-31. He insists that he is innocent and declares that his previous life does not deserve such suffering. He holds his own in the dialogue with his friends, but he does not really solve his own problem.

In Chapters 32-37 another friend takes up the debate. He acknowledges that the first three have not answered Job, but he is angry because he thinks Job has overstated his case. The proposed solution, however, is neither new nor helpful. After this Yahweh responds to Job. Read **Job 38:1-11** and **40:1-9**. Job's final answer is in **42:1-6**. He completely accepts Yahweh's will. In the epilogue (42:7-17, prose) everything turns out right, and Job lives happily ever after!

Personification of Evil

Satan appears in the book of Job as Yahweh's antagonist,[3] but he is portrayed as an "insider." The personification of evil in the Bible is a difficult matter to understand, and we shall deal with it only briefly here. Scripture generally assumes the existence of such a one in the spirit world, but his character is not analyzed nor are the practical implications of such a one considered.

The Judeo-Christian traditions, in contrast to many other religions, reject "dualism," the belief that two great cosmic powers are in constant conflict in the world with the outcome in the balance. The Bible everywhere assumes the almighty power and sovereign supremacy of God. God is somehow the source of everything, but "everything" is not equated with God. This means that the power of any personified evil is limited by God's absolute control. The texts never represent God as the creator of evil, but the remaining problem of the source of evil is never worked out in a rational way. This vagueness is not allowed to be a valid excuse for human sin. See Job 2:10; Luke 22:3, 22. The Gospels portray Jesus as the antagonist to and victor over the evil one. The stories of Jesus' "temptation,"[4] Matthew 4:1-11, and the Beelzebul controversy, Mark 3:20-27, illustrate this.

The book of Revelation emphasizes Jesus' victory as God's supreme act of deliverance (see Theme 1, Part 4). The complete and final overthrow of evil is the result, but the details are set in apocalyptic language. Read **Revelation 12:7-12**. Here is a dramatic portrayal of evil

---

3 "Satan" means "adversary" in Hebrew. The Bible has other names for the one who leads opposition to God.

4 The Greek word used is perhaps better translated "testing"; see NJB.

invading earth. Several names and labels of the evil one are brought together (verses 9, 10), and the seer implies that all opposition to God is one, however diverse it may appear. The final elimination of this evil is a major matter in Revelation, and Theme 10, Part 4, studies it in detail.

The Role of Faith

Job's final answer to his questions about evil is, after all, an answer of faith. This is striking because the book makes great efforts to find another solution. The prophet Habakkuk deals with the same problem in a different framework. He comes to the conclusion that evil will lose and God will win (as in Habakkuk 1:12), and *the righteous live by their faith*.[5] Two prophets use the imagery of *potter* and *clay* to illustrate the relationship between the Creator and humanity (see Isaiah 64:8; Jeremiah 18:1-6). Paul also uses this figure in Romans 9:19-24.

As covenant responsibility is not easy for God's people, neither is reliance upon God's love and justice. In Luke 17:7-10 Jesus uses a sharp illustration to make it clear that complete obedience to God's will is a minimum requirement for a faithful person. Indeed, minimum/maximum is probably an inappropriate distinction. As God's love and justice are totally one, so must be the response of God's people.

FOR FURTHER STUDY AND REFLECTION

Memory Bank

1. Exodus 34:6, 7.

2. Retell the story of Jonah (make only passing mention of the *large fish*).

Research

1. How do the teachings of your church define "sin"?

2. The heavenly scenes and the earthly speeches in Job seem to constitute two layers of tradition. Which do you think would be the older? Check the references to Job in Ezekiel 14:12-20 and in James 5:11.

---

[5] Notice the footnote: *faith* may also be translated *faithfulness*. The point, however, is the same, for the most important word is *live*. Perhaps our slang idiom, "hang in there," is an appropriate combination of faith and faithfulness.

3. Investigate the relationship of Milton's *Paradise Lost* to Genesis 3, 4; Job 1, 2; and Revelation 12:7-17.

4. Read Luke 13:1-5. How do Jesus' illustrations relate to the question of this theme? Try to work out an interpretation.

Reflection

1. Have you ever asked, "If God loves me, why is this happening to me?" What answer have you worked out?

2. What is your definition of justice? In what ways is it the same as or different from the biblical ideas we have studied in this part?

3. How may love be viewed as a manifestation of justice? Justice as an aspect of love?

PEOPLE REFLECT ABOUT GOD

Knowing the Unknowable God

PART 3

SUMMARY
When Israel reflected about God, they emphasized more and more the divine transcendence. They believed, however, that God continued to reveal. So they kept on using human terms about God. They recognized angels as divine messengers, but often revelation came by God's Spirit. People who accepted the Hebrew Scriptures as God's revelation had a problem when they became convinced that Jesus was making God known in a new and unique way. The Gospels present various aspects of this. Paul is the theological interpreter. The Holy Spirit is the key to what God reveals.

BASIC BIBLE REFERENCES
Isaiah 6:1-8
Ezekiel 37:1-14
John 1:1-18; 14:15-26
Acts 17:22-34
Philippians 2:5-11

WORD LIST
Immanence
Paraclete (Research 3)
Seraphim
Synoptic Gospels (Footnote 4)
Theophany
Transcendence

Mystery and Revelation

Most of the early efforts of God's people to understand the essential nature of God are expressed in terms drawn from their own life experiences. The more they reflected about God, however, the more mystery they encountered. Each revelation from God made evident how much more was unknown. God became more and more unknowable, more aloof. The theological term for this is "transcendence."

When Moses meets Yahweh and the divine name is revealed, the meaning of the name remains somewhat mysterious. Moses is told to keep his distance. Today we might describe the relationship that began there as "open-ended." At Sinai Israel receives new knowledge of Yahweh's will, but it is just there that Yahweh's "otherness" is dramatized. There is a display of clouds and fire, and only Moses is allowed to penetrate the mountain taboo (Exodus 24:12-18). Such a revelation is sometimes called a "theophany," a word that means "appearance of God." God becomes at the same time inescapable and unknowable—as Job and Jonah both found out.

But the people continue to learn more about God. Hebrews 1:1 says that this was *in many and various ways*. Anthropomorphic language is often used because so much of what God reveals comes in the people's everyday experiences. God's presence usually is marked by a voice or a vision or a natural phenomenon. A notable example is presented in **Isaiah 6:1-8**. What does Isaiah learn about God in this vision?

God is also revealed through messengers. These are sometimes called "angels" in our translations. The word is directly derived from the Greek word for "messenger." The word "angel" may suggest figures from medieval or renaissance art, so it can be misleading. The story of the strangers who met Abraham at Mamre[1] illustrates how shifty the terminology may be. What other instances can you recall?

In addition, God becomes known through the anointed king. The "royal" Psalms portray this. Examples are Psalms 2:6, 7; 21:1-7; 72:1-4. Nature also is perceived as a source of divine revelation, as in Psalm 19:1-6; Job 38:1-11.

The Spirit of God

Sometimes the messenger is referred to as the "Spirit" of God, and it is often hard to tell exactly what sort of experience is being described. In Genesis 1:2, that which *swept over the face of the waters* (NAB, *abyss*) is *a wind from God* (NRSV) or *the spirit of God* (REB). An older translation reads *breath of God*, for the same Hebrew word can mean all three—as can the corresponding Greek word.

In some instances God's Spirit is almost the same as God's "word." In Isaiah 61:1-3 the prophet declares that *the spirit of the LORD God is upon* him *to proclaim*. In Joel 2:28 Yahweh promises, *I will pour out my spirit*, and this will enable people to *prophesy*. *The spirit of God* takes possession of persons, as Gideon (Judges 6:34) and Saul (1 Samuel 10:10). Some kind of word regularly accompanies God's Spirit. *The word of Yahweh* is the power that authenticates and moves the prophets. God's word is powerful as God is powerful (see Isaiah 55:11 and Hebrews 4:12). *And God said* is the effective power in creation (Genesis 1:3, 5, 6, etc.).

The prophet Ezekiel in the second part of his book offers hope of restoration for the Jewish exiles in Babylon. He has a remarkable vision in which, by God's word, new life and breath come into dry bones. Read **Ezekiel 37:1-14,** which was also a Basic Reference in Theme 1, Part 2. Check the footnote on *breath* in verse 9. What is new in this view of God's word and Spirit? God's closeness or presence is referred to theologically as "immanence."

Old Scripture, New Revelation

New Testament writers believed that God was revealed in the Hebrew Scriptures. When New Testament texts mention *scripture(s)*, they are referring to parts of what we call the Old Testament. In Luke 24:44 Jesus speaks of *the law of Moses, the prophets, and the*

---

1 Recall the discussion in Part 1, page 70.

psalms. In Mark 12:10, 11 Jesus quotes Psalm 118:22, 23 and calls it *this scripture*. Paul declares twice in 1 Corinthians 15:3, 4 that the saving events of the gospel came about *in accordance with the scriptures*, even though we are not sure what specific texts he had in mind.

We have already referred to Hebrews 1:1, 2, where the writer sums up the varieties of God's communication *long ago*, and then says that God's final word is *a Son*, who is clearly Jesus (see Hebrews 2:9). The first-century Christian church was convinced that the climax of God's self-revelation is Jesus Christ and that in him the God who has always been beyond human description has become known in human form. Jesus Christ now defines how people are to think of God, and Jesus Christ becomes the unique way by which people are to become connected with God.

Jesus As Revelation of God

But now the old problem of describing the indescribable surfaces in a new form. Other gods are often portrayed as appearing in human form, but the God of the Hebrew people is different. This God is so holy that by the time of Jesus even the divine name is considered too sacred to utter. Thus the earliest Christians are pressed to find ways to explain and describe how God could appear as a human being.

The Gospels deal straightforwardly with Jesus' career. Very little is told about his life before the public ministry, and it appears to have been relatively simple and unassuming. His teaching brings him some prominence and is in some respects highly original. People address him as teacher or rabbi, and he becomes known as a healer, a wonder-worker, even a prophet. But if it had not been for the cross and resurrection, Jesus might have been scarcely remembered.

The problem does not become any easier when we ask how Jesus thought of himself. In the Gospels he refers to himself most often as *the Son of Man*.[2] There has been a lot of scholarly debate about this title, but we may at least conclude that (1) it is meant to emphasize the unique mission of Jesus, (2) it is part of a pattern of avoiding the title "messiah," and (3) the early church does not continue to use the title for Jesus, probably because other titles seem more appropriate after his death and resurrection.

Jesus uses familiar Old Testament stories to emphasize how he views his role. Elijah and Elisha are mentioned in the sermon at Nazareth. In Matthew 12:38-42 Jonah and the queen

---

2 For example, Matthew 8:20; 11:19; 16:13; Mark 14:21; Luke 22:48; John 8:28; 9:35-37. Old Testament background may be checked in Psalm 8:4; Ezekiel 2:1; and Daniel 7:13 in RSV. (NRSV changes the terminology to reflect inclusive language.)

of Sheba (*the South*)³ appear. An action of David is cited to justify what Jesus' disciples are doing (Luke 6:1-5).

The event known as "the transfiguration" connects Jesus with Old Testament revelation.⁴ Recall the exodus reference in Luke 9:31. *Moses* and *Elijah* represent the Law and the Prophets, that is, the great divisions of the Hebrew Scriptures at that time. A *voice from heaven* says, *This is my Son...listen to him!*, a message that combines Psalm 2:7 and Isaiah 42:1.

We have observed that the Gospel of John is quite different from the other three. **John 1:1-18** gives an unparalleled interpretation of the role of Jesus Christ in making God known.⁵ John 1:14 makes it clear that the familiar verses about *the Word* are intended to refer to Jesus as the embodiment of the Word. John appropriately captures the spirit and power of God's word in the Old Testament and subtly affirms that this has appeared in human life in the Word-become-flesh. Woven with this is another symbol of revelation, namely *light*. John 1:1 consciously copies Genesis 1:1, and John 1:4-9 picks up the association of God's word and light in Genesis 1:3.

Jesus and God's Spirit

The Spirit of God is associated with Jesus. The four Gospel stories of Jesus' baptism state this (Matthew 3:11-17; Mark 1:9-12; Luke 3:21, 22; John 1:32-34). *A voice from heaven* proclaims the same message as at the transfiguration. In the upper room discourse according to John, Jesus says that the Spirit will take his place and continue what he set out to do. Read **John 14:15-26** (see also 16:7-15).

The book of Acts shows that the first Christians believed this had happened. Recall how Peter associates the coming of the Spirit on Pentecost with the career and victory of Jesus. Acts 10 and 11 recount how Peter was involved in the conversion of a Roman centurion Cornelius. The Holy Spirit is prominent in the story, and Peter connects this with *the word of the* LORD (11:16, referring to 1:5). Later in one of Paul's mission travelogues, first *the Holy Spirit*, then *the Spirit of Jesus* gives instructions (16:6-8).

---

3 See 1 Kings 10:1-10.

4 Matthew 17:1-8; Mark 9:2-8; Luke 9:28-36. These are parallel accounts of the same event, each with a few distinctive details. The first three Gospels are called "synoptic," from Greek roots that mean "seeing together." Their passages are regularly closer to each other than any of them is to the fourth Gospel, John.

5 This passage is a prologue to this Gospel. Verse 19 introduces the ministry of John the Baptist, a point shared with the synoptics.

Paul and Jesus

In the story of Paul's conversion a vision of Jesus is instrumental in what happened (Acts 9:1-22; note verses 5 and 17).[6] Paul had been present at the death of Stephen, and Stephen's witness to Jesus may have been a strong influence in Paul's change (note Acts 26:14, 15). Immediately after his conversion Paul begins to proclaim that Jesus is the new way by which God is to be known (see 9:20, 22, 27, 28).

Read **Acts 17:22-34**, the digest of a sermon Paul preached to a curious audience in Athens. This is the only incident where he uses something like philosophical reasoning—he even quotes two Greek poets (verse 28). He uses this unusual approach to tell about Jesus, and the effort is somewhat successful.

Paul's letters repeatedly emphasize how God is made known through Jesus Christ. In Romans 8:3, 4, 11 he stresses that Jesus has accomplished what earlier revelations did not. In 1 Corinthians he says that *Christ Jesus...became for us wisdom from God* (1:30). *Jesus Christ and him crucified* is the substance of Paul's message (2:1, 2). *We have the mind of Christ* (2:16). In **Philippians 2:5-11** Paul expresses in lyrical language how Jesus Christ has made God known. Notice the progression: *in the form of God...emptied himself...in human form...death...exalted...LORD.*

Revelation beyond Jesus

New Testament writers are convinced that God will continue to become better known. This further revelation will come through the Holy Spirit, but the once-for-all revelation in Jesus Christ is to be the standard by which the future will be governed. John 16:12-15 states this quite clearly. Ephesians 1:22 says that Christ is *the head over all things for the church*. The seer of the book of Revelation associates *the word of God and...the testimony of Jesus Christ* (1:2).

FOR FURTHER STUDY AND REFLECTION

Memory Bank

1. Add to your "I-can-identify" list these passages from this part:

    Psalm 2:7   Acts 9:1-22
    Isaiah 6:1-8   Acts 17:22-31

---

[6] The story is repeated in Acts 22:4-16 and 26:9-18, which must indicate its importance. The details of the Peter and Cornelius story are also repeated, Acts 10 and 11.

Ezekiel 37:1-14
John 1:1-18
John 14:15-26

Philippians 2:5-11
Hebrews 1:1, 2

Research

1. What does "theophany" mean? How does it relate to this theme?

2. 1 Samuel 14:41 mentions "Urim and Thummim" as a way of learning God's will. Check it in a Bible Dictionary. What do you think of this?

3. In John 14 and 16, NRSV has the word *Advocate* in special reference to the Spirit. The Greek original is sometimes transliterated "Paraclete." Check the translation in KJV and several other versions. Also refer to notes in a study Bible or a Bible Dictionary. Which translation do you find most helpful? Why?

Reflection

1. How to "know" God is still a challenging problem today. What help can you get from the various sections of this part?

2. How do you think of angels? On what biblical material is your idea based?

3. How do you understand Jesus as a truly human being and yet the unique revelation of God?

4. How is Jesus present today? How can you relate this to the Holy Spirit?

PEOPLE LIVE IN GOD'S WORLD

THEME 4

Views of the World in the Hebrew Scriptures

PART 1

SUMMARY
The Bible has its setting in a particular part of the world, and there are reasons for this. Geography and archeology aid our understanding and appreciation of the biblical texts. God's concern for the whole world is evident from Genesis on, but Israel was slow to learn what this implies. Prophets urged an inclusive world view, and poets celebrated God's universal power. Nature was sometimes viewed as harsh, sometimes as benign.

BASIC BIBLE REFERENCES
Genesis 9:1-10
Psalms 19:1-4; 24:1, 2
Isaiah 45:1-13, 22, 23; 65:17-25
Amos 3:2; 9:7

WORD LIST
Anatolia
Day of Yahweh
Mesopotamia
Suffering Servant
Tell

Why Palestine?

Our study so far has assumed that the Bible has its setting in the world, but we have not paused to consider the significance of this setting. The Old Testament centers in a tiny land at the eastern end of the Mediterranean Sea. It is about the size of the state of Vermont. How could such a small territory become so important? What connection is there between the religious history of the people and their geographical setting? What was their view of the rest of the world? These and related questions must now claim our attention.

Palestine was precisely at the crossroads of the ancient world, at the point where three continents join. In Asia to the east important nations arose in Mesopotamia, the land of the Tigris and Euphrates Rivers. The old civilizations of the Nile valley in Africa lay to the southwest. The Asian lands of Anatolia (modern Turkey) and the European nations of Greece, Macedonia, and Rome were in the north and west. The routes from all of these toward the others met where the Hebrew people settled. When Alexander the Great set out to conquer the world, he passed this way, and the history of the Middle East was permanently changed.

Inevitably such a location affected the life and faith of the people who lived there. The people of God called this bit of geography their "Promised Land." In Ezekiel 5:5 Yahweh declares that Jerusalem is in the center of the nations. Do you think these people would have become so important if they had lived somewhere else? Probably that question is impossible to answer, but thinking about it will help us to get a broader understanding of the history of God's people.

What Sort of Country?

Along the Mediterranean Sea Palestine has a coastal plain. Here were the strongholds of the Philistines, persistent enemies of Israel. To the east this gives way to foothills, which in turn rise to the central highlands. Here are some low mountains famous in Scripture. *As the mountains surround Jerusalem, so the LORD surrounds his people* (Psalm 125:2). But the Mount of Olives, which overlooks the holy city is only about 2,700 feet above sea level. Texts usually speak of going <u>up</u> to Jerusalem.

Immediately to the east the land drops abruptly into the Jordan River valley. It is nearly 700 feet below sea level when it leaves the Sea of Galilee at the north. It empties into the Dead Sea (called by several names in Scripture), which is the lowest point on earth (1,294 feet below sea level). Jericho is just north of the Dead Sea, and you may remember that the man in Jesus' parable of the good Samaritan *was going down from Jerusalem to Jericho* (Luke 10:30).

To the east of the Jordan valley the land rises again to the eastern highlands. Here and to the north there are higher mountains. Southeast of the Dead Sea they reach nearly 6,500 feet, and Mount Hermon in the north is over 9,200 feet. These areas were inhabited mostly by nomadic enemies of Israel.

The northern limit of Israelite territory was often said to be the city of Dan. North of that were the Syrians. From there, in an arc to the east and southeast, was "the fertile crescent," leading to and from Mesopotamia. This was a principal trade route. The southern limit of Israel was said to be Beer-sheba (see, for example, 1 Samuel 3:20). Beyond this to the southwest is wilderness stretching to Sinai, and west of that is Egypt.

A general grasp of the geography of Israel and the ancient Middle East is indispensable in study of the Scriptures. Most Bibles have some maps with which you can make a modest beginning. Church and public libraries usually have Bible atlases for more detailed study. The geographical features of the land have changed little since Bible times. Modern visitors to Palestine usually remark about this. For instance, one sees today that the *wilderness* is for the most part quite barren and forbidding. The features that humans have constructed, on the other hand, are not changeless, and few of these are as they were in biblical times.

Archeology

We turn to archeology to help us recover much from the past. Cities in Palestine were rebuilt repeatedly on the ruins of earlier habitation. Thus there has been a settlement at Jericho since about 8,000 B.C. Towns and cities persisted in the same locations usually because they had a water supply and were readily defended. Sometimes elaborate tunnels were dug to provide access to water in case of siege. 2 Kings 20:20 mentions King Hezekiah's water tunnel. It was rediscovered in modern times, and an inscription on the wall verified the history.

"Tells" is the term archeologists give to the mounds produced by the succession of leveling and rebuilding.[1] Techniques for excavating these tells have been refined so that the ages of the succeeding layers can be determined and much about their history may be recovered. Archeology has become a complicated and exacting science, and much of the information it unearths is very valuable to biblical scholarship.

Small World / Large World

We may at first get the impression that the Old Testament people of God were not concerned about the world around their territory except when invasions forced their attention. A national, monotheistic faith might suggest that other peoples and lands were relatively unimportant. Since God created the world and then chose one people for the central role in sacred history, everything not Hebrew might be treated as a spin-off from this center.

But the relationship of God, people, and the world is prominent at the very beginning of Genesis. Notice what the creation stories in Genesis 1 and 2 imply about God and the world. The origins of the natural world are recounted because it is God's world. What does the text mean, *And God saw that [it] was good?* Humankind is the crowning act of creation in Genesis 1. What significance do you see in that?

The story of Abraham deals with Yahweh's choice of one family to be the channel of divine blessing upon humankind. The narrative develops against a backdrop of the whole Near Eastern world. Abram/Abraham emigrates from Mesopotamia and lives for a time in Egypt (Genesis 12). He camps at a number of places in Palestine, which was then settled largely by Canaanites.[2] The blessing by Melchizedek, Genesis 14:18-20, king of Salem (pre-Israelite Jerusalem), is a hint that Israel related Yahweh to the people around them. *God Most High*—in Hebrew *El Elyon*—is the name for the supreme Canaanite God. In

---

1 *Tell* is an Arabic word for a hill, natural or artificial.
2 Perhaps his "business" was caravans, as Professor W. F. Albright has suggested.

conversation with Melchizedek Abram combines this name with *Yahweh*. Here is early evidence that the God of Israel is indeed sovereign over the world. God's people are related to the world both by their place in creation and through the traditions of their ancestry.

Israel and the Promised Land

The promise of a land in which to settle implies that the world may be ordered in any way that God's chooses. The promise goes back to God's word to Abraham, *by your offspring shall all the nations of the earth gain blessing for themselves* (Genesis 22:18). Abraham himself owned only a burial plot, which he purchased (see Genesis 23), and his descendants became slaves in Egypt before the promise came to reality.

The defeat of Egypt's power and events at the beginning of the exodus gave evidence that Yahweh is sovereign over the world. The Egyptian magicians could duplicate some of the "wonders" that Moses performed, but only Yahweh was supreme over life and death. At Sinai Yahweh was revealed in natural phenomena. When Israel confronted hostile tribes and kingdoms during the wilderness wanderings, Yahweh's delivering power gave further evidence that the world they lived in is indeed God's world.

We must read the biblical narratives carefully to see whether they reflect the time that is being described or imply the later period when the narrative was written down. For example, at an early period some people thought that their gods could be persuaded to manipulate the forces of nature for their well-being. According to 1 Kings 20:23-28, an enemy thought that Israel's *gods are gods of the hills*, so Israel could be defeated *in the plain*. Such views reflect the world setting of the people involved.

Solomon introduced international sophistication to the Israelite scene along with territorial expansion, but late in life he *did what was evil in the sight of the LORD* (1 Kings 11:6). Elijah and Elisha both had varied and exciting conflicts with foreign peoples. Omri, king of Israel, was a very successful ruler from a political viewpoint, but the record in 1 Kings 16:25 says that he *did more evil than all who were before him*. The Israelites repeatedly forgot that God, who made the world, intended that they be the agency for divine blessing of the world. Ultimately, failure to come to terms with their proper place in God's scheme of things brought about the downfall of Israel and then Judah.[3]

---

3 Details of this history are provided in Themes 5 and 6.

Prophets and the World View

Throughout the Bible there runs a serious belief that the whole world is God's and that God is directly concerned with the whole world. Consequently God's people dare not ignore their relationship to this world or the responsibilities such a relationship imposes. Believing this is easier, however, than following its practical social, political, and moral demands.

The message of the divine destiny of God's people was prominent in the proclamation of the latter prophets.[4] Along with the fate of neighboring kingdoms, Amos pronounces Yahweh's judgment upon Israel. Read **Amos 3:2**, and notice *therefore*. In **Amos 9:7** the prophet goes a step further and declares that the migrations and relocations of Gentile nations are under Yahweh's will and control.

The prophets faced the question of how Israel was to be a blessing to the nations, for the Jews did not seek converts. Micah looks to a future *ruler in Israel*, who will *be great to the ends of the earth* (Micah 5:2-4). Isaiah 40-55, written during the period of the exile in Babylon,[5] says much about Israel and the nations. The key figure is called the *suffering servant* (as in 42:1). Sometimes it seems this is an individual (53), but elsewhere it is an elect remnant of God's people, who were designated to be the agents of hope in the world (41:8, 9; 49:6). The prophet repeatedly emphasizes the universal sovereignty of Yahweh. In 40:15 he says, *the nations are like a drop from a bucket*. Read **Isaiah 45:1-13, 22, 23**.

In exile many Jews must have been tempted to conclude that a Babylonian god had proven stronger than Yahweh, and they would find it hard to understand how Yahweh could allow them to suffer this terrible indignity. Sometimes they looked to a final reckoning referred to as *the day of the LORD* or simply *the day* (for example, see Joel 3:11-14). The theological achievement of Isaiah is therefore remarkable. Read **Isaiah 65:17-25**. The prophet has not given up on this world. He casts his hope in terms of *a new earth*, but it is not otherworldly.[6]

Facing a Dilemma

The Hebrew people found the world power of God troublesome, so it is a difficult subject in the Hebrew Scriptures. How can God's universal sovereignty be reconciled with the choice of one people for special, exclusive relationship? How can the world be the creation

---

[4] For the term "latter prophets" review Introduction, Part 1.

[5] Cyrus the Persian is referred to as Yahweh's *anointed* in Isaiah 45:1. This and other details indicate that the book of Isaiah contains portions that were not written by Isaiah, the son of Amoz (Isaiah 1:1) but were collected under his name. This point is not vital to this theme and will be taken up later.

[6] Note that the prophet also looks for *new heavens*. Hope is considered at length in Theme 10.

and possession of God and yet be alienated from and even opposed to God? How can people be God's agents in the world without becoming tainted from their contact with the world? There is no final resolution of these questions in the Hebrew Scriptures.

The book of Jonah is an example of this dilemma. The prophet is reluctant to go on a mission to Nineveh precisely because he fears he may be successful! He is unwilling to face the possibility that the Ninevites may share God's favor. Jonah speaks for a narrowly exclusive view of Jews who are unwilling to undertake the world role that Yahweh has set for them. But Yahweh is concerned for the pagan city, and the book becomes a dramatic call for God's people to fulfill the divine will.

The Maccabean rebellion freed the Jews from political power of paganism, but it did not solve the theological dilemma. The political freedom of the Jewish nation did not eliminate the demand for a workable relationship with the rest of God's world. When the Romans took over, they at first allowed the Jews some religious privileges, but finally Caesar could no longer tolerate their primary loyalty to God.

Nature and World View

We have been dealing with the relationship between God's world and Israel's national life and religion. There is a great deal more to be said about the world of nature. The Bible relates nature closely to faith and history. All human activity takes place in some relation to nature, and the destiny of the natural creation is under God's sovereign sway and purpose.

Adam and Eve are given responsibility for certain parts of nature. But the idyllic existence in Eden soon ends, and toil becomes necessary for human survival (Genesis 3:17-19, 23). There is no indication here that nature has become evil. The *curse* against the *ground* is the result of human failure. Responsibility for nature is renewed with Noah. Read **Genesis 9:1-10**. Although the world is pictured in other passages as the arena for the forces of evil, that is not God's intention. God maintains sovereignty over all creation in spite of the consequences of wrong human choices.

The grim side of nature is sometimes viewed as a sign of God's displeasure. Sometimes (but not always) disasters in nature are declared to have been sent as punishment from God. This is how the death of Egypt's firstborn is interpreted at the exodus. For other examples, see 2 Samuel 21:1; 1 Kings 8:35, 36. The great flood (Genesis 6-8) comes because of Yahweh's displeasure with evil humankind but is not directed against the whole creation. The rainbow covenant is related to all earth's creatures.

Yahweh's power over the created world is fully affirmed in the final chapters of Job. (Review Job 38:1-11.) Everything that Job beholds in nature is under the power of Yahweh. Even *Leviathan*, a creature representing ugly, evil nature, is subject to the divine will (41:1). Job is finally impressed and in a brief confession acknowledges Yahweh's sovereignty (42:1-6). Natural hardships are not always an indicator of spiritual failure.

Usually nature is benign. The Promised Land was *flowing with milk and honey*. Several of Israel's annual festivals are connected with the cycle of nature's productivity.[7] The Psalms are full of praise of nature and nature's God. See Psalms 65:9-13; 104:1-24. Many other Psalms repeatedly and beautifully express the conviction that God made the world, continues to rule it, and so possesses it completely. **Psalms 19:1-4** and **24:1, 2** are probably familiar. (See also 95:3-6; 103:19; 139:7-12.) Prophets often associate the future happiness of God's people with a wonderful increase of nature's bounty. See Isaiah 35.

We might expect that such concern with nature would be seen as sure proof of God's sovereignty and would lead people to recognize God's rule. There is no indication, however, that contemplation of natural phenomena produces sufficient revelation to lead people to become devoted to Yahweh God. Nature is a mighty witness but not a final proof.

FOR FURTHER STUDY AND REFLECTION

Memory Bank

1. Psalm 19:1

2. Psalm 24:1, 2

Research

1. Familiarize yourself with the maps at the end of this book. In addition to the principal topographical details, note the location of these Old Testament cities:

Beer-sheba	Gaza	Rabbah
Bethel	Hebron	Samaria
Damascus	Jericho	Shechem
Dan	Megiddo	Tyre

---

7 These are discussed in Theme 9, Part 1.

2. Ask a librarian to help you locate books about biblical archeology. Read about one or more topics mentioned in this part, such as Canaanite religion, Jericho, or Hezekiah's tunnel.

Reflection

1. If you should travel to the Middle East today, what would you want to see? Why?

2. What particular relevance does this theme have for God's people today with regard to: (a) our care of the earth? (b) our relationship to the world's peoples?

PEOPLE LIVE IN GOD'S WORLD

THEME 4

Good News in All the World

PART 2

SUMMARY

The Christian faith arose in the land of the Hebrew Scriptures, but it soon spread through the wider world. Almost all of Jesus' ministry was carried out in Palestine, but his outlook embraced all humanity. He was also intensely aware of the world of nature. His followers moved out of the confines of the Jewish world, at first hesitantly, then boldly under Paul's leadership and influence. Paul, a Roman citizen, took his mission to the west, confident that the whole world is God's. Some New Testament texts use "world" in a negative sense, but God's sovereignty is affirmed throughout. Christ's victory guarantees final renewal for the world.

BASIC BIBLE REFERENCES
Matthew 6:26-30; 28:16-20
Luke 12:54-56
John 3:16, 17
Acts 11:1-18; 13:44-48
Romans 8:18-23, 38, 39; 13:1-7
2 Corinthians 5:17-20
1 Peter 2:13-17
Revelation 21:1-5

WORD LIST
Beelzebul
Deacons
Gentiles
Hellenistic
Syrophoenician
World

Jesus and the World He Lived in

Jesus was born in the land where the Hebrew Scriptures had developed. The religious, social, and political impact of this fact can hardly be overemphasized. From babyhood through youth Jesus was initiated into Jewish religious life (see Luke 2:22-24, 39-47), and according to Luke 2:52 he adjusted very well. His mature ministry was in a land rich in associations from the lives of his ancestors.

Jesus' public career was affected by two political facts of the past. (1) Two hundred years before his time the Jews had gained independence, and the fervor of that Maccabean revolution was not forgotten. (2) One hundred years before Jesus' time the Romans had conquered Judea, and the Roman presence was deeply felt and resented by most of Jesus' hearers. After his resurrection, his followers asked, *Lord, is this the time when you will restore the kingdom to Israel?* (Acts 1:6).

The geographical movements of Jesus' public ministry appear to be deliberate. His instructions to the twelve disciples when they were sent on a mission include a charge to restrict their travel to Jewish territory (Matthew 10:6). In an encounter with a Syrophoenician woman (Matthew 15:21-28) Jesus implies that she is an outsider, but he softens this sharp edge by his kindly conversation. In his Nazareth sermon he used illustrations in which Elijah and Elisha cared for non-Jews. This proved to be very unpopular, but it reflects the breadth of Jesus' outlook (Luke 4:25, 26). A visit to Samaria and his conversation with a woman there at Jacob's well also reveal a wide horizon in his mission (see John 4:1-42).

Luke's Gospel includes the good deed of a centurion (7:4, 5), the parable of the good Samaritan (10:30-37), and the healing of ten lepers, one a Samaritan *foreigner* (17:11-19). Mark's Gospel gives explanations of customs and words to help non-Jewish readers. Matthew is perhaps the most Jewish of the Gospels, but it ends with "the great commission," which commands Jesus' disciples to *make disciples of all nations*. Read **Matthew 28:16-20**.[1] The risen Christ tells the assembled disciples that *repentance and forgiveness of sins is to be proclaimed in his name to all nations* (Luke 24:47).

In the New Testament the world is used with various shades of meaning. Sometimes it means heaven and earth; sometimes it indicates the inhabitants of creation.[2] It may refer to the environment in which people live.[3] It may express a negative contrast to God's way.[4] We must be careful, then, when we encounter the word "world" in the New Testament. It may be good, bad, or indifferent; the context must tell us which. Read **John 3:16, 17**, probably the best-known passage in the Gospels. What does it say about *God* and *the world*?

Jesus and Nature

Jesus spoke much about nature. His sayings and stories are full of references to the countryside. One of the best-known passages is **Matthew 6:26-30**, from the Sermon on the Mount. Much of his ministry is conducted out-of-doors. Recall how many incidents take place on or around the Sea of Galilee. In **Luke 12:54-56** he makes weather observations. A familiar parable tells about two men who built houses without regard to danger from weather (Matthew 7:24-27). His illustrations and lessons show that he is constantly close to the natural world around him.

In Luke 13:4, 5 Jesus refers to an otherwise unknown accident in which people *were killed when the tower of Siloam fell on them*. These were not *worse offenders than all the others living in Jerusalem*, he says. Natural events are not punishment from God, but they should cause people to *repent*, that is, to redirect their lives according to God's will.

There was an unusual darkness during the early afternoon hours when Jesus hung on the cross—as though nature felt the horror of the occasion (Mark 15:33). Matthew relates that

---

1 The Greek word translated *nations* may also be rendered Gentiles; TEV has *all peoples everywhere*. The point is strengthened whichever translation is used.
2 See Matthew 25:34; Acts 17:6; Romans 1:20; Hebrews 1:6
3 As in John 12:25; 17:15; 1 John 3:17; 5:4, 5.
4 As in John 15:18, 19; Galatians 6:14; 2 Timothy 4:10; James 1:27; 4:4; 1 John 3:1.

there were other strange phenomena including an *earthquake* which led the attending centurion to declare that Jesus was God's son (Matthew 27:54).

The Early Christian Mission

Jesus warned his followers that their mission in the world around them would not be easy. The presence of Judaism in the Hellenistic world was sometimes a help and sometimes a difficulty for the new movement. Translation of the Hebrew Scriptures into Greek had helped the Jewish faith survive outside Palestine, and that Septuagint version became the Bible of the Christian missionary church.[5] While Judaism was struggling to survive in the first-century world, Christianity moved deliberately into that world as a field for mission.

At Pentecost, after Jesus' resurrection, many people from other lands were in Jerusalem because of their relationship to Judaism, and they were immediately drawn to the Christian faith (Acts 2:5-11). Peter connects this with Jesus' plan and promise (Acts 2:38, 39). Thus the early church claimed the authority of Jesus for its mission (recall the Great Commission).

The universal outreach of the gospel caused friction among some of the first Christians. When the momentum of the faith led Christian leaders to accept Gentiles, difficult tensions developed because of the diverse backgrounds of the members. Conflict in one such situation led to the appointment of the first deacons (see Acts 6:1-6). Note that the names of these men are Greek. Two of them soon attracted attention and caused problems.

One deacon, Stephen, was opposed by Jews of non-Palestinian background because of his powerful preaching (Acts 6:9-11). His defense (which is told at length in Acts 7) infuriated his enemies, and this resulted in his being stoned to death. Philip, another deacon, engaged in a successful mission to Samaria (Acts 8:4-25), and brought the Jerusalem leaders to investigate the situation. Philip also preached effectively to an Ethiopian official in a chariot (a sort of hitch-hiking evangelism; see Acts 8:26-40). A milestone in the church's mission was reached when Peter visited a Roman centurion and was prompted by the Holy Spirit to baptize the soldier and his household. Read **Acts 11:1-18.**

Paul's Mission

When Paul grasped the worldwide intention of the gospel, he moved boldly to evangelize both Jews and Gentiles. His letters provide a theological foundation for world Christian mission. In **Acts 13:44-48** read how Paul took a radical step. During this same journey Paul

---

5 Scriptural quotations in the New Testament are frequently from the Septuagint.

and Barnabas had a remarkable brush with Greek religion at Lystra in Asia Minor; first they were treated as gods, then they were stoned (see Acts 14:8-19). During Paul's next journey he visited Athens, the very center of Greek religion and secular philosophy.[6] This marked another step of the Christian movement into the non-Jewish world.

Paul's letters reflect this advance into the Greco-Roman world. In Galatians 2:6-10 he recounts how the Jerusalem church approved his Gentile mission. In his correspondence with the Corinthian church he counters the pagan influence of their city. The moral environment shocks him (see 1 Corinthians 5:1; 6:9-11). Christians are to live in such a society without compromising their faith (see 1 Corinthians 10:23-29; 2 Corinthians 6:14-16). The list of personal greetings in Romans 16 contains Greek and Roman names.

The social structure of pagan society raised serious questions for Christian faith. Slavery was widely practiced and accepted, and Paul makes many references to the subject, sometimes very delicately. The letter to Philemon concerns a slave Onesimus. Paul does not mount protest movements, but he insists that Christian faith must make a difference in social relationships (see Ephesians 6:5-9; Colossians 3:11, 22-24; 4:1; 1 Timothy 6:1, 2; Titus 2:9, 10).

Paul's travels expand the geographical horizons of the first-century church. A map will help you gauge the extent of his travels. When he writes to the church at Rome, it has already been active for some years. He expresses his hope to visit them, *when I go to Spain* (Romans 15:22-24). Those plans did not work out, but he did reach Rome near the end of his career (Acts 28:11-16). This involved a hazardous sea voyage, from which we may learn much about navigation on the Mediterranean Sea in the first century. Theme 5, Part 3, will look at Paul's travels from a biographical perspective.

Rome and the Pagan World

Roman imperial power is always in the background of New Testament events, but that power is viewed in various ways. Roman authorities crucified Jesus, yet he prayed for those who carried out the sentence (Luke 23:34), and Paul implies that Rome acted in ignorance (1 Corinthians 2:8). There is evidence that Paul was somewhat proud of his Roman citizenship. At any rate, he took advantage of it (see Acts 16:37-39; 22:25-29; 23:26, 27). Prayer for civil authorities is enjoined in 1 Timothy 2:1, 2. The legitimacy of human governments is recognized in **1 Peter 2:13-17**.

---

6 Review Acts 17:22-34, a Basic Reference in Theme 3, Part 3.

The Roman Caesars, however, often did not merit respect. Several of the Caesars thought that they should be treated with divine honors. Since the Roman gods were thought to have human failings, and Roman moral standards were generally far below those of Jews and Christians, pagan Romans were not offended by such claims. But for those who believed that God is sovereign in the world, there was an inevitable conflict.

Read **Romans 13:1-7**, where Paul discusses his view of government at that stage in his career. He is on good terms with rulers, but human governments are not permanent fixtures in God's world. Paul's relationship with Roman authority finally turns bad. He exercised his right to appeal to Caesar, but tradition tells us that Paul was eventually put to death by the emperor's authority. 1 Peter 4:12-17 describes how it is when matters turn ill for the church.

Colossians 1:23 states that *the gospel...has been proclaimed to every creature under heaven,* but this is surely a rhetorical exaggeration. There were very many pagans that did not have an opportunity to hear the good news about Christ. What is their fate? Paul says that all people should be able to perceive God in the created world and therefore they should acknowledge God's power (Romans 1:18-25). He writes that there is law *written on their hearts*, which renders all people liable to God's judgment (2:12-16). God nowhere is *without a witness*, Paul says at Lystra (Acts 14:16, 17).

The World and Evil Power

Jesus recognizes the power of evil in the world. He speaks freely about it, but he uses terms and ideas that were current in his day. Thus the world may be the arena in which God is combatting evil. In John's Gospel Jesus refers three times to *the ruler of this world*, and it is clear he is thinking of an evil power (12:31; 14:30; 16:11). In each instance, however, he is bringing the power of that ruler to defeat.

In his farewell discourses Jesus speaks of the world much as we should refer to pagan society or secular circles. He contrasts this to the company of his chosen followers (see John 15:19; 16:20; 17:6, 14-16). He has no doubt about how his mission will turn out: *I have conquered the world!* (John 16:33.) His ministry challenges and will defeat the power of evil in the world. When he is accused of being in partnership with *Beelzebul, the ruler of the demons,*[7] Jesus insists that he is breaking the power of evil (see Luke 11:15-22).

---

7 You may find this name in your Bible Dictionary under *Beelzebub* or more probably *Baal-zebub*, which gives a clue as to the pagan origin of the name.

Occasionally there is a hint that the power of evil temporarily rules in the world. In Jesus' temptation the tempter[8] offers Jesus authority over *all the kingdoms of the world* (Matthew 4:8-10; Luke 4:5-8). Without discussing whether such an offer was at all possible, Jesus rejects it with a declaration of the absolute supremacy of God. Ephesians 6:12 speaks of *the cosmic powers of this present darkness...the spiritual forces of evil in the heavenly places,* but the same epistle declares that Christ is *far above all rule and authority and power and dominion* (1:21). While the power of evil is potent, it is ultimately subject to God's supreme rule. Indeed, it has already been doomed by the victory of Christ, and thus there is no dualism.[9] Paul states this beautifully in **Romans 8:38, 39**.

The Future of the World

The future of the world is directly related to what Christ has already done. Paul ties this to creation when he writes in **Romans 8:18-23** that *the whole creation* yearns for the fulfillment anticipated through Christ and *the children of God*. God purposes to form a *new creation* out of persons who will be *ambassadors for Christ*. Read **2 Corinthians 5:17-20**.

Theme 10 goes into detail about the future of the world. God will finally suppress all opposition and *be all in all* (1 Corinthians 15:28). Isaiah's expectation of a renewed world will be accomplished. This is part of John's vision in **Revelation 21:1-5**.

FOR FURTHER STUDY AND REFLECTION

Memory Bank

1. Matthew 28:18-20

2. John 3:16, 17

3. Romans 8:38, 39

Research

1. On the maps at the end of this book locate these New Testament cities:

Athens	Corinth	Lystra
Bethlehem	Ephesus	Nazareth
Caesarea (2)	Jerusalem	

---

[8] Do not get stuck on the character of *the devil* at this point. We shall consider this matter in other themes.
[9] See Theme 3, Part 2, page 78.

2. Make a list of references to nature in the sayings of Jesus.

3. Who was Zeus? Hermes? (see Acts 14:12); Artemis? (see Acts 19:24-28, 35-37).

Reflection

1. The text refers to the question whether God can be understood from nature. What difference does the answer make with reference to Christian mission?

2. In what ways does Christian faith lead to concern for the needs of the world?

GOD'S PEOPLE HAVE LEADERS

THEME 5

Early Leaders in the Rise of the Nation

PART 1

SUMMARY
Human leaders are prominent throughout the early history of God's people. Joseph plays a unique role among the patriarchs. Moses is a commanding figure in both religious and political spheres. Joshua is a national hero. Judges are chieftains, usually in tribal crises. Samuel leads in the transition into the period of the monarchy, where Saul and David rally the people into nationhood. Miriam, Hannah, Ruth, and lesser-known women make significant contributions in the society of God's people.

BASIC BIBLE REFERENCES
Genesis 45:1-15; 50:20
Exodus 18:13-26
Numbers 14:13-23
Deuteronomy 1:1-14
Joshua 24:14-28
Judges 4; 21:25
Ruth 1:16, 17
1 Samuel 3:1-18; 17

WORD LIST
Arabah
Expiate
Negeb
Shekel
Shephelah
Wadi

Another Start in the Pentateuch

We have already noted that God called men and women to communicate the divine will and appointed them to be leaders of God's people. Much of the Bible story can be told by surveying the lives of these leaders. We now turn our attention to how these leaders responded to God's appointment and showed the people God's way. Since this includes much story material, the Basic Bible References are lengthy. Other references are numerous. Read as much as you can manage.

God chose Abraham to be the first great patriarch of God's people. He founded a clan that grew with his son Isaac and grandson Jacob and their families. The story of Abraham's great-grandson Joseph leads to the change from a clan to the tribes that became the Israelite nation.

Joseph's remarkable rise to a position of power in Egypt is told in Genesis 37, 39-41. Scan these chapters if you are not familiar with the story. Eventually Jacob and Joseph's brothers go to Egypt to escape a widespread famine. Read about Joseph's meeting with his brothers in **Genesis 45:1-15**. In **Genesis 50:20** Joseph declares that the sequence of events has worked out God's will.

The Career of Moses

In previous themes Moses appears as a key participant in events and as God's agent in delivering great religious truth. Now we shall focus on the man himself and how he led God's people in response to God's call. Moses' birth and early life are recounted in Exodus 1:15-2:10. The story of how he was adopted by Pharaoh's daughter is familiar. In what ways would these early circumstances affect his later career? Notice the key role played by women: Shiphrah and Puah, *the Hebrew midwives*; Moses' mother; his sister; and Pharaoh's daughter.

Events that came to a climax with Moses' call at the burning bush are told in Exodus 2:11-4:23. As you will recall, he is reluctant to assume the awesome responsibility, and Yahweh promises him the aid of his brother Aaron. Moses' power struggle with Pharaoh is related in Exodus 5-11. You need not remember all the details; a general summary of what happened is enough for now. Yahweh is really the chief actor in the exodus; Moses and Aaron are agents (Exodus 12:50, 51). The close relationship between Moses and Yahweh is apparent in the story of the crossing of the Sea of Reeds (Exodus 14:10-31). When we remember that this material was preserved in oral tradition for many generations, the esteem in which Moses was held is remarkable: *So the people feared the L*ORD *and believed in the* L*ORD and in his servant Moses* (Exodus 14:31).

We have already referred to the story about water from the rock (Theme 2, Part 1). Another incident in Exodus 17:8-13 tells what happened in a battle with Amalek. It went well for Israel when Moses held up his hand in blessing; but when he got tired, he needed help. In **Exodus 18:13-26** Moses learns to share leadership responsibility. This may be how "elders" began to function in Israel.

Moses' part in events at Mount Sinai is recounted in Exodus 19; 24; 32; 33; 34:1-10, 27-35. Again there are many more details than you need for following the story line. Moses continues to lead through the wilderness. The story line is picked up in Numbers 11-14. Several times Moses intervenes when the people anger Yahweh. In Chapter 13 twelve Israelites go into Canaan to spy on the Promised Land. Ten of the spies bring a negative report, and the people are dismayed. Read in **Numbers 14:13-23** how Moses challenges Yahweh to forgive them. (Verse 18 quotes words we read in Theme 3, Part 2.) Joshua and Caleb are optimistic spies. Later on Joshua becomes Moses' successor in leadership.

The incredible difficulty of Moses' task is highlighted in a rebellion led by Korah, Dathan, and Abiram (Numbers 16). Moses keeps punishment from falling on all the people. A second story about water from the rock is in Numbers 20:1-13. In 20:12 Yahweh accuses Moses and Aaron of impatient lack of trust and declares that they will not enter the Promised Land. The story of the serpents, Numbers 21:4-9, was noted in Theme 2, Part 1.

You may be feeling somewhat overwhelmed at this point, but you will gradually gain skill at untangling and organizing passages that at first seem jumbled and confusing. The more you learn about the Bible in its wealth of detail, the more skillfully you will sort out what is most important to remember.

To round out our view of Moses as a leader of God's people, we look briefly at the book of Deuteronomy. Read **Deuteronomy 1:1-14**. The whole book is a second recounting of God's law, set in the form of a farewell address by Moses.[1] Verse 7 includes five terms that are used today by students of Palestinian topography. Check *Arabah , Shephelah , and Negeb* in a Bible Dictionary. There are significant differences between Deuteronomy and parallel parts of the other Pentateuchal books. For example, the reason for keeping the sabbath commandment in Exodus 20:11 is related to God's rest from creating; in Deuteronomy 5:15 it is related to Israel's slavery in Egypt. In the law for the release of slaves, Deuteronomy adds a provision to *provide liberally* for a newly freed person (Exodus 21:2-6; Deuteronomy 15:12-18). Deuteronomy includes passages about the end of Moses' career and his death (32:44-52; 34).

The place of Moses in Judeo-Christian tradition can hardly be overestimated. Deuteronomy 34:10, 11 says, *Never since has there arisen a prophet in Israel like Moses...He was unequaled....* In Deuteronomy 18:15 is a promise that *the LORD your God will raise up for you a prophet like* Moses. (Peter applies this prophecy to Jesus in Acts 3:22.) Moses' part in the Passover and wilderness events further enhances his significance in the New Testament. He may indeed be regarded as the Old Testament model of a God-appointed leader. Only Samuel and David come close to playing so many roles. As human mediator of the law, "Moses" is sometimes the equivalent of "Torah" in the New Testament. (See, for example, John 1:17, 45; Luke 16:29.)

Joshua and the Conquest of Canaan

Yahweh commands Moses to commission Joshua to succeed him as leader of the Israelites (Numbers 27:18-23). When he assumes this critical task, Joshua's first assignment is to lead the people across the Jordan River into the Promised Land (Joshua 1:1-7). They are approaching from the east. Their way through the wilderness led them south of the Dead Sea and north through what is now the Hashemite Kingdom of Jordan to a point opposite Jericho. Joshua sends two spies ahead, and in Jericho they are saved from capture by *a prostitute whose name was Rahab* (Joshua 2).

---

[1] The name of the book comes from two Greek words meaning "second law."

To celebrate crossing the Jordan twelve memorial stones are set up at Gilgal, the new generation is circumcised, and the Passover is observed (Joshua 3-5). The famous battle of Jericho is described in Joshua 6. The city and its population is destroyed, but Rahab and her family are spared.

The complete destruction of Israel's enemies and their possessions is mentioned rather often in this period of Israel's development. Our standards of justice and morality revolt against this. Remember three things. (1) Such action was not considered immoral at the time. (2) Our ideas of justice and morality have been indelibly influenced by the later prophets and particularly by Jesus' teaching. (3) The destruction was a visible reminder that Israel was to be absolutely separated from the pagan civilization of Canaan and its neighbors.

We need not cover all the stories of Joshua's conquest of the land. They are not necessary for a general understanding of the period. There is evidence that the conquest was not simple nor complete in Joshua's time (compare Joshua 11:16-23 with 13:1). Available archeological evidence leaves many questions unanswered. Joshua's final charge to the people reaches a climax in **Joshua 24:14-28**.

The Judges

After the death of Joshua and his generation there is a sharp decline in devotion to Yahweh. This brings on political disaster. (See Judges 2:6-15 for a summary of the situation.) Leadership in this period seems to be sporadic and sometimes limited to one tribe or another. The leaders who appear are called "judges," but their activity is usually more military than political or judicial. Except for Samuel their achievements have no permanent effect on the nation. There is a recurring cycle: disobedience to Yahweh, oppression by enemies, *groaning* of the people, deliverance through a judge. (See Judges 2:16-19 for a summary of this cycle.) What judge did we study in Theme 1, Part 2? How did he lead Israel?

Here we note two more judges. Deborah is one of the famous women of the Old Testament. Her story is told in **Judges 4**, and Chapter 5 contains poetry about her victory. (Check 5:19-21 for an additional detail of the battle.) Another woman, Jael, plays a gruesome part in the same story. Perhaps the best-known judge is Samson, whose heroic story includes both comedy and tragedy. Read as much of Judges 13-16 as you have time for.

The rest of the book contains an odd assortment of stories that need not detain us now. The last verse of the book, **Judges 21:25**, is an apt summary of the political and moral situation in those strange times.

5:1

Samuel

Samuel may be called the last of the judges and the first of the prophets.[2] Although Moses is called a prophet and a judge (along with his assistants), he lives long before the periods dominated by judges and prophets. Samuel's career covers the first 24 chapters of the books that bear his name.

Samuel's birth and childhood make a charming and challenging story (1 Samuel 1-3). The prayer-psalm of Samuel's mother Hannah (Chapter 2) strongly influenced Mary's "Magnificat" (Luke 1:46-55). Read in **1 Samuel 3:1-18** how Yahweh calls the boy Samuel.

Eli is the priest-judge during Samuel's growing years. Things go badly for Israel, and the Philistines are the constant enemy. At 1 Samuel 7:3 Samuel assumes leadership, even acting as a priest (7:9, 10). Probably his chief accomplishment is managing the transition from tribal confederation to monarchy.

Saul and David

Samuel expresses reservations about putting kings over Israel. (This matter is examined further in Theme 6.) Nevertheless at Yahweh's direction he anoints Saul privately, and Saul is publicly acclaimed at Mizpah. Later, after Saul leads a successful battle against Ammonites, a great gathering at Gilgal reaffirms him as king. Why is the location appropriate?

Samuel takes the occasion to deliver a kind of valedictory address. He recounts *the saving deeds of the* LORD and promises the LORD's blessing, conditional upon the people's faithfulness. These events are spread through 1 Samuel 10-12. (Samuel's death is not mentioned until 1 Samuel 25:1 and 28:3.)

Saul never consolidates his rule, and flaws of character threaten his effectiveness almost from the start. At Yahweh's direction Samuel anticipates the future and anoints David to be Saul's successor (1 Samuel 16:1-13). David's first introduction to Saul's court is as a musical therapist, soothing Saul's evil spirit by playing on the lyre.

Perhaps the best-known story about David is his encounter with Goliath. Read **1 Samuel 17**. David continues to be connected with Saul's family (references are scattered through to 2 Samuel 21). His friendship with Saul's son Jonathan is noteworthy. The deterioration of Saul's character brings David more and more to the fore, but royal jealousy soon

---

2 See 1 Samuel 7:15 and 3:20. We noted this double designation in Theme 1, Part 2. In 1 Samuel 9:9, 11 he is also referred to as a "seer." This term indicates that he received divine messages in visions, but it is practically equivalent to "prophet."

compels David to go into exile. Here we may identify traits that later make David Israel's ideal king.

David becomes a kind of Robin Hood. On one occasion he asks for a contribution for his troops from Nabal, a *very rich...surly and mean* man, but Nabal refuses. Nabal's wife Abigail is *clever and beautiful*, and she averts a bloody feud by taking provisions to David. Nabal dies soon after, and the story has a romantic ending with David's marriage to Abigail (1 Samuel 25).

Later Saul consults *a medium at Endor*. The narrative gives a strange glimpse of folk religion at that period. Saul meets an apparition of Samuel, which gives the king a grim prediction of his death (1 Samuel 28). 1 Samuel ends with a disastrous battle in which Philistines kill Jonathan and Saul commits suicide.

David becomes one of the most important figures in the Old Testament. Also, his name appears more than fifty times in the New Testament. Only Moses and Abraham are mentioned there more often. His career as king is covered in Theme 6 and his fame as a psalmist in Theme 9. In 1 Samuel 13:14 he is called *a man after [the LORD's] own heart*, which Paul quotes in Acts 13:22.

The Story of Ruth

The book of Ruth is one of two books in the Hebrew Bible that bear a woman's name. It is set in *the days when the judges ruled* (Ruth 1:1), but the story must have been recorded much later, for the last verse traces Ruth's family line to David (4:22). The book mentions quaint religious customs, but you can scan the whole story without research.

Ruth's admirable traits are revered in Judeo-Christian tradition. She was noble, loyal, wise, resourceful, and loving. Her words in **Ruth 1:16, 17** are often quoted. We should not overlook the fact that David's great-grandmother was not a Jew, but a Moabite. She is included in Jesus' family tree (Matthew 1:5).

FOR FURTHER STUDY AND REFLECTION

Memory Bank

1. Summarize these stories:

> Joseph and his brothers
> Moses, Jethro, and the elders

Joshua's charge to Israel
Deborah's victory
The choice of David to be king

2. Memorize Ruth 1:16, 17 and explain its setting.

Research

1. Where was Canaan? Read about it in a Bible atlas and dictionary.

2. Check Midian, Amorites, Edom, and Philistines in the same resources.

3. Why are there two books of Samuel? In the Septuagint and some other versions Samuel and Kings are called 1-4 Kingdoms. Explain why this might be appropriate.

4. In the story of the birth of Samuel identify parallels to the stories of Isaac and Moses.

5. List the important women we have met in the Old Testament thus far.

6. Begin to develop your own chronological chart of biblical persons and events, and add rulers and nations that affected biblical history. This may be an expansion of the chart in the Appendix. A librarian can help you.

Reflection

1. How can you judge whether a leader is appointed by God?

2. How many leaders studied here serve as role models for religious leadership today? Consider, for instance, how Moses was a mediator and reconciler.

3. Think of some modern leaders who have seemed right for their time. How do they compare with Old Testament leaders?

GOD'S PEOPLE HAVE LEADERS

THEME 5

Prophets and Later Leaders

PART 2

SUMMARY
Elijah, the model prophet, and Elisha, his successor, struggle against a corrupting, alien religion. Micaiah, Amos, and others appear in a variety of circumstances. Isaiah, Jeremiah, and Ezekiel play key prophetic roles at critical times in the life of Judah, extending through the exile. In the return from exile Ezra the scribe and Nehemiah the governor help the struggling Jewish community to meet the demands of their new life. At the end of the Old Testament period seven groups of leaders emerge in Judea: priests, rabbis, scribes, Pharisees, Sadducees, Zealots, and Essenes.

BASIC BIBLE REFERENCES
1 Kings 19; 22:1-28
2 Kings 4:38-44; 19
Ezra 1:1-8
Nehemiah 6:1-16
Jeremiah 1
Ezekiel 1:1-3
Amos 7:10-15

WORD LIST
Essenes
Hasideans
Pharisees
Rabbi
Sadducees
Scribes
Zealots

A New Focus

Most of the prophets were leaders in the time of Israel's kings. They labored under a driving sense of God's special guidance. We shall follow the prophets in a generally historical sequence rather than in the order of the Old Testament books. Chronology will not be as important here as it is in our study of the kings in Theme 6, but you may find it helpful to refer to the chronology chart in the Appendix.

You will recall that the Hebrew nation divided after Solomon's rule. Descendants of David were kings of Judah in the south. Several different dynasties ruled Israel in the north. Prophets were active in both kingdoms. There is more about the Southern Kingdom, Judah, for it is important long after Israel, the Northern Kingdom, has ended. The fall of the Northern Kingdom is recorded in 2 Kings 17. The exile of Judah begins in 2 Kings 25.

Elijah, the Model Prophet

Elijah's work was in Israel. His duel on Mount Carmel with the priests of Baal is perhaps the most striking story about a prophet in the ninth century B.C. We have already read the passage (1 Kings 18) in Theme 1, Part 2. We have also noted his stay with a widow in the Sidonian town of Zarephath (1 Kings 17). Now read **1 Kings 19** to get a broader view of Elijah's activity.

Because of his powerful relationship with Yahweh and the bold pattern he set for later prophets, Elijah becomes the model prophet. At Jesus' transfiguration Moses and Elijah appear—Moses representing Torah, Elijah representing Prophets. In later Jewish belief Elijah is expected as a forerunner of the messiah. So Malachi writes, *Lo, I will send you the prophet Elijah before the great and terrible day of the LORD comes* (Malachi 4:5). Some contemporaries of John the Baptist think that John is Elijah come back to life (John 1:21).

Micaiah and Elisha

Elijah is not the only prophet to confront King Ahab. Some time later, Ahab enlists the help of Jehoshaphat, king of Judah, in a joint military operation. Read **1 Kings 22:1-28**. The four hundred prophets are a kind of professional court guild. It is apparent that they are yes-men and not God-appointed leaders. Micaiah proves to be the true interpreter of Yahweh's will. This story gives important insights into how various prophets functioned.

In 2 Kings 2 *a chariot of fire* takes Elijah *into heaven*. Elisha witnesses the sight and takes up *the mantle of Elijah*. Then follow many stories of the awesome deeds of Elisha, many of them reminiscent of Elijah. Read **2 Kings 4:38-44**. What New Testament story does this bring to mind? In Theme 1, Part 2, we noted how Naaman the Syrian was healed through Elisha's intervention (2 Kings 5:1-16).

Amos

Amos is reckoned to be the first of the "writing prophets," who appear in the eighth century B.C. Their messages come to us about as originally delivered and not as recounted by others. As a result, their books give us more message than action, the opposite of the records in Samuel-Kings. We have already referred to Hosea, who comes from this period and had a very unusual career in Israel (Theme 2, Part 1).

Amos came from the Kingdom of Judah, but he prophesied in Israel. His book is one of "The Twelve," which make up the fourth scroll of the latter prophets in the Hebrew Bible. His stature among the prophets, however, should not be measured by the brevity of his book. The courage with which he denounced evil is intense, and the force of his ethical message is memorable.

Amos labored *in the days of King Uzziah of Judah* (Amos 1:1), whose death is noted in Isaiah 6:1. A capsule description of Amos' activity is given in **Amos 7:10-15**. We can only guess at the results of his powerful preaching. He lived about the middle of the eighth century, and the Northern Kingdom fell in 722/721 B.C. His preaching did not divert Israel from destruction.

Isaiah Son of Amoz

The prophet Isaiah, son of Amoz, was active in Judah in the latter half of the eighth century. His call is dated *in the year that King Uzziah died* (Isaiah 6:1), that is about 740 B.C. according to modern calculation. Judah and Israel are unhappy buffers between Assyria, where power is rising, and Egypt, where power is waning. Early in Isaiah's career Israel falls. Judah believes the dynasty of David can never end, but the political situation becomes precarious. The deliverance from Sennacherib's army in the time of Hezekiah was referred to in Theme 1, Part 2. Now read about Isaiah's part in the story, **2 Kings 19**.

2 Chronicles is a somewhat idealized review of the history of Judah. It credits Isaiah with writing records of the monarchy in his time (2 Chronicles 26:22; 32:32), but they have not survived—our book of Isaiah does not match the descriptions. We do know that Isaiah was married and had two sons. Both of them were given unusual names that were meant to convey messages to Isaiah's contemporaries; check the footnotes to Isaiah 7:3 and 8:1. Parts of Isaiah's message that are directed to the future (especially Chapters 9 and 11) are more appropriately taken up in later themes.

Jeremiah

Jeremiah's activities in the affairs of his day are more fully recorded than details of Isaiah's public life. In sheer word-content Jeremiah is the longest book of the Bible. Read **Jeremiah 1**. The time is roughly a century after the beginning of Isaiah's career. Note the similarities between the call of Jeremiah and that of Isaiah. Jeremiah's career extends through the downfall of Judah in 587 B.C.

Jeremiah plays an important role all during the last years of Judah. The Babylonians have captured Assyria, and a power struggle has developed between Babylonia and Egypt. Judah, of course, is caught in the middle.[1] Babylonia wins a famous battle at Carchemish (605 B.C.) and becomes the ruling power in the Middle East.

Jeremiah repeatedly urges the people to hold fast to the covenant with Yahweh and to follow wiser courses in their political dilemmas. More than once the prophet is in trouble. To dramatize how grim the future is, he does not marry (Jeremiah 16:1-9). Once when he prophesied coming disaster, *the chief officer in the house of the LORD...put him in the stocks*

---

1 We may note that Babylonia is the area that is Iraq in modern times.

(19:14-20:6). Later he was brought to trial but was acquitted because of his status as a prophet (Chapter 26).

Yahweh instructs him to dictate his message onto a scroll, and Baruch, his scribe, reads it in the temple and then before the council of princes. Eventually the king burns the scroll, but Jeremiah dictates it again and adds *many similar words* (36:20-32). Later he is arrested and imprisoned, but because of the king's friendship—or fear—he is placed under house arrest (37:11-21). When Jeremiah continues to proclaim doom, he is put into a cistern. The king again releases him and places him in protective custody, where he secretly advises the king (Chapter 38).

Not long afterwards, Judah revolts, but Nebuchadnezzar subdues Judah and sets up a puppet state. When another revolt develops, Jerusalem is leveled. Jeremiah is treated well by the conquerors (39:11-14). He is allowed to choose between good treatment in Babylon and staying in Judah, and he elects to stay. His message is really misunderstood both by his own people and by their enemies. The people who remain in Judah are uneasy and decide to go into voluntary exile in Egypt. Jeremiah vetoes this decision, but they force him to go along (Chapters 41-43). There he continues to be spokesman for Yahweh and vigorously opposes idolatry among the exiles.

Lamentations, Nahum, and Others

The book of Lamentations is credited to Jeremiah in ASV, but it is really anonymous. Five beautiful, touching poems express mourning after the destruction of Jerusalem. We have seen how the Jews attribute everything to the rule of God, so the poet says that *the LORD has made [Zion] suffer* (Lamentations 1:5). This is not, however, to accuse God of evil; *the LORD is in the right, for I have rebelled against his word* (1:18). Again, *the steadfast love of the LORD never ceases, his mercies never come to an end; they are new every morning; great is your faithfulness* (3:22, 23).

The books of Joel, Obadiah, Nahum, and Malachi all come from this period. We do not have time or space to study each of these. Brief summaries of their contents may be found in a study Bible or in a Bible Dictionary. These books are mentioned for the sake of completeness.

Ezekiel

Ezekiel's vision of the valley of dry bones was included in Theme 1, Part 2. Here we focus on his relationship to events of his time. Read about his call in **Ezekiel 1:1-3**. It appears that he is among a group exiled early to Babylon about 597 B.C. The chronology of his prophecies is not certain, but the book falls into three distinct parts. The first twenty-three chapters consist mainly of warnings about what is to come. In 24:1, 2 Ezekiel hears that Jerusalem is under siege, and he turns to woes against Judah's enemies. In 33:21 he hears that *the city has fallen*, and his message turns to comfort and hope for God's people. His last great vision is of a new, restored temple (Chapters 40-47).

Ezekiel's character is unusual, and his prophetic practice differs considerably from that of Isaiah and Jeremiah. His book opens with an elaborate vision filled with symbolic figures and culminating in an appearance of *the likeness of the glory of the L*ORD (1:4-28). He sometimes uses what we might call "object lessons." In Chapter 4 he makes a model of Jerusalem and portrays a siege. Then he lies down beside it for many days, first on one side, then on the other, signifying punishment of Israel and Judah.

Postexilic Leaders

Jeremiah foretold that the exile in Babylon would last seventy years (Jeremiah 25:11, 12; 29:10). When the chronicler tells how that period came to an end, this fulfillment is mentioned (2 Chronicles 36:21-23). Two leaders of the return from exile, Ezra and Nehemiah, give their names to books. We can identify Nehemiah's period approximately, for he appears to have been governor of Judah when Artaxerxes I was king of Persia, 464-422 B.C.

Begin your reading with **Ezra 1:1-8**. The rest of Chapters 1-6 deals with the return of the exiles. The chain of events in these books is very difficult to untangle, and most of the details do not concern us. Our focus is on the leaders. The prophets Haggai and Zechariah are mentioned in Ezra 5:1. Ezra is more concerned with religious affairs than is Nehemiah. He describes the rededication of the temple and the celebration of Passover (Ezra 6:16-22). He directs a movement to abandon marriages with *foreign women* (Chapters 9, 10).

Nehemiah's first task is to rebuild the walls of Jerusalem. There can be no political stability until defenses are in place. Nehemiah is opposed by Sanballat, who seems to be the official from whose territory the Jewish state is being carved out. The story is sketched roughly in Nehemiah 1-7. Read **Nehemiah 6:1-16**.

In Nehemiah 9:6-38 Ezra recounts a broad review of Israel's history. It is in the form of a national confession to Yahweh. In Nehemiah 9:17 we read familiar words: *you are a God ready to forgive, gracious and merciful, slow to anger and abounding in steadfast love.* The rest of the two books contains more about religious reforms than about political events. The times are extremely difficult, and the leadership of Ezra and Nehemiah is crucial.

The Maccabean Period and After

The Hebrew canon gives very little information about the period between Ezra-Nehemiah and Jesus. Nevertheless it is important to have some knowledge of these times so we can estimate what kind of leadership the Jews would be hoping for at the end of the period. There is a brief time of Hebrew national glory for nearly a century beginning about 165 B.C. The leadership of Judas Maccabaeus, of the Hasmonean clan, is especially important (noted in Theme 1, Part 2).

Following the return from Babylon, the Jews had no prophet-leaders. After the death of Judas Maccabaeus, *there was great distress in Israel, such as had not been since the time that prophets ceased to appear among them* (1 Maccabees 9:27). During the exile the priesthood goes into eclipse because there is no temple, but during the centuries immediately following the exile **priests** attain considerable influence. When the temple is rebuilt and its services and staff expand, the office of high priest becomes very powerful. Priestly writers play an important part in editing books of the Hebrew Bible. When Herod the Great gives new grandeur to the temple (late first century B.C.), the priests have increased prestige but are not popular leaders among the people.

Leaders at the End of the Old Testament Era

At about this same time experts in the study of Torah come into prominence. Already in the Maccabaean era persons devoted to Torah are known as *hasidim*, "pious ones." The natural leaders of these "Hasideans" are the **scribes**. Since the exile they have been responsible for copying the sacred books and are also experts at interpreting them as the law for God's people.

Some time in this period the synagogue develops as a religious institution. It fills the void left when the temple was destroyed, and it brings Jewish faith and practice closer to the people where they live. Lay teachers of the Law who become leaders in the synagogues are called **rabbis**. The word "rabbi" literally means "my great one," but it came to mean "master" or "teacher." Jesus is occasionally so addressed (see John 1:38).

About the middle of the second century B.C. two groups called Pharisees and Essenes emerge from a Hasidean background. Both groups are marked by intense dedication to doing the will of God as they believed it to be revealed in the Law, but they differ strongly in their interpretations of it. Along with the Sadducees and Zealots, these are commonly named as the major parties or sects within Judaism at the beginning of the Christian era.

The **Pharisees** come closest to being leaders in the style of the figures so far studied in this theme. The common people looked to them as standard-setters in religious matters. The Pharisees were concerned to make God's will clear for every area of life, so they developed an elaborate system of rules. They intended to put a "fence" about the Law to keep people from coming to ruin by transgression. This came to be regarded as "oral law" and was considered to have divine authority. By Jesus' day this Pharisaic doctrine holds a place alongside the written Torah. The scribes were natural allies of the Pharisees, and the two groups are often mentioned together in the Gospels. They were respected leaders but were not popular with the common people.

The **Essenes**, unlike the Pharisees, withdrew from the common life of the people and became, at least in some respects, monastic. The center of their activity was near the Dead Sea. There they produced and preserved what have come to be known as the Dead Sea Scrolls. Their influence on John the Baptist and early Christians in Galilee may have been considerable.

The **Sadducees** were mostly from priestly, aristocratic families. Jerusalem was their center, for the temple was their official responsibility. Their religious point of view was conservative. Politically they favored the status quo, and their public policy supported Roman rule. They had little direct influence among most of the people.

Zealots did not really form one party. The name is apparently applied to any cell of organized resistance to Rome, or more generally to any individual who resisted an enemy of Judaism. They appear early in the first century A.D. Many Zealots acted from deeply religious motivation, and they produced some prophet-like leaders.

FOR FURTHER STUDY AND REFLECTION

Memory Bank

Tell something important about each of the following:

Amos	Ezekiel	Pharisees
Babylon	Ezra	Sadducees
Elisha	Micaiah	Zealots

Research

1. Who besides Elijah was said to have avoided the experience of death?

2. Why is Elijah singled out for the role of forerunner of the day of Yahweh (See Malachi 4:4, 5)? How is this reflected in modern Jewish observance of Passover?

3. Choose one prophet and find out more about his life. A Bible Dictionary will help.

4. Read Ezekiel 20 to see how the prophet uses Israel's history to challenge her present.

5. In Hebrew *ben-* means "son of," and in Aramaic it is *bar-*. Thus we may call Isaiah "ben-Amoz." What other biblical names can you find that use this form? (What does "Benjamin" mean?) What parallels are there in modern languages?

Reflection

1. What leaders in the twentieth century might fit the pattern of leaders we have studied in this theme? What are your bases of comparison?

2. Religious groups may influence political decisions. What historical examples can you think of outside the Bible? Today?

3. How should religious leadership be exercised?

GOD'S PEOPLE HAVE LEADERS

THEME 5

The Baptist, Jesus, and Apostles

PART 3

SUMMARY

John the Baptist appears suddenly, and his prophetic proclamation creates a sensation. At John's death Jesus' public ministry begins, and he becomes famous as a powerful and unique leader. After his death and resurrection, apostles continue and extend Jesus' ministry. Peter is prominent. John, James, and others appear briefly. Paul emerges as the outstanding leader in the spread of the church. He travels widely and has many associates.

BASIC BIBLE REFERENCES
Mark 8:27-30; 11:1-19
Luke 3:1-20
John 2:1-11
Acts 1:15-26; 22:3-21
Galatians 1:13-2:14
2 Timothy 4:6-22

WORD LIST
Apostle
Aramaic
Disciple
Gospel parallels

John the Baptist

The Gospels all state that Jesus is preceded by a prophet-like figure, John son of Zechariah. Luke has two long passages about his birth (Luke 1:5-25, 57-80), and there are echoes of Old Testament stories we have read. A distinctive feature of John's ministry is *a baptism of repentance for the forgiveness of sins* (Mark 1:4), and he becomes known as *John the Baptist* (for example, Matthew 11:11).

Imagine the excitement when people begin to believe that a genuine prophet has appeared after so long a time! *The crowd... regarded [John] as a prophet* (Matthew 14:5). Some people even question *whether he might be the Messiah.* Read **Luke 3:1-20**.[1] Although John is so popular, he insists that someone *more powerful* is coming after him and will have proper qualifications for messiahship.

The synoptic Gospels tell that Jesus upon occasion identifies John with Elijah returned, as Malachi promises (see Malachi 4:5, 6; Matthew 11:7-11 and parallels).[2] In John 1:21 the Baptist denies that he is Elijah. Since both Jesus and John are interpreting the prophetic role, both can be right.

---

1 The term *Messiah* comes from a Hebrew word meaning "anointed." The equivalent Greek word gives us the term *Christ*. KJV, ASV, and RSV all read *Christ* in 3:15, but NRSV properly translates *Messiah*. These people were Hebrews, not Greeks.

2 Matthew 17:10-13; Mark 9:11-13; Luke 7:24-28. We shall not always list parallels, but it is profitable to examine them wherever they exist—a Gospel "harmony" gives them. You should note variations. They are useful for study and discussion.

John exercises a historic, prophetic function by denouncing the private life of Herod Antipas, and as a result he is imprisoned and eventually put to death (Mark 6:14-29). The biblical story has been much embellished in later times (for example, in the opera *Salome*).

Jesus' Early Career

Although Jesus' followers quickly came to believe that he was much more than a leader, most of the people who observed his public ministry thought of him as a teacher, a charismatic healer, and probably a prophet. It is appropriate, then, for us to look at Jesus' life from this leadership perspective.

Jesus' career is related to that of John at several points. Jesus comes to John to receive baptism. Matthew, looking at this from a later perspective, deals with a theological problem. John says that Jesus should baptize him, but Jesus replies, *Let it be so now; for it is proper for us in this way to fulfill all righteousness.* That is, Jesus wants to be completely identified with the whole religious tradition of God's people, and he accepts his destiny (Matthew 3:13-17). According to Mark 1:14,15 the end of John's life is a signal for Jesus to begin his ministry.

Luke writes that Jesus' and John's mothers were related (Luke 1:5,36). Mary plays a vital part in Jesus' life from start to finish (Luke 2:48, 51; John 19:26, 27). In *the first of his signs*, at the wedding in Cana, Jesus' mother is prominent. Read **John 2:1-11**. Jesus is reluctant to rush his ministry (*My hour has not yet come*), but his devotion to the needs of people is already evident.

A turning point in Jesus' career is described in **Mark 8:27-30**. At a retreat with his disciples they discuss his public image. Some people are saying that he is John the Baptist, or Elijah, or another prophet reincarnated. Herod entertains some such idea and says, *John, whom I beheaded, has been raised* (Mark 6:14-16). Peter boldly declares, *You are the Messiah.*[3]

Jesus as a Public Leader

Early in his ministry Jesus gathers an intimate group of followers. They are sometimes called "disciples," sometimes "apostles." Learn the meaning of these two terms. Why would Jesus choose **twelve** men? Jesus' leadership is often dramatic. He boldly challenges his disciples: *Follow me* (Mark 1:17, etc.). On one occasion he *was walking ahead of them; they*

---

3 Be sure you understand why NRSV translates "Messiah" rather than "Christ" (KJV, RSV). The parallels in Matthew 16:16 and Luke 9:20 give more elaborate replies.

were amazed (Mark 10:32). He claims, *I have set you an example* (John 13:15). Sometimes he uses striking figures: *I am the good shepherd* (John 10:11).

The twelve are part of a larger group (Luke 6:13), and a number of women are among Jesus' closest followers and supporters (Luke 8:1-3). He exerts widening influence by force of his actions and winsome words. When his popularity fluctuates, so does the number of his followers (John 6:66-68). Matthew notes that Jesus *had compassion for [the crowds] because they were harassed and helpless, like sheep without a shepherd* (Matthew 9:36).

Jesus often shuns publicity. He tries to hush excitement about his remarkable deeds. He expends his energy for the crowds, but he frequently retires for personal refreshment of spirit or for a private opportunity to teach his disciples (Matthew 14:23; Mark 6:31).

On one special occasion Jesus takes the spotlight; we call it "the triumphal entry" into Jerusalem. If he has political aspirations, this is the opportunity to make his move. But he does not capitalize upon the strategic momentum. Read **Mark 11:1-19**, where details are spread over several days. Jesus' movements hardly suggest a grab for power, but his enemies are worried. What does the narrative tell about Jesus' intentions?

In the Gospel of John the clearing of the temple is placed in Jesus' early Judean ministry (see John 2:13-17). In that setting it provides an early reason for the Jerusalem authorities to be concerned about a Galilean rabbi. But Jesus was not leading a revolutionary movement against Roman government, nor was he seeking power among the Jewish parties.

The Twelve[4]

Jesus' primary concern is not with otherworldly goals. Theme 7 studies how his teaching calls for results in the present life. Recall the meaning of the terms "disciples" and "apostles." Three from the circle of twelve form an inner-inner circle: Peter, James, and John (for example, at the transfiguration, Mark 9:2). When one of the original twelve is lost as a traitor, the infant church deems it necessary to select a successor. Read **Acts 1:15-26**. The symbolic importance of twelve as leaders is evident. What are the qualifications specified for the new apostle?

Tradition and legend record some details about the later lives of the twelve, but we are concerned only with New Testament data. This includes some information about Andrew, James, Philip, and Thomas. You may find the references in a concordance. Their qualities as leaders are more implied than demonstrated. Judas Iscariot is a special case. He was a

---

[4] A chart in the Appendix lists the names of the twelve.

sort of treasurer for the twelve, so he must have had ability. Indeed, we may assume that Jesus saw significant potential in each of those he chose, but we know nothing else about the other disciples.

Peter

Jesus calls Peter to leave his fishing business (Mark 1:16-18). According to John 1:40,41, Peter's brother Andrew hears John the Baptist point to Jesus as *the Lamb of God* and reports to Peter that he has *found the Messiah*. Peter's real name is Simon. Jesus promptly gives him a nickname: *Cephas*, from the Aramaic word meaning "rock," or *Peter* from the corresponding Greek word. (See the footnote in NRSV. Aramaic was the Hebrew-like language commonly spoken in Palestine.) This nickname appears to be somewhat ambiguous, for Peter was not always rock-like. What modern English nickname would be similar and appropriate?

Peter becomes the leader and spokesman for the twelve. For example, recall his confession in Mark 8:27-30 (above). When Jesus begins to say that his ministry will come to a drastic end, it is Peter who speaks out against this unwelcome declaration. (See Mark 8:31-33. Recall that this is a turning point in Jesus' career.) His speech and actions are often impetuous. Probably the worst instance is his denial of Jesus (see Mark 14:53-72).

Jesus anticipates that, whatever his failings, Peter will be a special leader. When Peter confesses that Jesus is the Messiah, Jesus tells him that he will be a foundation rock for the church and that he will give him *the keys of the kingdom of heaven* (Matthew 16:17-19). The same privilege of "binding" and "loosing," however, is granted to all the disciples (Matthew 18:18). The risen Christ tells the women at the tomb to report especially to Peter (Mark 16:7). Later Christ gives Peter a commission for the future (see John 21:15-19).

Peter's leadership in the early church is strong. He convenes the meeting to elect Judas' successor (Acts 1:15-22). He preaches a powerful sermon at Pentecost (Acts 2:1,14-40). He becomes a fearsome, charismatic leader and is treated with almost superstitious regard (Acts 5:14,15). He even brings to life Dorcas, a devout worker in the church at Joppa (see Acts 9:32-42).

Two other stories about Peter have already been studied. His experience with the Roman centurion Cornelius is noted in Theme 4, Part 2, and his deliverance from Herod's prison in Theme 1, Part 4. Two letters that bear his name are noted in later themes.

John, James, and Others

John and his brother James, fishermen-sons of Zebedee, are called to follow Jesus (Mark 1:19,20). Tradition has assumed that the disciple *whom Jesus loved* is this John. This description occurs in the Fourth Gospel (13:23, 19:26, etc.), and an apostle "John" is not mentioned there. The apostle John works with Peter for awhile in the early church. The three letters attributed to "John" are probably not by the apostle, for the author makes no apostolic claim. He probably is associated with tradition that stems from the apostle's ministry. The seer of Revelation gives his name as John, but we cannot tell whether or not he is the apostle.

John's brother James is one of the inner circle of Jesus' disciples. Aside from his prominence among the twelve, we know little about him except that he is the first martyr recorded from among the apostles (Acts 12:1,2). Several other men in the New Testament are named James.

Another James, whom Paul calls *the LORD's brother*, becomes an important leader in Jerusalem (Galatians 1:19; see also Mark 6:3). Paul implies that the resurrected Jesus appeared to this James (1 Corinthians 15:7), and we may infer that this brought him into active faith (see John 7:5 and Acts 12:17). In Acts 15 he serves as moderator of a church council. Paul refers to James, Cephas, and John as *acknowledged pillars* of the church (Galatians 2:9).

There are other persons who merit the title "apostle" because of their leadership in the early church. Find four names in Acts 14:14, Romans 16:7, and Galatians 1:19. Eleven disciples are named just after Jesus' ascension, and then *certain women, including Mary the mother of Jesus, as well as his brothers* are mentioned (Acts 1:13,14). It is not unreasonable to think of Mary as the first disciple.

Stephen is one of seven men chosen to be what we call "deacons" (Acts 6:1-6). He is a fearless preacher and, as we have already noted, becomes a martyr for his testimony. Philip, another of the seven, becomes an evangelist in Samaria and the coastal regions from Gaza to Caesarea Maritima (Acts 8:4-40). The only person actually called *deacon* in the New Testament is *our sister Phoebe*; see Romans 16:1.[5]

---

[5] Some versions read *deaconess* or *minister* or servant.

Paul

Without question the outstanding leader in the first-century church is Paul. His original (Jewish) name was Saul, but he becomes known by the Roman sound-alike Paul (Acts 13:9). We first meet him at the stoning of Stephen, which may have deeply impressed him (Acts 7:58, 8:1; see also 26:14). Paul's Christian career occupies most of Acts 13-28, but details should be checked and adjusted by reference to his letters wherever possible.

The story of his conversion is told three times in Acts. The reports supplement each other. Read the second one, given in a public speech when he is arrested in Jerusalem for the last time, **Acts 22:3-21** (the other versions are Acts 9:1-22; and 26:4-20). The longest biographical passage in his letters is **Galatians 1:13-2:14**. Other details of his life are collected in Acts and scattered throughout his letters.

He has no doubt that God has called him to leadership. Most of his letters begin by affirming that *he is called to be an apostle*, a claim he defends vigorously (as in the Galatians passage above). He goes head to head with Peter, but they remain friendly coworkers and divide areas of responsibility. He appears before the church council described in Acts 15, where all the leaders agree to a compromise.

Paul's Travels

Most of Paul's ministry was spent in what are often called his "missionary journeys." They are a notable achievement. The overland travel by foot would even today be extremely difficult. These trips are charted on maps in the Appendix. Acts recounts many details, but we need to study only general features now. At the beginning Barnabas was the team leader (Acts 13:1-3), but Paul almost at once becomes the most prominent. Here is an outline of the travels. The Scripture passages are for reference. Read as much as you can find time for.

First journey, Acts 13:4-14:28. The team leaves Antioch in Syria and sails to Cyprus and then to southern Asia Minor (Turkey, today). A circuit brings them back to the coast, and they return homeward by sea. Notable details are Paul's sermon in Antioch in Pisidia and the encounter with pagan religion in Lystra.

Second journey, Acts 15:36-18:22. Paul's associate now is Silas (a.k.a. Silvanus). They travel through Asia Minor to the northwest. At a spot near ancient Troy, Paul has a dream that he interprets as a call to cross into Europe.[6] They travel to Philippi in Macedonia, then

---

6 At Acts 16:10 the pronoun *they* changes to *we*. Perhaps at this point Luke joined Paul's group.

to Athens, and Paul spends a year and a half in Corinth. They return by sea and stop at Ephesus, Caesarea, and Jerusalem. Notable details are his imprisonment at Philippi and his sermon at Athens. In Corinth he works at his trade, tentmaking. Mention of Gallio in Acts 18:12 helps us date the incident: Gallio was proconsul in late 51 or early 52.

Third journey, Acts 18:23-21:17. Again Paul goes through Asia Minor to Ephesus, on to Greece (*Achaia*), and back to Ephesus for a two-year stay. After another swing through Greece he comes back to Asia Minor and sails to Caesarea. Details include his relationship with Apollos and other leaders, a riot in Ephesus, and the story of a young man who fell asleep while Paul was preaching in Troas.

The success of Paul's Christian missions brings strong opposition from Jewish leaders. Why would they be concerned about Paul when he was out of the country most of the time? Hostility comes to a head in Jerusalem. He is imprisoned at Caesarea (the Roman administrative capital), and when legal procedures drag on, he appeals to Caesar (the right of a Roman citizen).

Paul is sent by sea to Rome—sometimes called his fourth journey. See Acts 27, 28. The story of the shipwreck is famous. In Rome he is placed under house arrest, but he is able to conduct an effective ministry. The New Testament does not tell about the end of Paul's life. Tradition says he died a martyr in Rome. A letter that is addressed to one of his hand-picked associates contains the last message that may be from Paul. Read **2 Timothy 4:6-22**.

FOR FURTHER STUDY AND REFLECTION

Memory Bank

Identify each of the following by the indicated number of details:

John the Baptist (2)
Jesus (4)
Mary, Jesus' mother (3)
Peter (3)
Andrew (1)

James, Jesus' brother (1)
Stephen (2)
Philip (1)
Barnabas (1)
Paul (4)

Research

1. How may Jesus be considered a new Moses?

2. Find out all you can about the details in the Cana wedding celebration.

3. List all the women mentioned in this part and give information about each.

4. Prepare an outline of Paul's life.

Reflection

1. What kinds of leadership are demonstrated in this part? How may these be applied to life in the church today?

2. What modern Christian leaders have exerted significant influence in the world? Can you identify any who are affecting world life today?

3. How does a person's faith affect the ability to lead effectively?

THEME 6 — PART 1

GOD'S PEOPLE HAVE RULERS BUT ONE SOVEREIGN

Yahweh, Kings, and a United Kingdom

SUMMARY
From very early times God's people thought of Yahweh as king. When they acquire a human king, he does not replace but rules for Yahweh. Samuel anoints Saul and later David. David consolidates the kingdom, and his dynasty lasts four centuries. Israel's prosperity peaks in Solomon's reign, but under his son the kingdom splits.

BASIC BIBLE REFERENCES
*1 Samuel 8:4-9;
10:1, 9-13, 20-25;
11:14, 15; 12:14, 15;
15:22, 23
2 Samuel 2:1-11;
5:1-5; 7:4-16
1 Kings 3:1-15; 10:23-29;
11:9-13; 12*

WORD LIST
Apostasy
Royal theology
Theocracy

Yahweh and the Kings of Earth

We cannot be certain when God's people first thought of Yahweh as king. In Egypt they were under the pharaohs, who assumed the role of gods. When the power of Yahweh was pitted against the pharaoh, it would have been reasonable for the Israelites to conclude that Yahweh was their ruler as the pharaoh ruled the Egyptians. The song of Moses after the crossing of the Sea of Reeds ends, *The LORD will reign forever and ever* (Exodus 15:18).

Early Mesopotamian legends treat the rulers there as being under the particular, special favor of their gods. In Canaan Israel was surrounded by peoples who thought of their gods as monarchs. It would have been surprising if Israel had not come to associate royal terms and ways with Yahweh. This tells us that when we consider the beginning of monarchy in Israel and its later developments, we must not lose sight of the place of Yahweh as the ultimate ruler, the one sovereign.

While Israel was settling in the Promised Land, leadership was irregular. After the strength of Joshua, the times of the judges varied from near chaos to periods of hope. Yahweh is called *judge* in Judges 11:27, a sign that the human judges are Yahweh's subordinates.

After Gideon delivered some of the Israelites, they asked him to be king, but he answered, *I will not rule over you, and my son will not rule over you; the LORD will rule over you* (Judges

8:23). But one of Gideon's sons, Abimelech, set himself up as king, and he *ruled over Israel three years* (Judges 9:22). He ruled over only a part of Israel, however, and the whole grisly story soon ends.

Establishment of Monarchy—Saul

The circumstances that finally brought monarchy to Israel are like those that called forth several of the judges, but the story is given in much greater detail. After Samuel engineers a defeat of the Philistines (1 Samuel 7), the narrative skips to his old age. Here the transition to monarchy begins, and 1 Samuel 8-11 indicates that it happens in four steps.

(1) **1 Samuel 8:4-9**. The request for a king. Samuel warns of future trouble, but the people persist. Then follows the selection of Saul. A positive note in the process is given when Yahweh tells Samuel that Saul *will save my people...for I have seen the suffering of my people, because their outcry has come to me* (9:16). (2) **1 Samuel 10:1, 9-13**. Samuel anoints Saul. (3) **1 Samuel 10:20-25**. Samuel goes through the motions of choosing Saul again. Shortly thereafter Ammonite oppression comes to a head, and Saul leads Israelite forces to defeat the enemy. (4) **1 Samuel 11:14, 15**. Samuel and the people *renew the kingship*. Summarize this process in your own words.

From the outset, the rule of Israelite kings is evaluated on the basis of their relationship to Yahweh. Read **1 Samuel 12:14, 15** from Samuel's farewell address. His warning about the potential dangers of having a king (1 Samuel 8:10-18) has probably been edited in the knowledge of what happened later. Almost at once Saul's character weakness appears when he disobeys Yahweh. Saul and his son Jonathan have some military successes, but it is evident that the role of the king is not yet clearly defined. In one battle the command to *utterly destroy the sinners* (1 Samuel 15:18) was only partially obeyed;[1] some things were saved *to sacrifice to the* LORD. Samuel's oracle on this occasion is notable: **1 Samuel 15:22, 23**.

The shift of power from Saul to David is narrated in a series of stories. There is a sharp interplay of personalities and evidence of Saul's psychological breakdown. When a military parade celebrates David's victory, Saul goes into a jealous rage and tries to kill David (see 1 Samuel 18:6-12). Jonathan tries to protect David, but David finally flees into exile. David is forgiving toward the king. Saul's visit to the medium at Endor and his death at Mount Gilboa by the plain of Jezreel have been mentioned in Theme 5, Part 1.

---

1 This primitive practice is discussed in Theme 5, Part 1.

David

David's rise to prominence is described in Theme 2, Part 1, and in Theme 5, Part 1. The country was divided north and south, a rift that is reflected in the moves by which David becomes king. The first stage is told in **2 Samuel 2:1-11**. David is king in the south at Hebron (locate it on a map), but a son of Saul is ruling in the north. David's military leaders, especially Joab, and the northern forces under Abner play out a grim rivalry. *There was a long war between the house of Saul and the house of David: David grew stronger and stronger, while the house of Saul became weaker and weaker* (3:1).

Finally Israel comes over to David. Read **2 Samuel 5:1-5**. His capital at Jerusalem is strategically located near the border between Judah and Israel.[2] Subsequently the Ark is brought to Jerusalem, and the religious and political consolidation is complete. David has a fine palace, and he proposes to build a house for Yahweh. Read **2 Samuel 7:4-16**. Explain how the term house is used with more than one meaning.

David proceeds to organize his rule and neutralize his enemies. But the stories are not limited to glory and praise of the king. A sordid episode tells how he takes Bathsheba, another man's wife, and then arranges that the husband would die in battle (see 2 Samuel 11). The prophet Nathan helps David to realize the enormity of his deeds, and he repents sincerely (2 Samuel 12:1-15). Bathsheba's baby dies, but later she bears a son Solomon.

The king is hardly ruler in his own household. One of his sons, Absalom, is strong-willed, ambitious, unscrupulous, and badly spoiled. He leads a rebellion against his father. He is temporarily successful, but eventually dies in flight from battle. David is grief-stricken. The whole story is long (2 Samuel 13:1-19:15) but is not really important to the future of the kingdom. When another son puts himself forward to be David's successor, the writer remarks, *His father had never at any time displeased him by asking, "Why have you done thus and so?"* (1 Kings 1:6), which throws light on David's family problems.

Solomon

Upon David's death, Solomon succeeds to the throne and quickly establishes his position. Under his rule the kingdom becomes quite different. David acquired territory by warfare and welded north and south into a shaky union. Solomon consolidates the kingdom by political shrewdness and military organization. He takes full advantage of the period of peace. (His name comes from the same root as "shalom," which means "peace" and "well-being.")

---

2 From this point we use "Israel" to refer to the ten northern tribes and "Judah" to refer to the two in the south. The year 1000 B.C. is the approximate date of this union.

His reign has an auspicious beginning; read **1 Kings 3:1-15**. The building of the temple is a far-reaching achievement (1 Kings 5-7), and the dedicatory prayer attributed to Solomon is impressive (1 Kings 8). This temple and its successors become a focus for Jewish religion for all time. Solomon's reputation for wisdom, which is marked here, is considered in detail in Theme 8.

The writer hints at misgivings about Solomon's pluralism from the outset of his reign (note 1 Kings 3:1-3). This is related to his prolific marriages (1 Kings 11:3 says *seven hundred princesses*), which probably have political significance. This apprehension comes to a head in **1 Kings 11:9-13** (the religious peril in foreign marriages is specified in Deuteronomy 7:1-6). Solomon is laying a foundation for future disaster.

Try to distinguish in your mind the changes in the monarchy from Saul to David to Solomon. How far national power has developed may be seen in **1 Kings 10:23-29**. Now they are a nation with international relations. The king's court is pretentious. His political and military establishment is extensive. There is also a labor force of over 180,000, and 30,000 of them are *conscripted forced labor* (1 Kings 5:13-16). Remember that the narrative has been written by one who knows how it all turns out, so we may assume that the warning details are deliberately given.

Beginning about this time, a kind of "royal theology" develops. The king is explicitly portrayed as Yahweh's "son" or adopted vice-monarch. This shows up in what are now called "royal Psalms" (for example, Psalms 2, 21, 45, 72, and 110). These are balanced by other Psalms where the ultimate sovereignty of Yahweh is affirmed (for example 93; 95; 96:10; 97:1; 99:1-5). The Psalms are featured in Theme 9, Part 2.

All this magnificence appears to be more than the nation can bear. Only two generations back the people were a loose confederation of tribes. Rebellion is on the northern horizon, and the death of Solomon bodes ill for the future (1 Kings 11:26-43).

Division of the Kingdom

Intertribal rivalries seem never to have entirely ceased, and now they flare up. Solomon's son Rehoboam is unable to maintain the centralized power of his father. Read **1 Kings 12**. The division of the kingdom dominates the political picture and affects the religious situation from this time on. Though Rehoboam is not a good king, the dynasty of David continues and indeed survives as long as the Kingdom of Judah. Jeroboam's dynasty in Israel lasts only through his son's time. Israel has a succession of dynasties throughout its existence.

Jeroboam's success is short-lived. The narrative associates this with religious apostasy. The northern tribes are isolated from central worship in the Jerusalem temple, and Jeroboam institutes idolatrous worship: he sets up *calves of gold* at Bethel and Dan and himself participates in leading worship (1 Kings 12:25-33). His sin becomes a byword, and the narrative later stigmatizes him for it (among many examples, see 1 Kings 15:25, 26, 34; 2 Kings 23:15). The measure of royal success becomes *doing what was right in the sight of the LORD* (1 Kings 22:43).

Beginning with the story of David there are narratives in 1 and 2 Chronicles parallel to those in 1 and 2 Samuel and 1 and 2 Kings. Study Bibles note the parallel references. Sometimes the material is identical. In other instances there is substantial difference. Chronicles treats only the kings of Judah, so the story is told from a southern viewpoint. These parallels cannot all be read in the compass of this study. Part 2 includes some of the Chronicles narrative.

FOR FURTHER STUDY AND REFLECTION

Memory Bank

1 Samuel 15:22

Research

1. The friendship of David and Jonathan is often mentioned as a model. The story begins in 1 Samuel 18:1-4. Later (19:1-7) Jonathan tries to reconcile his father Saul and David. Chapter 20 is an extended narrative about the friendship. When Jonathan and Saul die, David's *lamentation* is a poignant masterpiece (2 Samuel 1:19-27). Read these passages and reflect on how this friendship heightens the drama of David's rise to the throne.

2. Jerusalem is a vitally important place throughout the rest of the Bible, so begin to familiarize yourself with its topography and history. Consult maps, a Bible Dictionary, and a Bible atlas if available.

3. Two of Solomon's administrative cities have been excavated by modern archeologists. If this interests you, look up Megiddo and Hazor in library resources.

4. What information can you find about Jeroboam's cult cities, Bethel and Dan?

Reflection

1. Few kings rule in today's world, and the role of monarchy has changed dramatically through the ages. How does this affect our idea(s) of God as "king"? How else could we picture God's rule in the universe as we perceive it now? How far can we modernize history? How do these problems relate to our study of the Bible?

2. The "Western Wall" of the temple area in modern Jerusalem is one of the most sacred sites for Jews today. Why is this so? Why was it formerly referred to as the "Wailing Wall"? What is meant by a "holy city"?

3. How are historical and geographical associations important in the Christian religion?

THEME **6**

PART **2**

GOD'S PEOPLE HAVE RULERS BUT ONE SOVEREIGN

Rulers and the Divided Kingdom

SUMMARY

The Northern Kingdom, Israel, undergoes many changes in dynasty, and many of the kings are not faithful to Yahweh. Israel is overthrown by Assyria, and the people are dispersed. In Judah, David's dynasty continues. Despite many dark days, there are some notable rulers. The kingdom ends with the fall of Jerusalem and exile in Babylon. The difficult postexilic period ends with a century of Maccabean freedom and hope for a new kingdom.

BASIC BIBLE REFERENCES
1 Kings 14:22-28; 21
2 Kings 17:1-24
2 Chronicles 22:10-23:21; 34:14-33
Psalms 89:19-21, 35-40, 46, 49; 132:11-18
Jeremiah 52:1-16
Daniel 6:25-28

WORD LIST
Assyria
Babylonia
Megiddo
Persia
Syria

The First Years of Division

Jeroboam's son rules Israel after him, but he is assassinated. The dynasty that succeeds him lasts only two generations. The details are somewhat difficult to follow, especially when the narrative jumps back and forth between Israel and Judah—and when kings' names are similar. We shall follow the highlights here, and the chronology chart in the Appendix will help you organize the details. It is more important to understand the message of the records than to memorize many particulars.

Sources that have not otherwise survived are often mentioned by the writer of Kings; for example, *the Book of the Annals of the Kings of Israel* or *of Judah* (1 Kings 14:19, 29). RSV translates these *Chronicles*, but these *Annals* could not be our books of Chronicles, which were produced after the books of Kings.

The moral and religious situation in Judah does not appear to be any better than that in Israel. Read **1 Kings 14:22-28**. Inroads by foreign powers ultimately bring to ruin the fortunes of both south and north. Although Rehoboam's grandson Asa *did what was right in the sight of the LORD* (1 Kings 15:11), he appeases the king of Syria, the policy that leads to final destruction.

Omri founds a politically strong dynasty in Israel though he *did more evil than all who were before him* (1 Kings 16:25). He comes to the throne in a chaotic time and establishes a new capital in Samaria. Years later, Assyrian records refer to Israel as "the house of Omri." Such international mention contrasts with

133 6:2

the terse record in Kings, where religious failure eclipses political success. His son Ahab marries a pagan, Phoenician princess, Jezebel.

Kings in the Times of Elijah and Elisha

Because he rules in the time of Elijah, Ahab receives considerable attention. During the same period Judah has a strong king, Jehoshaphat.[1] The careers of the two kings intersect when they becomes allies against Syria (studied in Theme 5, Part 2, because of the part played by Micaiah). It was a misadventure for Judah and fatal for Ahab.

Ahab and Jezebel are infamous, the epitome of opposition to the way of Yahweh in Israel. *Ahab did more to provoke the anger of the LORD, the God of Israel, than had all the kings of Israel who were before him* (1 Kings 16:33). The crucial confrontation with Elijah is studied in Theme 1, Part 2. Another story about the evil couple and Elijah is in **1 Kings 21**.

2 Kings contains a formidable amount of detail. The history is hard to reconstruct, and biblical experts do not entirely agree on details of the chronology. At this point in our study we need to remember only the material (1) that contributes to understanding the sweep of the biblical story and (2) that is important for "biblical literacy." Details given here will help you with this.

Elisha plays the role of king-maker, not only in Israel but also in Syria. He anoints Jehu, who puts an end to Omri's dynasty and deals a severe blow to Baal worship. The narrative says, however, that he did not abandon the sins of Jeroboam. Quite aside, it is noted that *he drives like a maniac* (2 Kings 9:20).

Evil family relations seem to spread at this time. Jehoshaphat's son marries Athaliah, Omri's granddaughter (so Ahab's daughter or niece). When her son, king Ahaziah of Judah, dies after a short reign, she kills all but one of the heirs and assumes rule over Judah. She is the only woman to become sole ruler in Judah or Israel, and her reign is a six-year break in the succession of David's line.

One son of Ahaziah escapes his grandmother's purge. The boy Joash becomes king. Read **2 Chronicles 22:10-23:21**. The reign of Joash is important because of the temple restoration. *A large amount of money* for this work is collected in *a chest* (2 Chronicles 24:8-14). On the negative side, Joash buys off the king of Syria from attacking Jerusalem, thus signaling the declining fortunes of the monarchy.

---

[1] Details of his reign are given briefly in 1 Kings 22 and more extensively in 2 Chronicles 17:1-21:1.

King Joash of Israel grieves at the bedside of Elisha, who is fatally ill (2 Kings 13:14-20; 14:23 indicates that both Israel and Judah had kings named Joash.) The resulting interview indirectly recognizes that Yahweh is the true King. The prophet uses an object lesson to convey Yahweh's message.

The End of Israel

The catalog of rulers in 2 Kings reflects the shifting circumstances in Israel and Judah. The two kingdoms actually go to war with each other, and on one occasion the wall of Jerusalem is breached. The territorial expansion of Israel reaches its zenith under Jeroboam II; he *reigned forty-one years* and recovered lost territory. He receives brief mention, however, for *he did not depart from all the sins of Jeroboam son of Nebat* (2 Kings 14:23-29). In contrast, his son reigns only six months.

The end of the Northern Kingdom comes swiftly. Kings follow in rapid succession and for awhile buy off the Assyrian king, Tiglath-Pileser III. In the changing fortunes of surrounding powers, Israel tries double-dealing, but it proves disastrous. Samaria falls to the Assyrians in 722/721 B.C.[2] Read **2 Kings 17:1-24**. The writer is sure that Israel's fall comes because of religious failures. The resettlement policies of the conqueror produce a population of mixed nationality in the area of the Northern Kingdom from this time on. Pagan religions mingle with Yahweh worship (see 17:24-41). This fosters the later antipathy between Jews and Samaritans.

The End of Judah

Judah has two more noteworthy kings. During the reign of Hezekiah the land is delivered from Sennacherib of Assyria—a story treated in Theme 1, Part 2, and in Theme 5, Part 2. 2 Chronicles gives lengthy attention to Hezekiah (Chapters 29-32).

Josiah, grandson of Hezekiah, comes to the throne as a boy. His immediate predecessors led in a deterioration of Yahweh religion in Judah. The Chronicler gives Josiah good marks for his early years (2 Chronicles 34:1-7). A momentous series of events begins with Josiah's decision *to repair the house of the L*ORD *his God* (2 Chronicles 34:8). During the work the priest in charge finds *the book of the law of the L*ORD *given through Moses*. Read **2 Chronicles 34:14-33**. A special Passover is kept to celebrate the renewal of the covenant relationship with Yahweh. Because of the details of the reforms, it is generally agreed that the book that

---

[2] Exact dates are extremely difficult to determine in these early times. The siege of Samaria began in 722 B.C. and probably extended into 721. You will find both dates in reference books.

was found was an early edition of our book of Deuteronomy. The year is usually reckoned to be 621 B.C., just a century after the fall of Samaria.

Josiah dies in a battle with the pharaoh of Egypt near Megiddo (2 Chronicles 35:20-27). He is the last notable king of Judah and is one of its best. The end of the kingdom, however, comes a little over twenty years later.

Four kings in rapid succession experience almost constant foreign interference, first from Egypt, then from Babylonia. Zedekiah, the last king, becomes a Babylonian puppet after his two predecessors have been deported to Babylon. He starts a futile rebellion, and King Nebuchadnezzar of Babylon besieges and overthrows Jerusalem. Jeremiah's relationship to these events is noted in Theme 5, Part 2. Read **Jeremiah 52:1-16**. The year is 587 B.C.

When There Is No King

This is the end of the Jewish national monarchy. After this, God's people are under other rulers, not their own kings. The promise to David has been overtaken by the warning about infidelity. People of lesser faith might have interpreted events as the defeat of their God Yahweh, and this would have issued in despair. But their firm belief in their God as the ultimate sovereign of the world and their strong sense of national identity and destiny causes them to think further in two directions.

(1) They can attribute some acts of foreign rulers to the direction of Yahweh's will. Thus the Persian king Cyrus is called Yahweh's *anointed* in Isaiah 45:1. What does this word indicate about his role in Jewish affairs? 2 Chronicles 36:22, 23 expands upon this idea. The prophets did not hesitate to claim such overrule by Yahweh, but here the new circumstances—especially the lack of a Davidic ruler—give the idea new importance.

A cycle of stories in Daniel 1-6 is about a young Jew and his friends in the Babylonian court during the exile. The purpose of the stories is to declare how their devotion to God triumphs in extreme peril and to strengthen God's people who are facing critical challenges of paganism. The point is clear in **Daniel 6:25-28**. The sovereignty of the God of the Jews is valid over the dominant powers of the world.

(2) The Jewish people expect a restoration of their national kingdom. God's covenant promise to David is the basis for this hope. The tension produced by the collapse of the Davidic monarchy is boldly stated in **Psalm 89:19-21, 35-40, 46, 49**. The vitality of the expectation appears in **Psalm 132:11-18**.

At the end of the exile there appears among those who return to Jerusalem a leader named Zerubbabel, who is listed as a grandson of one of the last kings of Judah—that is, a descendant of David. The prophet Haggai writes, *I have chosen you, says the LORD of hosts* (Haggai 2:23), but Zechariah declares that it is Yahweh's will that power should pass into priestly hands (Zechariah 6:9-14). We hear no more of Zerubbabel until Luke mentions him as an ancestor of Jesus (Luke 3:27).

The Maccabean Era

The years after Ezra and Nehemiah are not good times for the Jews. Various forms of oppression come to a head under the Syrian king Antiochus IV. The stories in Daniel were likely published about this time to strengthen the resolve of God's people to withstand paganism. The Maccabean revolution (introduced in Theme 1, Part 2) brings God's people a brief time of national freedom. For about a century there is a semblance of royal rule, but there is no move to reestablish the throne of David.

When imperial Rome subdues and occupies the land, the people turn to a desperate hope that somehow God will intervene under the leadership of an anointed descendant of David. Recall that the Hebrew word for "anoint" gives us the word "messiah," so the expectation of a royal restoration is referred to as "messianic." In the Roman period Jewish hopes are not uniform in detail, but the common expectation is strong. This is part of the background for the career of Jesus, and it is important in Part 3 of this theme.

FOR FURTHER STUDY AND REFLECTION

Memory Bank

Identify each of the following rulers by at least one important event:

Ahab	Jeroboam I	Josiah
Athaliah	Jeroboam II	Omri
Hezekiah	Joash of Judah	Rehoboam
Jehoshaphat		

Research

1. Omri is mentioned on "the Moabite Stone." Consult a Bible Dictionary or book on biblical archaeology about this famous record. What significance do such records have for Bible study?

2. Compare the narratives about Jehoshaphat in 1 Kings with those in 2 Chronicles (see footnote 1, page 134). What does the comparison tell you about the perspectives of the books?

3. The vision in Isaiah 6:1 may be dated about 742 B.C. What landmark(s) in secular history can you locate about this time?

4. Look up Hezekiah's tunnel (2 Kings 20:20 and 2 Chronicles 32:30) in a Bible Dictionary or encyclopedia. *The Harper Atlas of the Bible* has a translation of the inscription from the tunnel. What can you learn about the period from this project?

5. The battle of Carchemish, mentioned in 2 Chronicles 35:20, is known in secular history. Find out what you can about it.

Reflection

1. 2 Kings constantly judges Jewish rulers on religious grounds. Is this fair? Argue pro and con.

2. What modern examples can you think of where people have faced national or racial despair? How did they handle it?

3. The Daniel stories raise the question: how do individuals cope with absolute confrontation by a pagan government? With a government demand that is counter to personal religious belief?

GOD'S PEOPLE HAVE RULERS BUT ONE SOVEREIGN

Jesus and the Kingdom of God

THEME 6

PART 3

SUMMARY

The message of John the Baptist revives dreams of the restoration of the Jewish kingdom. Jesus, like John, proclaims the kingdom of God. Jesus teaches that God's rule is present in a special, new way in his own mission. Paul preaches that Jesus is uniquely the anointed one so long hoped for. The Revelation affirms that God's sovereignty, past, present, and future, is manifested in the victory of Jesus Christ.

BASIC BIBLE REFERENCES

Matthew 13:44-52;
22:1-14, 41-46
Mark 4:26-29
John 18:33-38
1 Corinthians 15:20-28
Revelation 11:15-17

WORD LIST

Kingdom of God
Kingdom of Heaven
Repent

The Message of John the Baptist and Jesus

When John comes on the scene, God's people have been under Roman rule for about a century, and it is more than twice that long since they have heard the voice of a prophet. John announces that a new era is about to begin, so it is no wonder he creates a stir.

The keynote of John's proclamation is *Repent, for the kingdom of heaven has come near* (Matthew 3:2). John declares that his ministry closely anticipates a *more powerful* one, who is to usher in the new time (Matthew 3:11). John claims that God has confirmed the connection between his proclamation and Jesus' new revelation of God. All the Gospels say this in various ways.

When Jesus begins his public preaching in Galilee, his message picks up what John announced: *The time is fulfilled, and the kingdom of God has come near; repent, and believe in the good news* (Mark 1:15). Jesus thus begins to demonstrate that in his person and mission the divine demands of God's sovereignty are confronting the people and require radical reordering of their lives. The urgency of the message is indicated by the phrase *has come near* (KJV, RSV, *is at hand*).

The Kingdom of God

Repent is connected with an Old Testament word the root of which means *to turn* or *return*. Thus the people are promised Yahweh's favor *because you turn to the LORD your God with all your heart and with all your soul* (Deuteronomy 30:10), and Joel exhorts the people to *return to the LORD* (Joel 2:12, 13). John's and Jesus' calls to repentance are connected with *the kingdom of God* because God's sovereignty demands that people harmonize their lives completely with the divine rule. For *repent*, TEV reads, *turn away from your sins* (Mark 1:15).

Here we must look more closely at the phrase *kingdom of God*. Bible scholars agree that *kingdom* in both the Old and New Testaments refers first of all to the exercise of rule and only after that to the place, the realm, where ruling is applied. The distinction between "rule" and "realm" may be plainly seen in the cases of Omri and Jeroboam II, whose rules are found wanting by the writer of Kings even though their realms were extensive and their lives long. So Jesus proclaims, not the end of Roman rule and the reestablishment of the Hebrew nation, but the mighty presence of God as the King so long eclipsed by the arrogance of earthly kings.

Matthew usually uses *kingdom of **heaven***, rather than *kingdom of **God***. If you compare Matthew 13:11 with Luke 8:10, where both Gospels quote the same saying, it is clear that the phrases render the same words in Jesus' original teaching. Jesus may well have used *heaven*, for Jews of his day were careful to avoid using God's name when possible, and *heaven* was commonly substituted for God.[1] If *by kingdom of heaven* Jesus means that a place called "heaven" *has come near*, he is plainly mistaken. No, he is announcing that God has begun to assume the rightful sovereignty that is obscured when people focus on a substitute ruler or on a place.

Jesus speaks about *the secrets of the kingdom of God*—the Greek word for *secret* gives us the word "mystery" (Matthew 13:11=Luke 8:10; see KJV). Read the parable in **Mark 4:26-29**. Jesus gives his message in stories that will be easily remembered. It may take awhile for the surprising meaning to grab the hearer. This is why he says *is as if* or *is like*. Read **Matthew 13:44-52**. The details of an illustration are not equivalent to what is being illustrated. Perhaps we should paraphrase, *The kingdom of God is like a situation in which....* Our familiarity with Jesus' parables may become a barrier to grasping their message. The misunderstanding of Yahweh's rule in Old Testament times should warn us to be careful how we understand Jesus' proclamation of *the kingdom of God / heaven*.

Jesus' attitude toward the role of the messiah is related to his use of the term "kingdom." The popular hope connected with "messiah" developed, as we have noted, from the covenant with David, and so it involved expecting a king. How this king would establish a kingdom is not always clear, for it depends somewhat upon the circumstances of the people

---

1 So we sometimes say "heaven knows" when we mean "God knows."

at a given time. In Jesus' day it must have included freedom from Roman occupation and establishment of a national, Jewish monarchy. Jesus makes it clear that this is inconsistent with his proclamation of the sovereignty of God and the purpose of his mission. After the feeding of the multitude, the Gospel of John says that Jesus' popularity soared and *they were about to come and take him by force to make him king*, but he *withdrew...by himself* (John 6:14, 15).

The title *son of David* appears to have been connected with messianic hopes, but it occurs sparingly in the Gospels. Read **Matthew 22:41-46**. The quotation comes from Psalm 110:1. Jesus' tricky question seems to hinge upon the idea already familiar to us that God is the true sovereign, and any earthly king rules by virtue of God's appointment whatever the human ancestry. This may in part explain Jesus' avoidance of the title "messiah." In Theme 3, Part 3, it is suggested that this also may be a reason for Jesus' preference for the term "Son of Man."

Kingdom, Present and Future

Jesus speaks of the coming of the kingdom, sometimes as though it is present, sometimes as though future. The most familiar words are in the "Lord's Prayer": *Your kingdom come.* This is followed by: *Your will be done, on earth as it is in heaven* (Matthew 6:10; this second part is not in the parallel Luke 11:2). The second clause is usually considered to be an expansion of the first. Jesus certainly taught that his followers are to do God's will as fully as possible here and now, but since this is not fully realized, we ought to think of the Kingdom of God as coming both now and in the future.

Some Gospel passages related to the timing of the kingdom are very difficult to understand. In Matthew 16:28 Jesus seems to be saying that his *coming in his kingdom* will occur in the lifetime of some of his hearers. In the parallel Mark 9:1 the statement is more general, *that the kingdom has come with power.* Luke's parallel, 9:27, says that they will *see the kingdom of God*. What do you make of these differences in what are plainly parallel statements? We must analyze carefully each statement of Jesus and interpret it in the light of all we know about his whole proclamation.

Jesus speaks about entering the kingdom, and it is evident that he means accepting a relationship, not coming into a place (for example, see Matthew 5:20; 7:21; Mark 10:15, 23-25; John 3:5). He also mentions receiving the kingdom (Luke 18:17), inheriting it (Matthew 25:34), giving it (Luke 12:32), seeing it (John 3:3), proclaiming it (Luke 4:43), and waiting for it (Mark 15:43). The conditions Jesus attaches are usually aimed at the present life—for example, *sell your possessions, and give alms* (Luke 12:33). Consider how the various terms may relate to the present or the future.

Several of Jesus' stories refer to a king, where it is evident that Jesus means God is the king. Read **Matthew 22:1-14**. When Jesus mentions the king's son, we probably connect the king's son with Jesus as God's Son. But we are looking back after centuries of theology about the passage. Jesus' hearers would have understood the reference to God and the marriage celebration (Isaiah 62:5, *as the bridegroom rejoices over the bride, so shall your God rejoice over you*). If they identified the son at all, it might be with the messiah.

As far as we can tell, Jesus avoided assuming any kingly titles or prerogatives. It is ironic—and the Gospel writers would know this—that at his trial Jesus is charged with claiming kingship. Read **John 18:33-38**. Pilate's final mockery is the title-board on the cross: *The King of the Jews* (Mark 15:26).

The Gospel of John mentions *the kingdom of God* only in Jesus' discussion with Nicodemus (3:3, 5). The idea, however, is present in other ways. Statements about "life" and "eternal life" are somewhat equivalent, particularly with reference to "having" life (so 3:16, 5:24, 20:31). In the same Gospel Jesus makes a number of statements beginning *I am...*, and some of these include indirect references to prerogatives of God. When he says, *I am the bread of life*, it is connected with God's gift of *Manna in the wilderness* (6:31-35). *I am the light of the world* (8:12) connects with God's creation of light. *I am the good shepherd* (10:11) may remind us of Psalm 23:1 and Ezekiel 34:15.

Paul, the Kingdom, and the Christ

While Paul is a prisoner in Rome, for two years he is *proclaiming the kingdom of God and teaching about the LORD Jesus Christ*, according to Acts 28:30, 31. In his letters, however, he mentions *the kingdom of God* only four times (Romans 14:17; 1 Corinthians 6:9, 10; 15:50—the last three with *inherit*). Perhaps he uses the phrase sparingly because it might convey wrong ideas in a pagan environment. Most of his churches have little Jewish tradition, and his ministry is in a Roman socio-political context where "kingdom" could readily be misunderstood.

We have seen that Jesus' proclamation of the Kingdom of God is related to his avoidance of the term "messiah." With Paul the situation is reversed. He uses the term "Christ" (the Greek equivalent of "messiah") nearly three-fourths of the times it occurs in the New Testament. Paul has made a connection that is not clear until after Jesus' death and resurrection. Jesus is indeed the messiah, but he did not fulfill the expected role and did not reestablish the Davidic monarchy. For Paul, the Christ (the new kind of messiah) is the embodiment of the Kingdom of God.

Paul goes one step further. He often uses the phrase *in Christ* to characterize the relationship of members of the church and God. So, *if anyone is in Christ, there is a new creation* (2 Corinthians 5:17). What Jesus has done becomes the means by which a new community of God's people is formed—that is, the way the Kingdom of God becomes present in human life. God's people are the presence of Christ in the world: *so we, who are many, are one body in Christ, and individually we are members one of another* (Romans 12:5). He illustrates this in a long passage, 1 Corinthians 12:4-27, concluding, *Now you are the body of Christ and individually members of it.*

Thus the long biblical theme of kingship has reached its critical point. God's people were at first a theocracy; Yahweh was king. Then kings represented the divine sovereignty, and David's line became the designated bearer of this privilege. From the exile on, this line was broken. Jesus proclaimed that in his person and his mission the kingdom of God entered a new time: God is sovereign, and people confront the divine will in Jesus. Paul ties all this together by proclaiming that *in Christ* the rule of God continues in the world embodied in the redeemed community, the church.

The Kingdom Forever

One step remains. God's sovereignty does not appear complete in our world, so we live in hope for the future. Paul writes, *hope that is seen is not hope* (Romans 8:24). Our detailed study of "hope" is in Theme 10. Here, however, we may give some completion to our study in this part. Paul writes briefly, almost cryptically, about the future reign of Christ. Read **1 Corinthians 15:20-28**. The finale will be when God is *all in all*—God's sovereignty will be complete and absolute. God's will is going to be *done...on earth as it is in heaven.*

The Revelation uses "king" and "kingdom" imagery often. Jesus Christ *made us to be a kingdom* (Revelation 1:6). Read **Revelation 11:15-17** and note the kingdom language. Jesus appears as *the Lamb* (first in 6:1) and later is declared to be L ORD *of lords and King of kings* (17:14). Again he appears as *the Word of God* and is designated *King of kings and* L ORD *of lords* (19:13, 16).

In 1 Timothy 6:15 similar language is applied to God: *the only Sovereign, the King of kings and* L ORD *of lords*. Another phrase, *King of the ages*, is ascribed to *the only God* in 1:17 of the same letter.[2]

---

2 Modern Jewish liturgy often uses the Hebrew equivalent of *King of the ages* in reference to God.

Speculation about details in the end-time of the kingdom of God on earth has little biblical warrant. The certainty of God's reign has been established *in Christ*, and finally God will be *all in all*. More than that we really do not need to know.

FOR FURTHER STUDY AND REFLECTION

Memory Bank

1. Make a list of what the Kingdom of God/Heaven is "like" in Jesus' teaching.

2. Jesus' "Beatitudes" (Matthew 5:1-12) are a basic portion of biblical literacy. Learn verses 3 and 10.

Research

1. Read what the angel said to Mary in Luke 1:32, 33. How does this fit into Theme 6?

2. Compare Luke 17:20, 21 in NRSV and TEV. What is involved here regarding the understanding of the Kingdom of God?

3. In Matthew 12:38-42 Jesus twice says *something greater... is here*! Why do you think he says *something* rather than *someone*?

Reflection

1. Which parables of the Kingdom help you most in understanding the Kingdom of God? How?

2. How can you reconcile the present and future aspects of the Kingdom of God?

GOD DEMANDS A RIGHTEOUS PEOPLE

The Law of God — PART 1

SUMMARY

The first five books of the Old Testament contain instruction that regulates the moral and religious life of God's Jewish people. The law codes in these books set requirements that become the basis for right living before God. There are stories of how the people respond to the requirements. Some regulations apply to times long gone by, as is shown by their social and historical setting.

BASIC BIBLE REFERENCES

Genesis 17:1, 2; 22:1-18; 31:49
Exodus 20:1-17; 24:3-8; 25:21, 22
Leviticus 19:2, 17, 18; 20:26
Deuteronomy 5:6-21; 6:4-9, 20-25; 30:11-20

WORD LIST

Book of the Covenant
"Code"
Decalogue
Kosher
Lex Talionis
Mediator
Mercy seat
Righteousness
Shema

Background of Torah

The first five books of the Old Testament are the most sacred part of Scripture for Jews. They call them *Torah*, which means "instruction" or "teaching." This instruction comes from God; it reveals God's will. In the rest of the Bible, Torah is often called "the law." We are apt to interpret this in terms of *laws* and to think of these as arduous regulations or unwelcome restraint. Jews did not—and do not today—so regard Torah. Rather the law formulates the responses that God's gracious covenant calls forth. Thus, while we may have difficulty in thinking of law apart from laws, Torah is more than laws. This distinction is important as we study this theme. Law is not an end in itself; its purpose is to produce in God's people a condition that Scripture refers to as "righteousness" (which means being *right* with God).

Torah is the gift of Yahweh; *I will give you...the law and the commandments, which I have written for their instruction* (Exodus 24:12). Read **Deuteronomy 30:11-14**. The relationship between God and people is a very personal one. Tangible rewards are promised to those who respond rightly to God's commands. The best-known part of Old Testament law is the Ten Commandments. The text calls the commandments simply *words*, spoken by God. Read **Exodus 20:1, 2**. The setting is at Mount Sinai. Note the exodus connection in verse 2.

Genesis

God's command and promise and the people's response are connected and are written into the earliest Hebrew traditions. *In the garden of Eden* Yahweh God *commanded the man* what Adam may and may not do (2:16, 17). Human accountability is plain in the narratives about Adam and Eve's sin (Chapter 3) and Cain's murder of Abel (4:8-16). God sends the destroying flood because of the wickedness of humankind (6:5-7) and saves Noah because he is righteous (7:1). The covenant that God makes for Noah's descendants includes demands upon them (9:1-17).

Abraham becomes the model of Old Testament righteousness. Abraham *believed the Lord; and the Lord reckoned it to him as righteousness* (15:6)[1]. In **17:1, 2** Yahweh confronts the patriarch and offers him a covenant. Stories about Abraham do not always show him in a good light. On two occasions he pretends that Sarah is his sister so that rulers would not kill him to get her for a wife (12:10-20; 20:1-18). His treatment of Hagar and her son Ishmael seems cruel, but Yahweh assures him that it will turn out well (16:1-9; 21:9-16).[2] To his great credit is the story of the three divine strangers, which is studied in Theme 3, Part 1 (Chapter 18). An *awe-full* moment in Abraham's life is when Yahweh challenges him to sacrifice his son Isaac. Read **22:1-18**. He trusts God absolutely, and God is merciful, gracious, and steadfastly loving.

The sure effects of failure to act righteously appear in stories about Jacob. He cheats his brother Esau out of the birthright blessing and repeatedly in later life suffers from the treachery of others and the consequences of his own acts. Jacob and his father-in-law Laban trick each other but finally reach what we may call a pact of nonaggression at Mizpah. Read **31:49** and interpret it in light of this setting. When he has to confront Esau he is *greatly afraid and distressed* (32:7), but the meeting turns out to be friendly.

In the Joseph narratives personal integrity is prominent. In God's view this is righteousness. When Joseph refuses the sexual advances of his master's wife and is wrongly imprisoned, *the Lord was with Joseph and showed him steadfast love* (39:21). In Theme 5, Part 1, Joseph's confidence in God's providence is emphasized.

The Law Codes

The law promulgated at Sinai is often called the Covenant Code. "Code" in this usage means an organized collection of regulations. The narrative setting of this code is clear: it is given

---

1 This is referred to in Romans 4:3, 9; Galatians 3:6; James 2:23. The James verse calls Abraham *the friend of God*, a term that appears in 2 Chronicles 20:7 and Isaiah 41:8.

2 Ishmael is the ancestor of Middle Eastern Arab tribes. As such, he is honored in the Quran, the sacred book of Islam.

when Yahweh establishes the first covenant with the newly freed people. Read **Exodus 24:3-8**. The Old Testament laws do not occur as abstract lists but in the midst of narratives about God's people.

Leviticus contains extensive regulations associated with ritual purity. These become the Holiness Code. The word holy occurs sixty-three times in the book. **Leviticus 19:2** and **20:26** summarize the basis for the holiness of God's people. The demand for holiness extends to many aspects of their life. See, for example, the requirements about animal offerings (27:9, 10). The records are candid: God's people do not always act holy; they do not always follow God's commands—even the leaders are fallible, as we have already noted.

The Deuteronomic Code comes from material in Deuteronomy. It was noted in Theme 5, Part 1 that "Deuteronomy" means "second law;" that is, it contains a second recounting of the law. Theme 6, Part 2, explains how the book is connected with the reforms under King Josiah.

Many details in these codes are time-bound; they relate specifically to the social and historical settings in which they were formulated. This is at the same time a unique wonder and a recurring problem for God's people. The Judeo-Christian tradition is like no other in its belief that God has always been directly involved in the history of a people. For this to be true, however, God deals with radical changes in the social history of the people. This means that some of the laws are related to a setting that has passed away. It has never been easy for God's people to differentiate between what is for all ages and what is for the time being. Thus a crisis arose when there was no longer a temple in which to perform the ritual, cultic demands of the law. The altar sacrifices have never been reinstated since the Romans destroyed the Temple.

The giving of the covenants and laws is usually associated with human mediators. Noah and Abraham were such, but Moses is the classic example. So the Gospel of John says, *the law indeed was given through Moses* (1:17). Part 2 of this theme shows how the application of the law becomes the task of the prophets. The editing of Torah into its final literary form is usually placed in the time of Ezra (see Theme 5, Part 2).

Exodus

We must now take a closer look at the books of Torah that contain the collections of laws. Begin with the Decalogue—a term from two Greek roots that mean "Ten Words." Read **Exodus 20:1-17**. Here is the nucleus of the law. The tradition says that these words were written on stone tablets, which Yahweh gave to Moses on Mount Sinai, and then they *were put into the ark of the covenant* (24:12; 25:16). The Ten Commandments are restated in

Deuteronomy 5:6-21. Study the differences. Echoes of these commandments are scattered throughout the law.

To help you get an overview of the rest of the Pentateuch, here are survey outlines and notes. You are not expected to read every chapter of these books. Sample them as your time allows, but do not miss the emphasized passages.

> Exodus 21. Treatment of slaves and other human beings. Verses 23-25 contain the *lex talionis*—the law of retaliation, often quoted today as "an eye for an eye and a tooth for a tooth." The practical wisdom in these laws is applicable in a society in many ways different from ours.
>
> Chapters 22, 23. Continuation of everyday laws. Festival directions. Instructions about the Promised Land and avoidance of its pagan peoples.
>
> Chapter 24. Moses as mediator with Yahweh.
>
> Chapters 25-28. Appointments of the tabernacle. Note **25:21, 22**. What is the function of *the mercy seat*?
>
> Chapter 29. Ordination of the Aaronic priests (also treated in Leviticus 8).
>
> Chapters 30, 31. Tabernacle matters. Summary of Sabbath regulations (also in 35:2, 3).
>
> Chapter 32. The episode of the golden calf.
>
> Chapters 33, 34. Leaving Sinai. Renewal of the covenant.
>
> Chapters 35-40. Execution of the orders given through Moses.

Leviticus

> Chapters 1-16. Directions for worship in the Hebrew community; associated laws.
>
> Chapters 17-26. The Holiness Code. The kind of life called for by the regulations in the text reflects historical, economic, and social backgrounds somewhat changed from those of the Covenant Code. Many of the regulations are related to the settled life in the Promised Land.

Chapter 17. Mostly laws about blood. "Kosher" (from a Hebrew word meaning "fit, proper") regulations relating to the ritual slaughter of meat and the avoidance of eating blood.

Chapter 18. Prohibition of incest and other sexual irregularities.

Chapter 19. Miscellaneous. Note **19:17, 18**. What New Testament associations do you see?

Chapter 20. False worship. Sex rules.

Chapters 21-24. Priests, festivals, worship. An incident *in the camp* leads to a repetition of the *lex talionis* (24:17-21).

Chapter 25. Sabbatic years and jubilee. Responsibilities for dependents.

Chapter 26. Laws and promises; *if...then...*

Chapter 27. Various vows.

Numbers

The book covers the journey of the Israelites from *the wilderness of Sinai* (1:1) to *the plains of Moab by the Jordan at Jericho* (35:1). Included are tedious details of various censuses of the tribes (whence the name of the book), and there are some laws and regulations. Some stories from Numbers appear in previous themes.

Deuteronomy

This book is referred to a number of times in previous themes. Remember that it is a restatement of Hebrew covenant religion. Its historical perspective is somewhat later than that of Exodus-Leviticus-Numbers. The regulatory portions are the Deuteronomic Code (Chapters 12-26).

Chapters 1-4. Moses reviews the way from Sinai—here called Horeb—to Moab on the east bank of the Jordan, concluding with a summary exhortation.

Chapter 5. The Ten Words and some attendant details.

Chapter 6. Exposition of Israel's relationship with Yahweh. Read. **6:4-9**. Verse 4 is called the *Shema*, from the first word in the Hebrew text. It is the central affirmation of Jewish faith. Jesus quotes verses 4, 5 as *the first of all* commandments, with Leviticus 19:17, 18 (above) as *the second* (Mark 12:29-31). **Deuteronomy 6:20-25** is a Basic Reference in Theme 1, Part 1 and is mentioned in Theme 3, Part 1.

Chapters 7-11. Instruction and warning about Israel's life in the Promised Land with historical recollections as examples.

Chapters 12-19. Centralization and regulation of worship. Conduct of justice.

Chapter 20. Rules for making war.

Chapters 21-25. Miscellaneous laws.

Chapter 26. Conclusion to this code. The liturgical creed in verses 5-9 is a Basic Reference in Theme 2, Part 1.

Chapters 27, 28. A dramatic ceremony to be enacted at Shechem. Blessings are to be pronounced from Mount Gerizim and curses from Mount Ebal opposite (also anticipated in 11:26-30). The section ends with a terrible threat for failure *to observe all the words of this law*.

Chapter 29, 30. Moses' final address. Note **30:15-20**.

Chapter 31. Transfer of leadership to Joshua.

Chapters 32, 33. Moses' *song*.

Chapter 34. The end of Moses' life.

FOR FURTHER STUDY AND REFLECTION

Memory Bank

1. Exodus 20:2-17. You should know the Ten Commandments word for word. Begin by learning the ten "words" without the explanatory material given with several of them.

2. Leviticus 19:18 (the second half).

3. Deuteronomy 6:4-9.

Research

1. The words of the Ten Commandments are divided in different ways to yield ten. Some of the commandments deal with duties to God and some with duties to people. What can you learn about these divisions? Consult a Bible Dictionary. If you can, also compare Jewish, Catholic, and Protestant usage.

2. The *lex talionis* is cited in the Sermon on the Mount in Matthew 5:38-42. Why was such a grim regulation in the Jewish law? How do you explain Jesus' attitude toward it?

3. Learn more about the *mercy seat* (Exodus 25:17-22). Check a concordance and Bible Dictionary. Explain the symbolism.

4. Many Jews take Deuteronomy 6:8, 9 literally. Find out what you can about ancient and modern practices.

Reflection

1. List a kind of law that affects us in each of the following combinations of categories (for example, As local governments...In concern for the environment):

    a. As individual persons
    b. As family groups
    c. As local governments
    d. As a nation
    e. As a world community

    i. In respect to health
    ii. In religious life
    iii. In regard to school
    iv. In social relationships
    v. In concern for the environment

2. What place does the *lex talionis* have in the administration of justice today? How is this in tension with Judeo-Christian concepts of mercy?

3. The Torah codes offer many rewards. Is reward an adequate basis for law enforcement? How should justice, righteousness, and holiness each be related to reward?

GOD DEMANDS A RIGHTEOUS PEOPLE

THEME 7

Prophets' Call for Righteousness

PART 2

SUMMARY
The law codes are intended to bring about morally and spiritually righteous people of God. Samuel emphasizes the ethical demand of the law, and other prophets continue the call in the times of the monarchies. The writing prophets—Isaiah, Jeremiah, Amos, and others—call for righteousness in a variety of circumstances, and the requirement is applied in the postexilic period. This call is also clear in the Psalms.

BASIC BIBLE REFERENCES
Joshua 8:30-35
1 Samuel 12:16-25
1 Kings 2:1-4
Psalms 1, 19:7-13;
119:9-11, 18, 97, 105, 165, 176
Isaiah 1:16-20; 8:16-20; 52:13-53:12; 55:6-9
Jeremiah 7:1-11
Amos 2:6-8; 5:24
Micah 4:1-4; 6:6-8
Malachi 3:16-18

WORD LIST
Acrostic
Justice
Prophecy
Righteousness
The Day of the Lord

Torah before the Prophets

We have stressed the importance of the development of monotheism in earliest Hebrew faith. This belief in one God leads naturally to the conviction that God's people are ruled by divine law. This is expressed in a covenant relationship, which God's people accept. This biblical faith is unique in the religions of the world.

The law codes in Torah affect all the life of the Israelite people. Although the recording and editing of these codes come long after the time of Moses, the substance of Torah comes from the intervening years. Laws are usually known and in force long before they become codes, that is, written collections. To illustrate: the ceremony of curses and blessings prescribed in Deuteronomy 27, 28 is performed under Joshua's direction. Read **Joshua 8:30-35**. Thus Torah in the Pentateuch is linked to the history of the people in the Promised Land.

The period of the judges was unsettled politically, and the moral level of the people was mostly low. The generation after Joshua *did not know the Lord* and *did what was evil in the sight of the Lord* (Judges 2:10, 11). The law is not mentioned, but God does issue commands. Worship of *the Baals* and *other gods* (2:11, 12) breaks the first two of the Ten Commandments, but the sins are described without mentioning the commands that were being broken.

Samuel, Sin, and the Monarchy

Covenant law is regularly assumed in the books of Samuel and Kings, but it is seldom referred to. This is partly because much of the books consists of narrative. David's charge to Solomon includes words related to *the law of Moses*. Read **1 Kings 2:1-4**. (Identify the different words related to law.) In the reign of Josiah there is a stir about the law (recall the circumstances). 1 and 2 Chronicles make frequent reference to the law. This stems from their theological concerns in history.

Samuel, as the first great prophet, emphasizes the call to righteousness, which is a characteristic of all the prophets. Read **1 Samuel 12:16-25**. Samuel dramatizes the demand that the people *serve [the LORD] faithfully*. So with Nathan and David, Elijah and Ahab, Elisha and Joash of Israel, and others. Introduction, Part 1, notes that the Jewish canon refers to the books of Joshua, Judges, Samuel, and Kings as "the Former Prophets." Prophets, chiefly Elijah, were believed to have been responsible for the collection of these books.

The kings of Israel and Judah are judged in the records according to their performance of *what was right in the sight of the LORD*. The sins of Jeroboam I, *that he caused Israel to commit*, point to the close connection between law and righteousness. The standards are appropriate for the times. We must not underestimate how much Jesus' teaching has influenced our ethical sensibilities. The prophets and those they advised acted according to how they perceived Yahweh's will, and we should not expect to find Christian sensitivity there. It is true, to be sure, that the moral standards of Israelite law were far higher than those of neighboring peoples.

The Message of the Prophets

The prophets were called by God to speak and write directly and forcefully to their contemporary situations, and they claimed divine authority for their messages. A characteristic preface to their proclamation is, *Thus says the LORD* (for example Jeremiah 17:5). Sometimes they begin, *The word of the LORD* (as Joel 1:1) or *Hear this word* (Amos 4:1). Sometimes their message is called *an oracle* (as Isaiah 15:1). They do not mean that their word is taking the place of the law. They exhort the people to be righteous, and this presupposes the law. The law is the deposit of Yahweh's will for the people, and keeping it will prevent them from going astray by their own errors or the influence of their pagan neighbors. The prophets deal with the close connections of law, sin, covenant, and righteousness.

"A righteous people" implies more than a people who are right with God. The Hebrew word for "righteousness" (as well as the corresponding Greek word in the New Testament) may also be rendered "justice." To be righteous is also to be just. Another word for "justice" is often paired with the word usually rendered "righteousness." See Isaiah 5:16; Jeremiah 22:3, 13. The prophets were careful to proclaim that righteousness involves establishing justice among people, for the two terms are not separable in God's sight.

This brings us to the so-called "writing" prophets (which the Jewish canon refers to as "the Latter Prophets"). Read **Isaiah 8:16-20**. The word translated *teaching* is *torah* in the Hebrew text. In Jeremiah 31:31-34, which was a Basic Reference in Theme 2, Part 1, Yahweh says, *I will put my law within them*, and here the word *law* translates *torah*. The passage closely associates law with covenant and ends with a promise to *remember their sin no more*.

Read **Micah 4:1-4**, a well-known prophecy about future peace. The condition is that *out of Zion shall go forth instruction (torah)*.[1] The demands and promises that the prophets proclaim are closely connected with the law of God. We shall look at passages from a number of the prophets to observe their call for righteousness.

Isaiah

The book called Isaiah is a collection of prophecies. It takes its name from the prophet of the first 39 chapters, whose political career is studied in Theme 6, Part 2. Chapters 40 through 66 are concerned with the exile and the period just after it. The whole book deals with the righteousness of God's people. Some passages speak of the way to be righteous; some passages reproach unrighteousness; some passages look forward to a time when God will reward and enjoy a righteous people.

This calls attention to the shades of meaning that "prophecy" may have. Today many people think that the word means forecasting the future. An examination of the books of the biblical prophets quickly shows that they are mostly concerned with proclaiming God's will to their contemporaries. Sometimes this involves looking into the future, but the emphasis is usually upon what the prophets' hearers or readers may expect in their own future. Because some of these expectations were not fulfilled in or just after the prophets' times—or indeed until now—there is a temptation to think that the prophets were looking into the far future. This is rarely the case. Many such prophecies, however, deal with God's demands and promises, so it is quite proper to look for those meanings and applications for later ages and for our own time.

---

1 NRSV; RSV and earlier versions read *the law*.

Read **1:16-20**. The prophet begins by reproving the sins of Judah. In other passages the denunciation is very specific: idolatry, drunkenness, greed, lying, ill treatment of the poor, bad leadership, treachery, insincere worship. Isaiah uses vivid imagery: Judah is a *vineyard*, but it yields *wild grapes* (5:1-7). He can be very hard on the women for their preoccupation with clothes and beauty (3:16-4:1). On the other hand, he strongly denounces Judah's enemies.

The second part of the book is markedly different. It has been pointed out that the mention of Cyrus in 45:1 shifts the scene to the time of the exile. The people are not righteous, but God is intent on restoring them: *return to me, for I have redeemed you* (44:22). A figure called *my servant* is the agent of Yahweh's saving purpose. We are not sure whether the prophet understood this to be an individual or a collective group of God's people. Read **52:13-53:12**, a passage in which Christians have seen the figure of the suffering Christ. The Gospels indicate that Jesus was deeply influenced by the "servant" passages. The call to repentance in **55:6-9** is memorable.

Jeremiah

From the beginning of Jeremiah's book he assails the wickedness of Jerusalem-Judah. Sometimes he refers generally to *the house of Israel* (2:4), but in 3:6-10 he refers to the Northern Kingdom as *that faithless one, Israel*, and to the Southern Kingdom as *her false sister Judah*. He also compares Judah to *faithless children* (3:14) and to Yahweh's *bride* (2:2) and *faithless wife* (3:20). The prophet, in Yahweh's name *(says the* LORD*)*, appeals for *return* to the LORD and urges, *wash your heart clean of wickedness so that you may be saved* (4:1, 14). Like Abraham interceding for Sodom (Genesis 18:23-33—recall Theme 2, Part 1) Yahweh will *pardon Jerusalem* if *one person* may be found *who acts justly and seeks truth* (5:1). People *swear falsely* (5:2), thus breaking the third Commandment.

We can only sample the prophet's call for righteousness. Read **7:1-11**. This sermon in the Temple deals with righteous and unrighteous conduct. Chapter after chapter contain complaints of Judah's wicked ways. Many lines are memorable; for example, *Is there no balm in Gilead?* (8:22). The prophet laments, *I was like a gentle lamb led to the slaughter* (11:19). What saying of Isaiah does that remind you of?

The Covenant Code requires that slaves should be freed after six years service (Exodus 21:2). Zedekiah, the last king of Judah before the exile, and the people of Judah made a covenant to grant such liberty, and the covenant was ratified with the slaughter of a calf. But king and people reneged, and Jeremiah announces that Yahweh will bring on them the fate of the sacrificed animal (34:8-20). A group of people called the *Rechabites* kept intact a unique tradition of abstaining from wine and living a nomadic life. Their righteousness becomes an example to Judah (Chapter 35).

The So-Called "Minor" Prophets

Hosea dramatizes the covenant relationship between Yahweh and the Israelite people by his own domestic tragedy (Theme 2, Part 2). The prophet's love for his unfaithful wife becomes the basis for proclaiming Yahweh's determined love in the face of Israel's unrighteousness. The divine love is accentuated by severe warnings. *They sow the wind, and they shall reap the whirlwind* (Hosea 8:7). *Return to your God, hold fast to love and justice, and wait continually for your God* (12:6).

Amos is nearly contemporary with Hosea. No prophet has a stronger call for righteousness than Amos. The book begins by denouncing the transgressions of Israel's neighbors, even Judah. No doubt his hearers in Israel would applaud. But then in **2:6-8**, he unexpectedly enumerates awful sins of Israel and denounces them. Moreover, the people could not be righteous before God when there was such terrible injustice in their society. Read the often-quoted heart of the prophet's message: **5:24**.

Later chapters deal with coming judgment. The people expect *the day of the LORD* to be a good time for them, but Amos declares that *it is darkness, not light* (5:18, 20). Divine justice will deal impartially with their wickedness. Yahweh will deal with Israel by the same standards that are applied to other nations. *Are you not like the Ethiopians to me...? Did I not bring...the Philistines from Caphtor and the Arameans from Kir?*(9:7). The books ends, however, with a promise that *the booth of David* will be restored in a wonderful new age (9:11-15).

Micah lived about the same time as Isaiah the son of Amoz. Micah's denunciation of Judah's wickedness is scathing—*you who hate the good and love the evil* (3:2). **Micah 6:6-8** is a great summary of what it takes to *come before the LORD*. Note the requirement *to do justice*, the social aspect of righteousness. Like most of the prophets, he has words of hope; God *will again have compassion upon us* (7:19).

Habakkuk is a poetic *oracle* (1:1). He addresses the problem of evil, but he has no easy answer. Theme 3, Part 2, notes his important observation, *the righteous live by their faith*— or *faithfulness*, the reading of the footnote (2:4). Chapter 3 is a prayer-psalm, which declares, *God, the LORD, is my strength* (3:19).

Zechariah, after the exile, calls for righteousness. *Thus says the LORD of hosts, Render true judgments, show kindness and mercy to one another...and do not devise evil in your hearts against one another* (7:9, 10). There are also visions, which are studied in Theme 10.

Malachi (the name means "my messenger") also writes during the restoration after the exile and is particularly concerned for the righteousness of the priesthood. He employs an unusual question and answer form; for example, *Will anyone rob God? Yet you are robbing me!* (3:8). The note of hope is sounded in **3:16-18**.

Daniel

Daniel is not a prophet like those studied above. (Recall that the Jewish canon places this book among the Writings.) There is no emphasis on law and righteousness like that of the prophets. But Daniel and his companions-in-exile are diligent to please and obey God. They insist on following Jewish dietary rules. These are not specified, but Daniel does not want to *defile himself with the royal rations* (1:8). His companions are *thrown into a furnace of blazing fire* because they will not worship a *golden statue*, but God delivers them (3:14-27). At a feast of king Belshazzar a hand writes a mysterious message on the wall. Daniel interprets this as a judgment because the king has *exalted [himself] against the LORD of heaven...You have been weighed on the scales and found wanting* (5:23, 27). Daniel's jealous enemies plot against him *in connection with the law of his God*, and they get him *thrown into the den of lions* because he will not pray to the king instead of God (6:5-16). The emphasis upon righteousness responding to God's law is quite evident.

Psalms

The book of Psalms gives a prime place to the law in the lives of God's people. Read **Psalm 1**. Notice the two ways in verse 6. Read **Psalm 19:7-13**. List the synonyms and metaphors that refer to *the law of the LORD*. For the psalmist, law was much more than rules and regulations.

Psalm 119 is the supreme poem about the law: every verse—each two-line couplet—refers to some aspect of Yahweh's law. Each stanza of eight verses begins with a letter of the Hebrew alphabet in order, twenty-two sections in all. This form of poetry is called "acrostic." Read **Psalm 119:9-11, 18, 97, 105, 165, 176**. Again, list the words and phrases that expand the idea of the law.

FOR FURTHER STUDY AND DISCUSSION

Memory Bank

Learn: Isaiah 53:5, 6; 55:6-9
             Amos 5:24
             Micah 6:8

Research

1. Under what circumstances did Jesus quote Jeremiah 7:11?

2. *Mishnah* and *Talmud* developed as oral interpretations of Torah and eventually were collected in written form. Study about them in a Bible Dictionary or encyclopedia. How does interpretation of a law differ from the law itself?

3. Psalm 1 serves as a kind of covering preface to Israel's worship book. How do law and righteousness relate to worship?

Reflection

1. Explain the relationship between the call to be "holy" and the demand for "righteousness."

2. The prophets called for behavior that their times required. How do we receive such calls today? Where do they come from? When we do not receive such calls, why not?

3. How does God's demand for justice as proclaimed by the prophets apply to God's people today?

GOD DEMANDS A RIGHTEOUS PEOPLE

Jesus and the Law

PART 3

SUMMARY

The law is prominent in New Testament times though its role differs from that in the Old Testament. John the Baptist revives the prophets' call for righteousness. Jesus' ethical teaching is consistent with the spirit of Torah but goes beyond it. His approach is simple and direct, yet his meaning is complex and open-ended. He is compassionate toward the poor, the outcasts, and sinners. He embodies good news for all.

BASIC BIBLE REFERENCES

Matthew 5:17-48; 7:12; 11:28-30; 22:34-40
Mark 7:1-13
Luke 3:7-18; 6:31; 10:25-37; 18:9-14
John 1:17; 3:1-21; 13:34, 35

WORD LIST

Fulfill
Gospel
Sabbath
Targum

Law and Hebrew Scriptures

Torah has been central in Jewish life ever since *Ezra brought the law before the assembly* after the return from Babylonian exile (Nehemiah 8:2). The law was in Hebrew, and the people spoke Aramaic, which was like Hebrew, but enough different that it was not readily understood. So Levites *read from the book, from the law of God, with interpretation. They gave the sense, so that the people understood the reading* (Nehemiah 8:8). Since few people learned Hebrew, these translation-interpretations continued and were later written down. They are known as *Targums*.

"Law" in the New Testament usually refers to the Pentateuch. This and the eight "books" of the Prophets and the Psalms were considered sacred Scripture (see Luke 24:44). Probably most of the other Writings were also accepted, and other similar books were widely read. We have noted that a body of oral tradition developed, which by Jesus' day was held to be authoritative and in following centuries was collected in the *Mishnah* and the *Talmud*.

Jesus disputed with the *Pharisees and the scribes* about these traditions. Read **Mark 7:1-13**. The purpose of these oral laws was to *make a fence for the law*, as one of the books puts it; that is, they were to guard people from careless misuse of the law. It seems, however, that most Jews could not keep these regulations. Only a professional leader had the knowledge and time to do this. On one occasion Jesus accused *the lawyers*, that is, the religious professionals: *you load people with burdens hard to bear, and you yourselves do not lift a finger to ease them* (Luke 11:46).

All of Jesus' Jewish contemporaries doubtless thought of themselves as God's people, and to the limit of their ability they kept God's law. The Pharisees, scribes, and lawyers (to use all of the New Testament terms) tried to be the professional law-keepers. The bad impression of them that we find in the New Testament comes partly from the confrontations that are recounted in the Gospels and in Paul's career. The Sadducees, conservative priests, were proud that they accepted only the written Torah and rejected the oral law. The Essene people of the Dead Sea scrolls had their own written interpretations of Scripture, and they also accepted additional writings as authoritative. The Samaritans used only the Pentateuch, and they had their own version of it. How the rest of the people—clearly the large majority—thought of Scripture we can only infer from the writings of the others.

Law and the Gospels

In its first years the Christian church developed within the bounds of Judaism. Almost from the start, however, it was becoming free from legal extremes of the law. We must remember that Torah contains much more than legal regulations. The Passover deliverance, for example, is a part of Torah, and that event is very important in Jewish faith and becomes an essential feature in Christian worship. When the New Testament refers to law, then, it does not necessarily mean the complicated codes. We should avoid generalizing about "law in the New Testament."

Jesus Christ is at the heart of the New Testament. *The law indeed was given through Moses; grace and truth came through Jesus Christ*—**John 1:17**. Soon his followers were *called "Christians" (in Antioch...first;* Acts 11:26). Because Jesus was so central, his followers wanted to know all about him: what did he say? how did he live? how did he deal with people? Answers are given in the Gospels, not out of mere biographical interest, but to help people understand and follow Jesus.

The Gospels are the deposits of what the earliest church proclaimed. We are dealing with the material really at third hand. First there were the events of Jesus' career. Then there were the oral reports of eyewitnesses and the spreading proclamation based upon them. Finally there are the Gospels, the documentation of the church's revered traditions. The closest we come to an organized summary of this whole process is in the two-volume work Luke-Acts. The church has always been confident that this developing process was guided by God's Holy Spirit, but the diversity evident in four Gospels is testimony that the inspiration is beyond the human words.

John the Baptist

The immediate backdrop of Jesus' public ministry is the career of John the Baptist. John proclaimed *a baptism for the forgiveness of sins* (Luke 3:3). Read **Luke 3:7-18**. Consider carefully each part of the message. John says that repentance will have practical effects in each individual's life. People must be righteous in their particular circumstances. *Do those things that will show that you have turned from your sins* (Luke 3:8 TEV). This is not a grim, threatening message. Luke calls it *good news*—that is, God's forgiveness is readily available if one begins a new life and proves its sincerity by righteous acts.

The Law in Jesus' Teaching

We may be surprised at how much Jesus had to say about the law. The most striking and sustained passage is part of the Sermon on the Mount. Read **Matthew 5:17-48**. Jesus comments explicitly on three of the Ten Commandments. Identify and list them. Note also 6:24 and check your study Bible references.

Other laws are referred to, most of which we have already mentioned. (A study Bible will give you the Old Testament references.) Jesus claims that he does not intend *to abolish the law or the prophets...but to fulfill* them. After reviewing Old Testament laws, he announces, *But I say to you*. This is both an announcement and a claim: this is how the commandments should be interpreted, and Jesus has the right to interpret authoritatively. Is this somehow what he means by *fulfill*? His interpretations are rigorous, for they are directed at the inner intent of the law rather than at its literal prescription.

On one occasion a Pharisee-lawyer asked Jesus about the relative importance of the commandments. Read **Matthew 22:34-40**. In Luke's version the question is different and leads to one of Jesus' best-known parables. Read **Luke 10:25-37**.

One of Jesus' most often quoted statements is known as "the golden rule." Read **Matthew 7:12** and **Luke 6:31**. (Luke's larger passage is sometimes called "the Sermon on the Plain." See Luke 6:17). In Luke the saying is in a context of how to treat others who ill-treat you. In Matthew the saying is a reflection upon how God treats people and is offered as a summary of *the law and the prophets*.

Jesus and Righteousness

Jesus' proclamation has a strong ethical emphasis, particularly in Matthew and Luke. When Jesus speaks about the law, he invariably applies it to right conduct. The Beatitudes (Matthew 5:3-12; Luke 6:20-23) describe how Jesus' followers are to live if they want to be *blessed*. He calls his followers *the salt of the earth* and *the light of the world* (Matthew 5:13, 14). In Luke the Beatitudes are followed by words of *woe* (Luke 6:24-26. What Old Testament story is similar?).

Jesus' teaching goes beyond morals. He is proclaiming that GOD DEMANDS A RIGHTEOUS PEOPLE. Matthew and Luke note that *he spoke with authority* (Luke 4:32; see Matthew 7:28, 29). It becomes steadily clearer that this authority is not a matter of "do as I say" but is a declaration that he intends to support his followers with his own strength. Read **Matthew 11:28-30**.

Jesus Interpreting the Law

According to John's Gospel, laws regarding the Sabbath are a principal cause of the clash between Jesus and Jewish authorities. They said, *he does not observe the sabbath* (John 9:16; so also 5:10, 16; 7:23). Jesus, however, believes that he is not breaking the law. Rather, he accuses his antagonists of this (John 7:19; so also Mark 7:9; Luke 13:14-17). He declared, *The sabbath was made for humankind, and not humankind for the sabbath; so the Son of Man is lord even of the sabbath* (Mark 2:27, 28). This is part of what he means by "fulfill."

Jesus constantly confronts people with the law's demands, yet he focuses their attention on God as the ultimate judge of the law. In the story of "the prodigal son" (Luke 15:11-32) it is evident that the father shows something about God: when the most thoughtless of sinners return from their alienation, they are warmly welcomed by the heavenly Father.

Jesus' most striking word about the law is probably his *new commandment, that you love one another*. Read **John 13:34, 35**. His own love for his disciples is to be the measure of this love, and obedience to this commandment is to be the mark of his followers. *To lay down one's life for one's friends* is the supreme gauge of this love (John 15:12-14).

Jesus and the Unrighteous

Jesus often associates with those who in his day were commonly known as "sinners." No one is excluded from his call to discipleship. He said, *I have come not to call the righteous but sinners* (Mark 2:17). Perhaps he is implying that *the righteous* are scarce. Read **Luke 18:9-14**. (*Justified* in Greek comes from the same word-root as "righteous.")

Jesus shows a remarkable tenderness toward the nobodies of his nation. He declares that a person will go to great lengths to recover one lost sheep. So *there will be more joy in heaven over one sinner who repents than over ninety-nine righteous persons who need no repentance* (Luke 15:3-7). Twice he says, *I am the good shepherd* (John 10:11, 14). We have mentioned his attention to Isaiah 40-55; here he is probably thinking of Isaiah 40:11.

On the other hand, some of his harshest words are directed against the religious leaders who behave as though they have a corner on righteousness. He calls them *hypocrites!* They *lock people out of the kingdom of heaven* (Matthew 23:13). He pronounces woes upon them.

Jesus' Good News

Jesus announces that a new era is breaking in with his message and mission. *The law and the prophets were in effect until John came; since then the good news of the kingdom of God is proclaimed* (Luke 16:16). In the synagogue at Nazareth Jesus reads from Isaiah 61 about *good news* for the nobodies and then says, *Today this scripture has been fulfilled in your hearing* (Luke 4:18-21).

The church in the New Testament believed unequivocally that Jesus himself provides the way for his followers to become righteous. Read **John 3:1-21**. Do not let familiarity with the passage keep you from digging for its deepest meaning. *The kingdom of God, the Spirit, the serpent in the wilderness*, believing, *light* versus *darkness*, and God's determination *that the world might be saved through [the Son]* are all combined into one magnificent presentation of the good news. John 3:16 is probably the best-known verse in the New Testament. Believing in God's Son is the way to righteousness. In John's Gospel the noun "belief/faith" never occurs; always it is the verb "believe/have faith in." Faith is something you do. *To perform the works of God... believe in him whom he has sent* (John 6:28, 29). To believe is to *do what is true* (3:21).

FOR FURTHER STUDY AND REFLECTION

Memory Bank

1. Know where to find the Sermon on the Mount, Matthew 5-7, and the parable of the good Samaritan, Luke 10:30-37.

2. The Beatitudes are important for biblical literacy: Matthew 5:3-12.

3. Learn the golden rule, Matthew 7:12; Jesus' call in Matthew 11:28-30; and the two great commandments, Matthew 22:37-40 or Mark 12:29-31.

4. Learn John 3:16 (3:14-17 if you memorize easily), and John 13:34, 35.

Research

1. If you can get a copy of the *Mishnah*, find examples of how Torah law is treated, particularly the Sabbath laws. Use the index. (The public library or a synagogue library should have this book.)

2. Luke 2:22-24, 39-42 show that Jesus was brought up according to the law. Why would this be important to the early Christians?

3. How does the parable of the good Samaritan answer the lawyer's question that precedes it?

Reflection

1. Suppose you had been a law-teacher in the time of Jesus. How would you have responded to his teaching?

2. Can love really be "commanded"? Why or why not?

3. How may Jesus' teaching about law and righteousness influence your life?

GOD DEMANDS A RIGHTEOUS PEOPLE

THEME 7

Righteousness in the Church

PART 4

SUMMARY

Jesus left no legal code, but his teachings were treasured, and the demand for repentance and righteousness continued in the church. The church in Jerusalem tended to be legalistic. Paul opposes legalism though he has a place for law. He insists that righteousness comes through faith, not through the law. The development of this emphasis is traced through New Testament letters.

BASIC BIBLE REFERENCES
Acts 3:12-26; 15:1-35
Romans 1:16, 17; 2:12-14; 8:35-39
1 Corinthians 13
Galatians 5:13, 14, 22, 23
Ephesians 6:10-17
Philippians 4:8, 9
Colossians 3:18-4:1
1 Timothy 6:9, 10
James 1:22; 2:14-26

WORD LIST
Imperative
Justified
Pastoral letters
Works

Jesus' Legacy

Jesus left no law like the Old Testament legal codes. In a manner of speaking, however, he did leave new Torah. His teaching established guidelines for the lives of his followers. This teaching was repeated and finally collected in written form because the first Christians believed that through Jesus God had brought about a radical, new deliverance.

Jesus' first followers had difficulty reconciling the law and his ministry and his reinterpretation of the law. Gradually they did understand how he supremely fulfills the law, and this becomes a cornerstone of their proclamation. Read **Acts 3:12-26**. How does Peter explain "fulfill"? What response is required?

Stephen, in his lengthy defense (Acts 7), rehearses Hebrew history, accuses his accusers of often missing the point, and concludes, *They killed those who foretold the coming of the Righteous One, and now you have become his betrayers and murderers* (7:52). That is the flip side of the good news.

The two-volume work Luke-Acts brings together the teachings of Jesus in the setting of his life career and ties them into a kind of historical narrative about the people and events that immediately formed the earliest church. In keeping with Jesus' nonlegalistic approach, the book of Acts shows little concern with law. In keeping with his clear demands there is much said about righteousness.

167   7:4

Apostolic Witness

The preaching of the apostles, according to Acts, follows Jesus' high requirement for righteousness. Peter's sermon on Pentecost leads up to the climax, *Repent*. He exhorts his hearers to save themselves *from this corrupt generation* (Acts 2:38, 40). His next sermon, in Solomon's Portico in the temple area, urges the people, *Repent...and turn to God so that your sins may be wiped out* (3:19). He calls Jesus *the Holy and Righteous One* (3:14).

The story of the fatal deceit of Ananias and Sapphira (5:1-11) is a startling example of the total commitment expected from members of the early church. Peter learned from his experience with the conversion of the household of the Roman centurion Cornelius that God impartially accepts *anyone who fears him and who does what is right* (10:34, 35).

The early church develops in two ways. On the one hand, a congregation centered in Jerusalem is led by some of the original apostolic band and tends to have a conservative, Jewish outlook. Their preaching, as reported in Acts, stresses continuity with the Old Testament. In his Pentecost sermon Peter quotes Psalms 16 and 110, and in the Temple speech he says, *The God of Abraham, the God of Isaac, and the God of Jacob, the God of our ancestors has glorified his servant Jesus* (3:13).

On the other hand, a group with Hellenistic background (that is, from Greek-speaking Judaism) develops a broader outlook. The first deacons of the church are from this circle (Acts 6:1-6). Their ecumenical attitude displeases some Jewish-Christian leaders and raises problems in Jerusalem. Stephen's preaching leads to *a severe persecution...against the church in Jerusalem* (8:1). Philip's mission in Samaria is checked out by Peter and John (8:14). From this outward movement comes the church at Antioch in Syria, where *the disciples were first called Christians* (11:19, 26). This church is the springboard for the missionary efforts of Paul and his associates (13:1-3).

Enter Paul

Paul becomes the special apostle to the Gentiles. In the New Testament this places him in the center of a church struggle that grows out of the question: what is the relation of the church and Judaism? Paul believes that the very nature of the church is at stake. He tells of confronting Peter in Antioch when Peter, out of deference to Jewish Christians from the Jerusalem congregation, *drew back* from the Gentiles (Galatians 1, 2). Paul says that this has to do with whether a person *is justified* (footnote: *reckoned as righteous*) by the works of the law or through faith in Jesus Christ (Galatians 2:16).

This dispute is often focused on the rite of circumcision. Paul can describe his mission as being *entrusted with the gospel for the uncircumcised, just as Peter had been entrusted with the gospel for the circumcised* (Galatians 2:7). Disagreement becomes so strained that a conference is held. Read **Acts 15:1-35**. What *prophets* are quoted in 15:16, 17? The requirements placed upon Gentile converts are derived from laws in Torah, but it is a compromise decision.

Later the conflict flares up again. The Jerusalem Christians are glad for Paul's success with the Gentile mission, but they quote the decision of the conference and urge Paul to try to pacify the law-conscious people. Further misunderstanding leads to a near riot in the Temple grounds, and Paul is finally rescued by Roman soldiers, who hold him in protective custody. The series of events that follows leads to his being sent to Rome for a hearing before the emperor (Acts 21:15-26:30).

The second half of Acts deals with law and righteousness in connection with the mission of Paul. Paul's letters deal with actual situations in the local churches, and he applies his understanding of Scripture. Three factors must be kept in balance. (1) He emphasizes freedom from the law. (2) He demands righteousness, which is on the one hand the gift of God but on the other hand a response to God's goodness. (3) He insists on regulations for Christian living. In his first recorded sermon, at Antioch in Pisidia, he concludes, *by this Jesus everyone who believes is set free from those sins from which you could not be freed by the law of Moses* (Acts 13:39). In his letters he usually includes summaries of practical directives for Christian living.

Galatians

The radical limit to which Paul can move away from Judaic legalism is evident in Galatians. *For freedom Christ has set us free. Stand firm, therefore, and do not submit again to a yoke of slavery* (5:1). He is contrasting *works of the law* and *faith in Jesus Christ*. Faithful Christians have moved beyond the old law. Almost immediately, however, he insists that this does not free them from responsibility. Read **5:13, 14**. (Review the connection with Jesus' teaching.) He wants Christians to *live by the Spirit* and this means rejecting *the desires of the flesh* (5:16). *By contrast* read **5:22, 23**, a noteworthy summary of Paul's ethical emphasis.

So Paul does not intend to do away with law altogether. He is ordering priorities. He argues that if one puts obedience to law first, one is doomed to fail in Christian living, but if one begins with *faith in Jesus Christ*, one will respond in love by living in accord with Jesus' revelation of God's will. Paul counsels a disciplined life.

Paul is not neatly consistent in his use of the term "law." His thinking is not unclear, but we must exercise care to note the context in which he uses the term. The law served a good purpose as *our disciplinarian until Christ came* (3:24), but now relying on it *to be justified* cuts one *off from Christ* (5:4). As we study Paul, we should in all cases be wary of generalizations.

Romans

Paul had not yet visited Rome when he wrote his letter to the Christians there. This is probably why this is the most orderly presentation of his theological views. It is helpful to read the letter at one sitting. The following outline and notes will help.

1:1-17. An introduction. Read **1:16, 17**, a theme-text for the whole letter.

1:18-3:20. The situation of people under the control of sin. Law is meant to foster faithfulness to God and provide a standard for conforming to God's will, but it really becomes the evidence of people's downfall. Read **2:12-14**. Paul leaves room for those who have not had the advantage of knowing God's law.

3:21-4:25. How righteousness becomes effective through Jesus Christ. Abraham's faithfulness is an example.

5:1-8:39. The life freed from sin by faith-relationship with Jesus Christ. His life becomes the basis for our life. Law has been replaced by God's grace (6:14). Paul is careful not to equate the law with sin; law provides *an opportunity* for sin to take over (7:8). The psychology of sin is analyzed in 7:13-25. Read **8:35-39**, a declaration of the power of God's love in Christ.

9:1-11:36. Noticed in Theme 1, Part 3, and Theme 2, Part 2. This passage deals with the special place of Israel (Jews) in God's plan for humanity. The relation between the old Israel and God's new people is not easy to formulate. Paul is quite sure that God still has a saving destiny for the Jews. *All Israel will be saved*, and God's ultimate purpose is *to be merciful to all* (11:26, 32), but Paul does not know the details.

12:1-15:13. Specifics of Christian living—like the last chapter and a half of Galatians. Though Christians do not live under the law, there are certain things they ought to do. Old Testament precepts appear, and there is some reflection of Jesus' teaching. Mutual responsibility among God's people is prominent: *we, who are many, are one body in Christ, and individually we are members one of another*

(12:5), so *we who are strong ought to put up with the failings of the weak* (15:1). Civil responsibilities, treated in 13:1-7, are discussed in Theme 4, Part 2.

15:14-16:23. Personal postscripts, which contribute to our knowledge of Paul's career and the history of the early congregations.

16:24-27. An ascription of praise to God.

First Corinthians

Paul's Corinthian correspondence tells us a lot about that church and his relationship with it. Corinth was a cosmopolitan, seaport town, where there were many pagan influences, so it was inevitable that Paul would have much to say about morality and ethics. He has received direct information about the church, and his responses form a kind of loose outline.

The basic flaw in the Corinthian congregation is a divisive spirit that destroys its effectiveness as a Christian community. Some of this division arises out of misguided pride of knowledge. Paul remarks that *the wisdom of this world is foolishness with God* (3:19). Some division comes from differences in social status in the church. Thus at the Lord's supper *one goes hungry and another becomes drunk* (11:20, 21).

Immorality is a serious problem (5, 6). *Wrongdoers will not inherit the kingdom of God*, Paul writes (6:9). He discusses sex and marriage at some length (Chapter 7). His principle of mutuality is remarkably advanced for his day—and is important today—*the wife does not have authority over her own body, but the husband does; likewise the husband does not have authority over his own body, but the wife does* (7:4).

Some problems are tied to the customs of the times. Thus meat sold in the public markets was routinely *sacrificed to idols*—a kind of pagan "kosher." Eating this meat could raise problems of conscience. Paul lays down an ethical principal of responsibility: we must not become *a stumbling block to the weak; they are believers for whom Christ died* (8:9-11).

In Chapter 12 Paul develops the concept of the Christian community as *the body of Christ and individually members of it* (12:27. Where else in Paul's writing?). Here is one of Paul's longest analogies. This becomes part of his discussion of corporate life and worship, especially *concerning spiritual gifts* (12:1). In the midst of this comes his famous hymn declaring that love is the supreme aim and gift in all Christian living. Read **Chapter 13**. Other details in this letter are considered in Theme 9, Part 3, and in Theme 10, Part 3.

Other Pauline Material

Other letters written by Paul or associated with his mission deal with God's demand for righteousness. Several passages are well known and should be studied. Read **Ephesians 6:10-17** (*the whole armor of God*) and **Philippians 4:8, 9** (*think* and *keep on doing*).

Lists of household responsibilities were fairly common in first-century literature. Read **Colossians 3:18-4:1**. Paul's list has a distinctly Christian flavor. There is a longer version in Ephesians 5:21-6:9, and a non-Pauline example appears in 1 Peter 2:13-3:8.

1 and 2 Timothy and Titus are called "pastoral" letters because they address problems of church officials. Some details of church life reflect situations different from those in other Pauline letters. The reasons for this are somewhat technical and do not affect our discussion here. Exhortations to righteousness are abundant. Wrangling is wrong; contentment is good—*have nothing to do with stupid and senseless controversies—there is great gain in godliness combined with contentment* (2 Timothy 2:23; 1 Timothy 6:6). There is a kind of "household" list in Titus 2:1-10. Jesus warned about the dangers of wealth (as in Mark 10:23-27), but probably the best-known quotation about money comes from **1 Timothy 6:9, 10**.

James

The book of James is really a sermonic essay. It begins as a letter, but there is no letter ending. (The book is considered in another connection in Theme 8, Part 2). It is a kind of collection of Christian laws. There are nearly sixty imperatives in the book (that is, verb forms giving commands). The commandment from Leviticus 19:18 is called *the royal law*. Two of the Ten Commandments are quoted in 2:11. James emphasizes action. Read **1:22** and **2:14-26**. Sometimes this passage is thought to be directed against Paul's emphasis on salvation by *faith apart from works*. Careful study shows, however, that James and Paul differ more in emphasis than in substance. James also has harsh words for *rich people* (5:1-6).

Other books of the New Testament have passages on the demand for righteousness, but time and space limit us to these.

FOR FURTHER STUDY AND REFLECTION

Memory Bank

1. Romans 8:35-39

2. 1 Corinthians 13

3. Galatians 5:22, 23

Research

1. In Romans 8:15-17 and Galatians 4:6, 7 Paul uses the Aramaic term *Abba*. What does it mean? How may it relate to Paul's view of law?

2. Read 1 Corinthians 13 in as many versions as you can. Why do you think KJV *charity* was replaced in modern versions by *love*? What does the Greek word *agape* mean?

3. Compare the lists of virtues in the Pauline letters: Galatians 5:22-24; Philippians 4:8, 9; Colossians 3:12-17. Also the lists of vices: Romans 1:29-31; 1 Corinthians 5:11; 6:9, 10; 2 Corinthians 12:20; Galatians 5:19-21; Ephesians 4:31; 5:3-5; Colossians 3:5-9. Why is the list of vices longer?

4. Read Revelation 14:13, often quoted at funerals. What does it mean when it says *their deeds follow them?*

Reflection

1. Do you think it is valid to distinguish sections in Paul's letters as "practical" rather than "doctrinal" or "theological"? Give reasons for your decision.

2. If Paul were writing to your group today, what would he likely say about law? About freedom? About righteousness? Could he address God's people as a whole on these topics today? Why or why not?

GOD'S PEOPLE LEARN WISDOM

THEME 8

Wisdom in the Jewish[1] Scriptures

PART 1

SUMMARY

Jewish Scriptures share the widespread interest of the ancient world in "wisdom." This includes insights and advice about the natural world, human life and conduct, and good judgment. Solomon is regarded as the patron of wisdom in the biblical tradition. After the exile a wisdom movement in Judaism produced a wide variety of literature. There are the sanctified common sense of Proverbs and Sirach, the skeptical questions of Ecclesiastes, the painful probing of Job, the beautiful poetry of The Song of Solomon, and the elaborate reflections of The Wisdom of Solomon. All seek deeper meaning in life and find that meaning closely connected with the creator God.

BASIC BIBLE REFERENCES
1 Kings 3:16-28; 4:29-34
Job 28:12-28
Proverbs 6; 8
Ecclesiastes 3:1-8
Wisdom of Solomon 3:1; 7:15-30
Sirach 44

WORD LIST
Ben Sira/Sirach
Ecclesiasticus
Parallelism
Qoheleth
Wisdom Literature

Wisdom in the Ancient World

Wisdom was highly regarded throughout the ancient world. Wise persons were sought out for their insight into the meaning of life and the conduct of affairs. The courts of kings drew advisers who could be consulted on difficult matters. Villages and clans held in high esteem those whose judgment was regarded as worthy of acceptance by the community.

Some of these persons were hardly the kind of experts we expect. In the court of the Egyptian pharaoh *the wise men* were classed with *sorcerers* and *magicians* (Exodus 7:8-12). King Nebuchadnezzar *commanded...the magicians, the enchanters, the sorcerers, and the Chaldeans* to interpret his troubled dreams (Daniel 2:1, 2). We feel more at home with the wisdom of Moses' father-in-law Jethro, whose wise counsel helped strengthen Moses' leadership (Exodus 18:10-24).

Wisdom enabled persons to cope effectively with their particular environment. Wisdom passed along common sense and skill, and these know no national boundaries. Wisdom included not only political ability but the fine crafts of artisans. Wisdom covered knowledge of animal life as well as of the heavens. It was a keen observer of human limitations and was concerned for the stability of the coming generation. In general, wisdom was optimistic, for human nature could be guided and could learn to live in kind and just relationships.

---

[1] "Jewish Scriptures" is used here rather than "Hebrew Scriptures," as in Themes 2 and 4, because in this theme two deuterocanonical books are studied. These two books were used by Jews but were never part of the Hebrew canon.

Wisdom in Israel

It should be no surprise that God's people shared in this concern for wisdom. Skill at crafts is attributed to wisdom from Yahweh in Exodus 31:1-6. Well adjusted living was a common goal of those who shaped Israel's thought and practice. Certainly this was one of the ends of Torah: observing *statutes and ordinances...will show your wisdom and discernment to the peoples, who...will say, "Surely this great nation is a wise and discerning people!"* (Deuteronomy 4:5, 6). The prophets shared this aim: *Those who are wise understand these things* (Hosea 14:9).

Torah regulated much of Israel's life, but this does not mean that her sages expressed all their counsel in religious terms. In fact, much of it is common sense advice (as the words of Jethro). Wise women appear in special roles from time to time. Joab employs *a wise woman* to persuade David to bring Absalom from exile, (2 Samuel 14:1-21). Later another wise woman plays a fearsome part in helping Joab crush a rebellion (20:16-22). *The wise woman* is praised in Proverbs 14:1.

Israel put a distinctive stamp on her wisdom writings. This came about because of the unique religious, cultural, and social environment of Israel. Magicians and sorcerers were banned by Torah (Leviticus 19:31; Deuteronomy 18:9-14); there were clear limits to where Israelites should seek advice. *The LORD gives wisdom* (Proverbs 2:6). Human judgment alone is not finally to be trusted. *There is a way that seems right to a person, but its end is the way of death* (Proverbs 14:12; also 16:25). So the principle governing Israel's wisdom is repeated, *The fear of the LORD is the beginning of wisdom* (Psalm 111:10; Proverbs 9:10); *the fear of the LORD, that is wisdom* (Job 28:28).

Solomon

One name stands out in Israel's wisdom tradition. Solomon's prestige was so great that he becomes the patron-figure for wisdom much as Moses is the embodiment of lawgiving and David symbolizes psalms. As we shall see, Solomon's name was associated with a number of wisdom writings.

Solomon's wise judgment in resolving difficult problems was celebrated; see, for example, **1 Kings 3:16-28**. His reputation is elaborately described in **1 Kings 4:29-34**. *The queen of Sheba* made a long journey to test his wisdom (10:1-7). His extraordinary endowment is a gift of God (3:5-12)—as indeed is all Israelite wisdom.

A Wisdom Movement

In the period from Elijah to Ezekiel the place of the prophets in national life was to the fore (reflected in the second major division of the Jewish canon). At the end of that period prophet, priest, and wise man were sometimes rivals. Jeremiah bitterly denounces the wise men whose optimistic forecasts are being accepted by the king. The prophet is sure that their assessment of the international situation is dead wrong (Jeremiah 8:8-11). Following the return from exile the influence of the prophets declined, and the priestly guardians of the law and the teachers of wisdom were the principal influences in the life of the people.

Wisdom as a distinctive kind of expression is scattered among Old Testament books. Such literature evidently had a lengthy development. There are few identifiable historical allusions in wisdom books, and scholars have great difficulty in dating them. Wisdom did become a distinctive movement as may be seen in some of the Writings in the Jewish canon and in deuterocanonical books that are explicitly called "wisdom." A look at wisdom books will help us understand better the thinking of Israel's sages and their function in her life.

The Book of Proverbs

Proverbs is a collection of collections. Most of the divisions are identified by introductory markers. A simple survey-outline of the book may help you manage its structure:

1:1-7	Prologue to the collection
1:8-9:18	Discourses on wisdom, many addressed to *my son*
10:1-22:16	Miscellaneous proverbs, attributed to Solomon
22:17-24:34	A collection with parallels to Amenemope; 24:23-34 is called *sayings of the wise*
25—29	Attributed to Solomon but collected by officials of King Hezekiah (about 715-687 B.C.)
30—31	Two collections bearing the names of otherwise unknown wise men, Agur and Lemuel, plus a poem in praise of *a capable wife* (31:10-31).

Proverbs 1:1 appears to attribute the whole book to Solomon, but this is not really appropriate. Within the book some sections are credited to Solomon, but some are clearly not his. Some of the sayings are ancient, but the collections are meant for the instruction of young Jews in the post-exilic period. Wisdom by this time was conventionally attributed to Solomon, but pre-exilic editors are noted in 25:1.

Proverbs 22:17-24:22 bears close resemblance to an Egyptian wisdom writing, *Instruction of Amenemope*, which may be dated some time after 1000 B.C. Chapter 30 contains *the words of Agur* and a series of sayings that involve numbers. Chapter 31 begins with *the words of King Lemuel...that his mother taught him.* 31:10-31 is well known for its praise of an ideal wife-mother. The role of the teacher and the function of moral precepts are emphasized throughout the book and become a prominent motif in Jewish education.

Except for such a general outline, Proverbs is hard to systematize. The writing is in poetic form, mostly as couplets or series of interrelated verses. A common feature of Hebrew poetry is parallelism. In Proverbs two lines are most often either "synonymous," with the second line building on the first, or they are "antithetical," with the second line contrasting to the first[2] (see, for example, 4:14 and 10:1).[3] Read **Proverbs 6**. Here is a strong interest in the world of nature (6:6-8). Numbers are used in unique ways (6:16-19). Striking figures of speech are frequent (6:27, 28).

In Jewish life the family was of central importance, and instruction by parents was a backbone of society (6:20; see also 2:1-5). The sanctity of marriage is often implied by warnings against infidelity (6:23-29). Wisdom's *house* with its *seven pillars* is described in 9:1-6. There is instruction to faithful courtiers, and proverbs about the king and his people are mixed in with instruction for family and community life (see 20:7, 8).

In two passages wisdom becomes a woman-figure, addressing all who will hear her urgent message. Read **Proverbs 8** (see also 1:20-33). In 7:4, 5 Lady Wisdom (as she is sometimes referred to) is contrasted to the evil woman who appears so often. Since so much of the book is male-dominated, these passages and the role model of mother-wife elsewhere in Proverbs are particularly important.[4] The book closes with the description of *a worthy woman* (ASV), *a capable wife* (NRSV).

Many of the proverbs appear to be secular, and they often appeal to enlightened self-interest. The person who lives in *the fear of the LORD* will be rewarded in this life. There is no mention of Israel's covenant relation with Yahweh. For the Israelite wise man, however, life was not compartmentalized, so common sense, good living, and the divine will appear in a comfortable mix in Proverbs.

---

2 Hebrew poetry is treated in more detail in Theme 9, Part 2.
3 Many illustrative references are given in this part. Read as many of them as you have time for. Chapters 10-16 have many examples of antithetical parallelism.
4 The Greek and Latin word for "wisdom" is *sophia*, a feminine noun. In the eastern arm of the Christian church this figure assumes great importance. Thus the great cathedral in Constantinople was known as *Santa Sophia*, "Holy Wisdom."

Ecclesiastes

The wisdom of Ecclesiastes is not as optimistic as that of Proverbs. The author writes like a worldly-wise and somewhat cynical philosopher, but he is really a Jewish sage who deals with main themes of the wisdom movement. His Greek title means "leader of the assembly." Often the book is known by its Hebrew title *Qoheleth*, a term that KJV translates *preacher*, and NRSV translates *Teacher* (1:1)—the precise office of the person is unclear. He has tried everything life has to offer and finds it all disappointing; so he concludes that *all is vanity* (1:13, 14).

The negative skepticism of the book may cause surprise that it is in Scripture at all. Perhaps the association with Solomon's name helped, but the Hebrew of the author and some of his remarks are evidence that the book is post-exilic. Likely the final words (12:13, 14) made the earlier questions and doubts acceptable. The author acknowledges that life is not simple, that there are contradictions we cannot always explain. This probably accounts for the popularity of **3:1-8**.

There are statements that remind us of Proverbs; for example, *Wisdom gives strength to the wise more than ten rulers that are in the city* (Ecclesiastes 7:19). The writer, however, does not consistently support wisdom: *All this I have tested by wisdom; I said, "I will be wise," but it was far from me* (7:23). God is in control, but *no one can find out what is happening* (8:17). This leads to a kind of fatalism: *the same fate comes to everyone and the dead know nothing...time and chance happen to them all* (9:3, 5, 11). Human self-enjoyment is *God's gift* (2:24, 25; 3:13).[5] The book has many quotable gems; for example, *a living dog is better than a dead lion* (9:4).[6]

Job

The wisdom movement was not narrowly confined either in geography or in time, so for us the important relationship among the books is how they deal with similar problems. Ecclesiastes wrestles with the problems of life in its own way. So does Job. The literary form of Job is different from Ecclesiastes, so Job deals with his problem in a different way. He struggles to understand how God could be just and yet allow him to become so miserable (Theme 3, Part 2). Although it is unique in approach, Job is one of the great wisdom books.

Read **28:12-28**, which speaks broadly about the nature of wisdom. It is characteristic of wisdom to express concern for the individual. In Torah and the prophets God's people are

---
5 Jesus' reference to this is familiar, Luke 12:19.
6 Others: Ecclesiastes 5:1, 12; 10:1, 11; 11:1; 12:1, 12.

mostly treated in their collective, covenant relationship with God. Proverbs, however, speaks often of *my son*, and Ecclesiastes is mostly concerned with the welfare of *a man*. Job focuses on one person and his individual misery: "Why has this happened to me?"

The glib answers that Job's friends give to his questions are rejected though they claim to be the response of wisdom. They have assumed that one gets about what one deserves in this life. "Not in my case," Job retorts, and the nature of human life is argued out. Finally, Job finds his answer in the speeches of Yahweh, which are full of questions about nature that Job cannot answer. Thus the ultimate wisdom of God is vindicated.

The prose sections, Chapters 1, 2 and 42:7-17 form a kind of "envelope" for the book, which makes the difficult discussions in Chapters 3-41 more palatable to most readers.[7] Job's repentance (42:1-6) and the restoration of his fortunes are, as it were, a happy ending to the book.

The Song of Solomon

The Song of Solomon is also known as The Song of Songs from its title in the Hebrew (1:1).[8] The book is really a collection of lyric love poems with no explicitly religious content. The connection with Solomon is literary, made perhaps because of his reputation as a composer of songs (1 Kings 4:32) plus the tradition about his prolific marriages (1 Kings 11:3). The description of a wedding procession of Solomon in The Song of Solomon 3:6-11 is usually understood as a figurative poem celebrating a (much later) bridegroom's arrival at his wedding.

The date of the collection is usually placed after the exile. Thus it falls in the period of the wisdom movement, and it is regularly listed with the wisdom books though it is quite different from the ones we have just studied. It has maintained its place in the Jewish and Christian canons largely because it has been interpreted as a figure of the relationship between God and people—Yahweh and Israel, Christ and the church.

If you read the book without a conscious attempt to make a religious analysis, you will find it full of very beautiful expressions of human love, even the erotic. The poetry presents dialogues between a man and a woman, and there is also a kind of chorus, *daughters of Jerusalem*, who are repeatedly addressed and who sometimes respond. There are phrases that have found their way into our literary vocabulary; for example: *a rose of Sharon, a lily*

---

7 In Ecclesiastes 1:1 and 12:13, 14 provide a similar envelope.
8 The phrase in Hebrew is a superlative, *the greatest song*.

of the valley (2:1), *the voice of the turtledove* (2:12), *the little foxes, that ruin the vineyards* (2:15), and *many waters cannot quench love* (8:7).

Two Deuterocanonical Wisdom Books

In Theme 1, Part 2, we used the deuteroncanonical book of 1 Maccabees to read how God saved a people two centuries before Jesus' ministry. Now we take a brief look at two more deuterocanonical books that were produced late in the wisdom movement. The first is Sirach. Its author is identified as *Jesus..son of Sirach* (50:27), and the book is often referred to as The Wisdom of Ben Sirach.[9] Perhaps the author was a teacher in a wisdom school. Information in Chapter 50 fixes the date of the book as around 180 B.C. The book is also known as Ecclesiasticus ("the church's book") probably because of an early Christian feeling that this was the most important of the Jewish books outside of the Palestinian canon.

Much of the content of the book is similar to Proverbs. There is an important difference, however: the separation of wisdom from covenant law has given way to their union (Sirach 24:23). Wisdom is here neither secular common sense nor is it secret. Wisdom is at last at home in the temple (24:1-12). The best known passage is **Chapter 44**, which begins a survey of Hebrew history that continues through Chapter 49. In Jewish wisdom literature Sirach is unique in the attention given to the covenant history of God's people.

The Wisdom of Solomon is not like the other wisdom books you have read. Although there is some wisdom language, the style is more flowing, and the content shows its contact with Hellenistic Greek culture. The book received its traditional name because the author appropriates Solomon's prayer for wisdom (see Chapter 9 and 1 Kings 3:6-9). The author was a pious, somewhat traditional Jew, but he is influenced by cultural change. He wrote in Greek, probably in Alexandria shortly before the Christian era.[10]

Read **The Wisdom of Solomon 7:15-30**. The atmosphere is different from the Hebrew wisdom books. There are philosophical ideas and many poetical metaphors. There are other important details in the book: it identifies God's Spirit with wisdom (7:7; 9:17); it affirms a future life, as in **Wisdom 3:1** (also 5:15, 16); and it attempts to blend Hebrew and Greek wisdom (6:12, 24; 13:1-3). In 15:14-19:21 there is an elaborate series of contrasts related to the exodus: God helps the Israelites and plagues the Egyptians.

---

9 *Ben* is Hebrew for *son (of)*. The book was first written in Hebrew but was translated into Greek about fifty years later by Ben Sira's grandson (see The Prologue of the book). Sirach is the Greek form of Sira. Both Ben Sira and Sirach are used.

10 This excluded it from the Jewish canon, but it was included in the Greek Bible. In the third century A.D. it appeared in one list as "Wisdom, Written by the Friends of Solomon in His Honor."

FOR FURTHER STUDY AND REFLECTION

Memory Bank

1. Select and learn three sayings from Proverbs.

Research

1. Solomon had connections with Egypt (see 1 Kings 4:30; 11:1). How might these be related to his reputation for wisdom?

2. Argue for and against the proposition: The author of Ecclesiastes is inconsistent in the presentation of his thought.

3. The deuterocanonical book Tobit is a sort of romantic novel. In Chapter 4 a father gives advice to his son. Compare it to similar teaching in Proverbs and to Polonius' advice to Laertes in *Hamlet* (Act 1, Scene 3).

Reflection

1. Which wisdom book do you think is most congenial to popular thinking today? What functions as a replacement for "wisdom" today?

2. The secular elements of biblical wisdom may pose a problem for some people just because "it is in the Bible." Prepare a response to this difficulty.

3. Try your hand at writing an original proverb.

SUMMARY

The role of wisdom changed in New Testament times. Jesus used wisdom-like sayings and was considered a wise man. The influence of the traditional role of wisdom may be seen in the prologue to the fourth Gospel. Among the New Testament writings, James is closest to Jewish wisdom. In moving into the Greco-Roman world the church confronts new kinds of wisdom, and Paul meets this challenge. He is familiar with Greek philosophy, but he emphasizes wisdom that comes from God's Spirit, and he carefully relates it to Jesus Christ. In 1 John knowledge becomes a kind of wisdom that challenges faith, and the Revelation shows two other developments.

BASIC BIBLE REFERENCES
Matthew 11:28-30; 16:1-3
Luke 7:31-35; 11:45-52; 12:54-56
John 1:1-18
1 Corinthians 1:17-31; 2:6-13
James 1:5-11, 22, 3:13-18

WORD LIST
Gnostic
Logos
Mystery
Sign

GOD'S PEOPLE LEARN WISDOM

THEME 8

Wisdom in the New Testament

PART 2

Introduction

We have seen that wisdom in the Jewish Scriptures means first of all the sensible and consistent handling of contemporary life in one's environment. Much of this is similar and sometimes related to the thought of non-Jewish neighbors, but there is an emphasis on the creator God as the ultimate source of wisdom.

There is no wisdom movement as such in the New Testament, but wisdom is nonetheless present in several important ways. In the Gospels there are passages that show a definite connection with wisdom in the Jewish Scriptures. This we should expect since the teaching of Jesus was so deeply rooted in the Old Testament. When the Christian movement spread beyond Palestine, however, the intellectual and religious environment was mostly rooted in Greek thought. The influence that we meet in The Wisdom of Solomon is everywhere, and wisdom in international garb becomes a challenge to Christian faith. What we have learned about wisdom then becomes a helpful bridge as we try to sort out what is distinctive in Christian wisdom.

Wisdom in the Gospels

Wisdom appears in the Gospels in several forms. The simplest kind occurs in sayings of Jesus that we might call "folk wisdom." Read **Matthew 16:1-3**. Jesus points out that his listeners are able to forecast the weather from observation of nature, yet they miss the more serious *signs of the times*. In the parallel **Luke 12:54-56** the weather signs are different. Often his terse comments are very similar to sayings in Proverbs. Mark 3:24, 25 is in synonymous parallelism: *If a kingdom is divided against itself, that kingdom cannot stand. And if a house is divided against itself, that house will not be able to stand.* Mark 7:15 is in antithetical parallelism: *there is nothing outside a person that by going in can defile, but the things that come out are what defile.*

Upon occasion Jesus mentions wisdom. Read **Luke 7:31-35**. Here Jesus uses a homely picture of children's play to make a point about his contemporaries. Luke has just observed how Jesus' hearers were divided over John the Baptist (verses 29, 30). Now smug antagonism has confronted Jesus' own ministry. He concludes that he and his followers are wisdom's *children* and are thereby *justified*. In Matthew's parallel it is *deeds* that justify wisdom (Matthew 11:19), but the point is the same.

Read the familiar words in **Matthew 11:28-30**. Recall that Proverbs portrayed wisdom as calling to those who would hear. Among many references to heavy yokes in the Old Testament, note Isaiah 14:25: *[the Assyrian] yoke shall be removed from them, and his burden from their shoulders*. On the other hand, Jesus' pronouncement of woes is reminiscent of wisdom words against folly. Read **Luke 11:45-52**. In verse 49 *the Wisdom of God* is mentioned as though it were a quotation, but no definite literary source can be identified. In the parallel, Matthew 23:34, almost the same words are attributed to Jesus himself, so perhaps Luke means "God's wisdom." Since wisdom is considered to be a gift of God, Jesus would here be claiming to have that gift.

We should not assume that Jesus or the Gospel writers were consciously copying wisdom forms. The tradition and substance were already present in first-century Judaism. Luke tells how the twelve-year-old Jesus *amazed* those who heard his conversations in the temple, and the text adds, *Jesus increased in wisdom* (Luke 2:47, 52; so also 2:40, *filled with wisdom*). Later, many in his Galilean audience *were astounded* at *this wisdom that has been given to him* (Mark 6:2). He did not pose as a wise man, but his mastery of the Scriptures clearly included the wisdom books.

Occasionally Jesus' sayings reflect words from a wisdom source. The "Golden Rule"[1] is connected to *the law and the prophets*, but see how it is a positive extension of Proverbs 24:29. A parable that Jesus uses in Luke 14:7-11 includes an adaptation of Proverbs 25:6, 7.

In discussing his mission and message on one occasion Jesus mentions the visit of the queen of Sheba *to hear the wisdom of Solomon*, and then he says, *Something greater than Solomon is here* (Matthew 12:42). Jesus' interview with the Syro-Phoenician woman (Mark 7:24-30)

---

[1] A Basic Reference in Introduction, Part 1, and in Theme 7, Part 3.

and his decision about taxes paid to Caesar (Mark 12:13-17) may remind us of Solomon's wisdom, but Jesus insists that his good news is more important than wisdom, however great.

Theme 3, Part 3 studies the prologue of the fourth Gospel in its relationship to how Jesus revealed God. Read again **John 1:1-18**. Jesus embodies *the Word* (Greek, *logos*), and this is connected with God's word in creation (Genesis 1:1, 3). Now we may see further how this is related to Jewish wisdom thought. The association of *the Word* with God at creation reminds us of the role of wisdom as the expression of God's being and the agent of God's creating and communicating; for example, *The LORD created me at the beginning of his work.... When he established the heavens, I was there...I was beside him, like a master worker* (Proverbs 8:22, 27, 30).

The Word in John, however, is more than this. All that God seeks to communicate, *the Word* is. Wisdom in the Jewish Scriptures is not intended to be a separate being though it is hard to see how this is avoided. John 1:1 seems to risk this when it states that *the Word was with God*, but having distinguished the identity of *the Word*, it affirms that *the Word was God* (REB, *what God was, the Word was*). In John 1:14 there is a radical move: *the Word became flesh* proclaims God's ultimate communication with the human creation. The rest of the Gospel seeks to show that Jesus is not a created spirit but *the Son of God* (20:31). Being a son intends to declare a relationship completely different from that of a created being. Thus Jesus can say of his unique relationship to *the Father* (the term he usually uses for God), *The Father and I are one* (10:30).

James

One book of the New Testament comes close to being wisdom literature: the book of James. Theme 7, Part 4, notes that the book begins like a letter, but it has no epistolary ending. In its question-and-answer sections and in some other ways it resembles a Greek literary form known as "diatribe." (This is not exactly what we mean today by "diatribe"; the Greek form was used by the Stoic philosopher Epictetus, among others.) Common-sense subject matter is evident throughout. Couplet parallelism occasionally appears, but illustrations from nature and everyday experience are scattered throughout the book.

There are only four explicit references to wisdom. Read **1:5-11** and **3:13-18**. The author offers practical advice and can become very severe. *Come now, you rich people, weep and wail for the miseries that are coming to you* (5:1). Control of the tongue is emphasized; it is compared to *bits* in the *mouths of horses*, a ship's *rudder, a fire, a world of iniquity*, and *a restless evil* (3:3-10). There is a quotation from Proverbs 3:34 in James 4:6, and James 3:12 reminds us of Jesus' observation in Matthew 7:16-18—*a grapevine* bears grapes.

James 2:14-26, which is a Basic Reference in Theme 7, Part 4, deals with the relationship between *faith* and *works* (REB, TEV, *actions*). James approaches life from a wisdom-like, practical viewpoint, and there is no real conflict with Paul's views, which are more theological. Paul would concur that a do-nothing faith is ineffective, so he writes, *All must test their own work; then that work...will become a cause for pride.... Do not be deceived; God is not mocked, for you reap whatever you sow* (Galatians 6:4, 7). Compare this with **James 1:22**.

Paul and Wisdom

"Wisdom" is mentioned twenty-six times in the Pauline letters, but each reference must be studied in its context, for wisdom may have different shades of meaning. Keep in mind that it was a drastic move when Paul went from the Near East to Europe. The traditions of the great Greek philosophers were already five hundred years old, and their thought world was quite different from that of the Old Testament. But this was not new to Paul. He was a native of Tarsus, a university town in southeastern Asia Minor (Acts 22:3), and the rabbinic training that he mastered in Jerusalem already reflected contact with Greek thinking. His speech in Athens shows his ability to deal with such philosophy (Acts 17:16-34).[2] He is quite convinced, however, that philosophical wisdom is too speculative and secular for God's people.

Paul's most sustained treatment of wisdom is woven through the early chapters of 1 Corinthians.[3] Read **1 Corinthians 1:17-31; 2:6-13**. Note that *wisdom* is used in more than one sense. Human wisdom is contrasted to God's wisdom and is sometimes negative, sometimes neutral. The *Greeks* especially *desire wisdom*, but many people consider God's wisdom to be *foolishness*. God's wisdom may come to humans as a gift *through the Spirit* (12:8).

The effective center of this whole treatment is *Christ crucified*. This is *a stumbling block to Jews* because they could not think of their messiah coming to such an end. Besides, it is *foolishness to Gentiles* (*Gentiles* here is interchangeable with *Greeks*); they cannot make sense of worshiping a God who appears impotent to prevent such an unjust and cruel event. Paul's Old Testament citations are from Isaiah, a hint that wisdom influence may come from outside the wisdom books.

In Romans 11:33-36 Paul enthusiastically praises God, and he pointedly includes *wisdom and knowledge* as divine attributes. Several times in Colossians the phrase *in all wisdom*

---

2 See the NRSV footnote to Acts 17:28.

3 Almost a third of the occurrences of the word *wisdom* in the New Testament are in 1 Corinthians.

occurs, but the meaning goes beyond the wisdom-literature background. *All the treasures of wisdom and knowledge* are hidden in *Christ*. This is *God's mystery* (Colossians 2:2, 3). In Paul's day there were pagan religions that made much of "mysteries," and they initiated persons into those mysteries. In Colossians 2:20-23 *self-imposed piety, humility, and severe treatment of the body give an appearance of wisdom*, but Christ separates one from all of this. *With Christ* one dies *to the elemental spirits of the universe*, a phrase that may be taken to refer to earth, air, water, and fire, which, according to some Greek religious thought, must be overcome in order for one to gain immortality.

Christians are urged to be *wise*, not *foolish* (Ephesians 5:15-17). Timothy is told that *the Holy Scriptures...are able to give you the wisdom that leads to salvation* (2 Timothy 3:15, TEV). 2 Peter 3:15, 16 refers to *the wisdom given...our beloved brother Paul*—and comments that *there are some things in [his letters] hard to understand*.

What a challenge for Paul! He becomes a chief advocate of a new manner of understanding God's wisdom in a new environment. A measure of the success of his undertaking is the history of Christian thought in the West, where the old and the new were fused in the worldwide mission of God's people.[4]

1 John, Revelation, etc.

The First Letter of John[5] does not use the word "wisdom," but the verb "know" occurs twenty-six times. The people addressed seem to have been proud of what they say they know, but the author implies doubt about their understanding. The center of the problem is their confession of Jesus. *Who is the liar but the one who denies that Jesus is the Christ?* They are trusting in what they say they know rather than abiding *in the Son and in the Father* (1 John 2:22, 24). This has a practical side: *Whoever says, "I have come to know him," but does not obey his commandments, is* a liar... Wh*oever says, "I am in the light," while hating a brother or sister, is still in the darkness* (2:4, 9).

A dangerous challenge to Christian faith was developing in which people looked for salvation by knowledge. This is why 1 John is so concerned that a claim to "know" will not be an occasion for pride but will be proved by God's Spirit and by love (4:13-16). A pattern of thinking that offered deliverance from involvement with material existence by knowledge became known as "gnostic," from the Greek word for "knowledge." A century later it became a dangerous heresy in the church. It may already have started to be a problem in several of Paul's churches.

---

4 Think of the connection with Theme 4, Part 2.

5 This book is really not a letter but a kind of sermon. No mention is made of "John." It seems to be written by the author of 2 and 3 John, who calls himself *the elder*.

Wisdom is mentioned in the Revelation in two ways. In Revelation 5:12 and 7:12 it is included in sevenfold ascriptions of praise to God and to the Lamb, that is, *wisdom* is one of the attributes that belong uniquely to God. In 13:18 and 17:9 it functions as a signal that what immediately follows is written in a kind of coded language that requires a key to understand—*this calls for wisdom*. The word *mystery* is used in a similar way. These matters are examined more closely in Theme 10, Part 4.

In the development of liturgy in the church, wisdom has played a prominent role in the Eastern branches. So in the Russian Orthodox church today one may hear a solemn invocation of *Wisdom*.[6]

In summary, we may conclude that the theme of wisdom is not as easy to follow as other themes in the Bible. It is important, however, for two reasons. First, there is a body of literature that is best classified in this way. Second, it is a significant point of contact with nonbiblical religion and secular thought. We emphasize what is unique in the Judeo-Christian traditions, but we must remember that there is truth outside our Scriptures. Recognizing what is common will help us to recognize and describe what is different and distinctive.

FOR FURTHER STUDY AND REFLECTION

Memory Bank

1. Become thoroughly familiar with the prologue of the Gospel of John, and memorize John 1:1-5, 14.

2. Memorize James 1:22.

Research

1. Which parts of the Sermon on the Mount (Matthew 5-7) seem like wisdom sayings?

2. In Romans 1:14 Paul intimates that he is a *debtor...to Greeks...to the wise*. Relate this to 1 Corinthians 9:22. What is Paul's relationship to secular knowledge?

3. What does 1 Corinthians 1:26-29 suggest about the makeup of the Corinthian congregation?

---

[6] Review footnote 3 in Part 1.

4. There are a number of allusions to Gospel sayings in *James*. Find as many as you can. The notes in a study Bible will help you.

Reflection

1. Think of some modern wisdom-type sayings. In what way do they influence behavior?

2. Respond to the interpretation of the relationship between Judeo-Christian and secular wisdom presented at the end of this part. In what ways do you agree or disagree?

GOD'S PEOPLE WORSHIP

Early Backgrounds and National Rites

PART 1

SUMMARY

A study of the history of the Jewish people must include an account of their worship. From the patriarchs to the Passover to the giving of the law to the establishment of the Temple, worship is vital to Jewish identity. Exile and restoration brought far-reaching changes. The major festivals have always marked the cycle of the year. The Jewish experience of worship is essential to an understanding of the Bible.

BASIC BIBLE REFERENCES

Genesis 22:1-14
Leviticus 23
Numbers 3:5-10
1 Kings 6:20-30; 8:1-13, 22-30;
8:1-13; 22-30
Ezra 3:1-13
Esther 9
Psalm 137:1-6
Isaiah 6:1-8

WORD LIST

Festival of Weeks
Hanukkah
Levite
New Moon
Purim
Rosh Hashannah
Succoth
Tabernacle
Tithe
Yom Kippur

Worship and Beginnings

When Moses first appeared before the pharaoh, he announced, *Thus says the LORD, the God of Israel, "Let my people go, so that they may celebrate a festival to me in the wilderness"* (Exodus 5:1). Thus a worship request led to the events that overshadow all of the subsequent history of God's people. Passover, with all its memories and meaning, became central in Hebrew national consciousness. It is not too much to say that worship has been essential to the existence of God's people.

But even as far back as the prehistory, worship was a part of the traditions. Cain's anger against Abel arose because Yahweh *had regard for Abel and his offering, but for Cain and his offering he had no regard* (Genesis 4:3-5). When Noah *went out of the ark...Noah built an altar to the LORD...and offered burnt offerings on the altar* (Genesis 8:18-20).

Read **Genesis 22:1-14**. This is an important story. The word worship first occurs in the Bible in 22:5. The Hebrew word means "bow oneself down." Later tradition (nonbiblical) believed that this took place on the low mountain where the Jerusalem Temple eventually was built. When Abraham sent a servant to find for Isaac a wife from their clan, that servant *bowed his head and worshiped the LORD* several times (Genesis 24:26, 48, 52).

The story of Jacob's dream at Bethel is a Basic Reference in Theme 2, Part 1 (Genesis 28:10-22). God's people again and again experience that sense of the presence of God. The erection of memorial stones, the pouring of oil, the making of vows, and the giving of a tenth (a "tithe") are all practiced in later Israelite worship.

From Moses to Samuel

When God calls Moses from the burning bush (Exodus 3), two features affecting worship are involved. First, the spot is made holy by the special presence of God. Second, the revelation of the sacred name offers a new relationship between Yahweh and Moses and the people he was to lead.

The Sinai stories tell how Yahweh instructed Moses about the equipment, staff, and exercise of Israel's worship. The place of worship is the *Tabernacle*. This word has come to us from the Latin word for "tent." TEV translates, *the sacred Tent, the Tent of my presence*. It was portable, for the Israelites were nomadic in the wilderness period. The record of these stories reached their final form long after the people were settled in Palestine, so details occasionally reflect the later situation.

The furnishings and construction of the Tabernacle are described in Exodus 25-30. Some matters are important long after the tent was no longer used, but there are many details that we need not remember. The *ark* with its *mercy seat* appears as late as Revelation 11:19. The *lampstand* and *altar* are also important.

The priests and Levites play a prominent role in Israel's worship. These groups are not identical, but at times they are not distinguished in the texts. Read **Numbers 3:5-10**. The descendants of Aaron became the principal officials in the Jerusalem Temple. The Levites, a much larger group, performed prescribed Temple duties. Before the exile they were practically Temple servants.

No particular area of the Promised Land was set aside for the Levites. They lived in various towns throughout the land and had certain privileges that are spelled out in Deuteronomy 18:1-8. Their principal place of service, however, was in Jerusalem. After the exile both priestly orders became more important. Zechariah, the priest-father of John the Baptist, served when *his section was on duty* (Luke 1:8).

From early boyhood Samuel served as an attendant in the sanctuary at Shiloh. His mother had prayed for a child, so when he was old enough, she lent him to the Lord and he remained to minister to the Lord , in the presence of the priest Eli (1 Samuel 1:28; 2:11). The call of Samuel is a familiar story (Chapter 3). In later life he performed priestly functions, especially prayer and sacrifice. Not all priests, however, were reliable. *Eli's sons were scoundrels* (2:12).

The Ark and the Temple

The making of the Ark is described in Exodus 25:10-22. Here it is called the *ark of the covenant*, presumably because the tablets of the law were kept in it (see Deuteronomy 10:2, 5). The *mercy seat* came to represent the actual presence of Yahweh. The cherubs (Hebrew plural, *cherubim*) were fanciful, winged creatures that attended Yahweh's presence and were perhaps guardians of the mercy seat. The Ark was designed to be portable, and the places where it was kept during the settlement of the Promised Land became worship centers. David brought it to Jerusalem (see 2 Samuel 6:1-19), and it was eventually placed in *the most holy place* (often called "the Holy of Holies"). Read **1 Kings 8:1-13**. The Ark was the connecting link between the wilderness period and settled worship in Israel.

The building of Solomon's Temple had far-reaching consequences for Israel and the history of Jewish worship. Most Bible dictionaries have pictures of how it probably looked. Much of the design was adapted from Phoenician models—not surprising when we remember that the architect was Hiram, a Phoenician (1 Kings 5:1-6). To get an idea of its magnificence, read **1 Kings 6:20-30**. Sample Solomon's dedicatory prayer. Read **1 Kings 8:22-30**.

The Old Testament gives much attention to the practice of worship and to the leaders and beliefs that shape worship. Elijah's contest with the prophets of Baal tells us that the inroads of alien religious cults was an early concern. Remember also that Joash, Hezekiah, and Josiah felt compelled to institute religious reforms (Theme 6, Part 2).

The Prophets

Threats from powers outside Israel were more than political and social. The prophets saw clearly the drastic dangers that would come with corruption of Israelite worship. When Hezekiah showed Temple treasures to envoys from Babylon, more than politics was involved, and Isaiah scolded the king and predicted that captivity in Babylon was coming (see 2 Kings 20:12-19).

The call of Isaiah is one of the classic passages on worship in the Bible. It was a Basic Reference in Theme 3, Part 3. Read again **Isaiah 6:1-8**. Most of the elements of worship are included. Try to identify the parts of this pattern.

Other prophets complained about faults in worship and scolded those who were responsible. Amos declares Yahweh's displeasure: *I hate, I despise your festivals, and I take no delight in your solemn assemblies.* This is because the lives of the people do not match their religious words (Amos 5:21-24). Hosea complains that *multiplied altars to expiate sin...became...altars for sinning* (Hosea 8:11). Zephaniah says that *priests have profaned what is sacred* (Zephaniah 3:4). Malachi accuses the priests of *offering polluted food* on Yahweh's altar (Malachi 1:6, 7).

Exile and Restoration

Exile posed particular problems for Jewish worship. How could their rites be performed without the Temple, which had been destroyed? Read **Psalm 137:1-6**, which poignantly reflects the dilemma. Probably this situation influenced the development of the synagogue as an alternative way of worship.

Ezekiel ministered to exiles in Babylon. He assures them that God will restore them *into their own land* (Ezekiel 39:25-29). He describes visions of the rebuilding of the Temple (see Ezekiel 40-46). Although the details are idealized, the description is reminiscent of Solomon's temple, where Ezekiel may have served before the exile.

Ezra, Nehemiah, and Haggai tell about the rebuilding of the Temple after the exile. Read **Ezra 3:1-13**. This second Temple is important because in it were developed the practices that influenced Judaism in subsequent years. It suffered damage and desecration by the Greeks in the fourth century B.C. and by the Romans in the first century B.C. Herod the Great (37 B.C. to A.D. 4) rebuilt the Temple in lavish style. It was this building that Jesus knew. It is the one finally destroyed by the Romans in A.D. 70.

Features of Worship

The Temple was the focal point of Jewish national religion. Sacrifice was a major activity in the Temple and was a central act in the worship of Yahweh. Offerings of several kinds and for various purposes are specified in Leviticus, Numbers, and Deuteronomy. Life is God's gift; *the earth is the LORD's and all that is in it* (Psalm 24:1). The sacrifices and offerings are tangible acknowledgment of this belief.

Although the sacrificial system came to an abrupt end with the destruction of the Temple in A.D. 70, the spiritual ideas that underlay it still endure. The symbolism and meaning run through the New Testament, and they are adapted to help explain the death of Jesus. We still use vocabulary of the Temple today, especially "sacrifice," "altar," "offering," and "service."

The structure of Israel's worship was—and is today—developed around the High Holy Days. Indeed, it may be said that the Jewish calendar is the Jewish catechism. Read **Leviticus 23**, where the oldest appointed festivals are outlined. Several other festivals were added later and are celebrated in Judaism today.

The Major Festivals

The Sabbath is the most frequent and regular observance. Recall the commandment requiring that the Sabbath be hallowed and review the reasons given in Exodus and Deuteronomy. Isaiah urges the people to *call the sabbath a delight...not going your own ways, serving your own interests, or pursuing your own affairs* (Isaiah 58:13). Jeremiah complains specifically about the profaning of the Sabbath in his day (Jeremiah 17:19-27). In recalling the giving of the commandments at Mount Sinai, Nehemiah mentions particularly only the *holy sabbath* (Nehemiah 9:13, 14).

Along with the weekly observance of the Sabbath, there was a monthly observance of *the new moon*. The official calendar of Judaism has always been lunar, so the cycle of the year is regulated by the new moons. Monthly offerings are specified in Numbers 28:11-15, and *trumpets* are blown (10:10). *The sabbaths and the new moons* are mentioned together in 2 Chronicles 2:4 (also in Isaiah 1:13, Ezekiel 46:1, Hosea 2:11, Amos 8:5).

No observance is related specifically for the beginning of a new year, but *on the first day of the seventh month* a special observance is marked by rest, offerings, and the blowing of trumpets—the rams' horns (Numbers 29:1, 2). This later becomes *Rosh Hashannah*,[1] "the head of the year." The months are counted, however, from Nisan at the beginning of spring. Thus *seedtime and harvest*, the cycle of nature, are marked in the calendar (Genesis 8:22).

On the *tenth day of the [seventh] month* a special Day of Atonement, *Yom Kippur*, is observed. Elaborate instructions are spelled out in Leviticus 16. Only on this day did the high priest go into *the holy place*, and particular offerings are prescribed. Also a special goat was selected, the priest laid his hands on its head and confessed *all the iniquities of the people,* and it was sent *away into the wilderness*—the origin of "scapegoat."

Five days later is the *festival of booths*[2]—in Hebrew, *Succoth*. The people are to live for eight days in rustic booths in memory of the temporary shelters of their ancestors in the wilderness. It was a kind of thanksgiving time with offerings from the grape and olive harvests.

---

1 Sometimes spelled Rosh Hashanah. It is also called the Festival of Trumpets.
2 In KJV *tabernacles*. Think about the connections with Israel's history.

At about the same time when Christians celebrate Christmas, Jews celebrate *Hanukkah*.[3] It commemorates the rededication of the Temple after the Maccabean victory. The story is in 1 Maccabees 4:52-59. In the Gospel of John 10:22 it is called *the festival of the Dedication*. It is later referred to as the "Feast of Lights," connecting it with the relighting of the Temple lamps.

In late winter the festival of *Purim* is held. Read **Esther 9**. It is more a national than a religious holiday. See a study Bible for more information. We do not deal with the book of Esther again in this course, so you may want to read the whole story now.

Passover is the most notable festival of the Jewish year. It is highlighted in Theme 1, Part 1, and you should review that material. It is also known as *the festival of unleavened bread* (Exodus 23:15; 34:18). Why? On the last day of this festival, *first fruits* are offered; it is the beginning of the spring harvest. The very close connection between Hebrew history and worship is quite evident here.

The full grain harvest is celebrated seven weeks later—*the festival of weeks* (Exodus 34:22). Leviticus 23:16 notes that it is seven weeks plus one day, and the Greek word for "fifty" later yields the name "Pentecost" (as in Acts 2:1). In much later times the day commemorated God's giving the law to Moses, and the book of Ruth was also read.[4]

From earliest days three festivals are designated as special. They are noted in Exodus 23:14-17, and 2 Chronicles 8:12, 13 gives later names. You may want to list them. Pilgrimage to Jerusalem for these festivals became customary (see Luke 2:41; John 11:55; Acts 20:16).

Thus Israel's worship includes her history, her praise, and her festivals. The people of God are unique in combining their life experiences in such unity. When they have lost this sense, their identity is in peril. Precisely this ability to render all life holy has given Judaism its continuity and is an important legacy to Christianity.

FOR FURTHER STUDY AND REFLECTION

Memory Bank

1. Isaiah 6:3.

2. The cycle of Jewish festivals.

---

3 Also spelled Chanukah.
4 Notice that two books bearing the names of women are associated with festivals.

Research

1. Using a Bible atlas and other resources study the structure, furnishings, and appearance of the Jerusalem Temple. Most of this information will deal with the building Jesus knew.

2. Why is it reasonable to think that the synagogue developed in the period of the exile?

3. When the Jewish authorities were considering which writings belong in sacred Scripture, they hesitated about Esther. Find out why. Why was it finally included?

4. The Hebrew word for Passover is *pesach*, from which the Greek derived *pascha*. Check the English dictionary for "paschal." What is the significance of the association?

Reflection

1. Details of worship in the Old Testament imply certain things about how the people thought about God. How do our forms of worship imply our understanding of God?

2. In what ways has Christian worship been influenced by Jewish practices?

GOD'S PEOPLE WORSHIP

THEME 9

Devotional Life, Public and Personal

PART 2

SUMMARY

From earliest times Israel's worship included poetry. The book of Psalms expresses the devotion of individuals and of the assembled people. The poems range from intimate beauty to fierce nationalism and from simple to complex form. They are a fundamental resource for the worship language of God's people, and familiarity with many of them nurtures religious experience.

BASIC BIBLE REFERENCES
Psalms 1, 2, 8, 19, 22, 23, 24, 27, 46, 51, 72, 84, 90, 91, 95, 100, 103, 110, 121, 122, 136, 137, 139, 150

WORD LIST
Psalter
Metaphor
Simile
Parallelism
Antithetic
Climactic
Synonymous
Synthetic

Liturgical Poetry in Israel

We observe Hebrew poetry in other themes. Miriam's song of triumph, Exodus 15:21,[1] is considered one of the oldest bits of literature in the Old Testament. Jacob's blessing for his sons (Genesis 49:1-27) is in poetic form. Deborah and Barak celebrate their victory in Canaan with a long song (Judges 5). David welcomes the coming of the ark to Jerusalem with *dancing..., with songs*, and musical instruments (2 Samuel 6:5).

Leaf through the prophets, and the printed format will show how much of their messages is cast in poetic form. No doubt this made it easier for the people to remember.

Other Near Eastern peoples produced religious poetry, but Israel outstripped them in the development and intensity of her expression. The spirit of Israel's worship is best understood from a study of the Psalms. The detailed regulations for offerings and observances are readily forgotten, but the Psalms remain a living resource for both Jewish and Christian worship today.

The collection of the Psalms grew across the years as Israel's religious experience evolved. Many of the Psalms had their origin during the period of the monarchy, but we noticed in Part 1 that **Psalm 137** is clearly from the exile. Tradition attached David's name to the whole Psalter (another name for the book

---

1 In the Basic References of Theme 1, Part 1.

of Psalms), and the inspiration for such a collection may go back to him. Writers other than David, however, wrote many of the Psalms (see, for example, Psalms 73-83, which are ascribed to *Asaph*[2]). The Psalter can fairly be described as the worship book of Israel, particularly in the second and third temples.

Organization of the Psalter

There are various ways of dividing the Psalter. As finally edited, it is in five "books," probably in imitation of the Torah. The divisions are I. Psalms 2-41; II. 42-72; III. 73-89; IV. 90-106; V. 107-149. **Psalm 1** is an introduction to the whole collection, and **Psalm 150** is a final anthem of praise.[3] Psalms 42-83 and 108 use the Hebrew word elohim for "God"; the rest prefer the divine name *Yahweh*. Some Psalms occur twice, not always quite identical; 14 = 53 (note the different ascription); 40:13-17 = 70 (note *God and* LORD); 108 = 57:7-11 + 60:5-12. Psalm 18 is almost identical with 2 Samuel 22:2-51.

Various Psalms were written for particular uses. These classifications are helpful in our application of the Psalms. Introductions in study Bibles usually give more details. Here are some of the groupings. Hymns: **Psalms 95** and **100**. Thanksgiving: 92, 118. Personal meditation and reflection: **23, 27, 90, 91, 139**. Laments or entreaties, which may be collective, as 83 and **137**, or individual, as 22, 31, 42, **51**.[4] Historical: 78, 105, 106, 136. Nature; **8, 19**, 29, 104.

A number of Psalms reflect their use in public liturgy. Read **Psalms 24** and **84**. Note the antiphonal response throughout **136**. Some, such as **2** and **110**, are related to the monarchy and are often referred to as "royal" psalms.[5] Some are prayers for the king, for example, **72**. Psalm 45 may be a bridal ode for a royal marriage. Psalm 68:24-27 describes *solemn processions...into the sanctuary*.

Psalms 120-134 are called "Songs of Ascent." They are pilgrim hymns, which were evidently sung on the way to Jerusalem festivals. Read **Psalms 121** and **122**. About half of the Psalms in Book V (plus 104, 105) contain the Hebrew cry, *Hallelujah = Praise the* LORD! These "hallel" Psalms were sung at festival times (for examples, see 113-118). Jesus and his disciples probably sang one or more of these at the Last Supper (see Mark 14:26).

---

2 The ascriptions at the beginning of the Psalms are not part of the original text, but many of them are quite ancient. Seventy-three ascribe authorship to David. Much of the information in the ascriptions is related to use in the temple liturgy.

3 In this revision of *Kerygma: The Bible in Depth* I seriously considered whether we could reduce the number of Basic References, but I do not see how we can claim to have studied the Psalms unless we are familiar with this minimum list. Other Psalms are mentioned here by number; most of these are for reference. Read as many as you have time for.—Author.

4 Note the ascription, which relates this Psalm to an event in David's life.

5 Both of these are often quoted in the New Testament.

A few Psalms are unique and are hard to classify. Psalm 119 is noted in Theme 7, Part 2. It is an elaborate acrostic: it has an eight-line stanza for each letter of the Hebrew alphabet, and each line of each stanza begins with the same letter.

Literary and Poetic Characteristics

The Psalms employ much literary adornment. Nearly every Psalm has some figure of speech, particularly simile and metaphor. *A thousand years in your sight are like yesterday when it is past* (90:4—simile); *From the womb of the morning* (metaphor), *like dew* (simile), *your youth will come to you* (110:3).

The Psalms reflect the deep questions people ask about God and about their lives. There is the ethical question, "What is right?" (24:3, 4; 119:9). And the theological question, "If God is just, why...?" (13:1, 2; 74:1, 10, 11)[6] There is the search for faith; read **Psalm 22**. And there are affirmations of faith; read **46** and **103**.

The form of Hebrew poetry is introduced in Theme 8, Part 1. Unlike most English poetry, Hebrew poetry does not have meter or rhyme. It does have rhythm, but this is very hard to show in translation. A prominent feature is parallelism (which also occurs in other Near Eastern literatures).

In parallelism, lines of poetry—usually clauses or their equivalents in length—are balanced in various ways. In synonymous parallelism an idea is repeated in somewhat similar words:

> *The heavens are declaring the glory of God;*
>> *and the firmament proclaims his handiwork* (19:1).

Synthetic parallelism adds to the thought of one line a different line with a similar thought:

> *He makes me lie down in green pastures;*
>> *he leads me besides still waters;*
>> *he restores my soul.*
> *He leads me in right paths...* (23:2, 3).

---

6 This question is considered at length in Theme 3, Part 2.

These may be skillfully combined:

> 1   *The LORD is my light and my salvation;*
> 2   *whom shall I fear?*
> 3   *The LORD is the stronghold of my life;*
> 4   *of whom shall I be afraid?* (27:1).

Lines 1 and 3 are synthetic parallelism; lines 2 and 4 are synonymous.

Antithetic parallelism presents contrasting lines or half lines—often but signals the antithesis:

> *the LORD watches over the way of the righteous,*
> *but the way of the wicked will perish* (1:6).[7]

Synthetic and antithetic may appear together:

> *A thousand may fall at your side,*
>   *ten thousand at your right hand,*
>   *but it will not come near you* (91:7).

Climactic or step parallelism adds to the initial line in a step-by-step progression:

> *For the LORD God is a sun and shield;*
>   *he bestows favor and honor.*
> *No good thing does the LORD withhold*
>   *from those who walk uprightly.*
> *O LORD of hosts,*
>   *happy is everyone who trusts in you* (84:11, 12).

Significance of the Psalms

The Psalms provide very valuable insight into the worship life of the people who first used them. The real feelings of the people find utterance here, feelings of grief and joy, of despair and hope, of anger and penitence, of passionate entreaty for help or calm assurance of trust. Here are prayers and praises to suit the changing needs of the soul.

---

[7] In Theme 8, Part 1 it is noted that many of the couplets in Proverbs 10-16 are in antithetic parallelism.

The Psalms help us appreciate the religious pilgrimage of Israel in a way that the national cult of the Temple could never do. They help us understand why the prophets sometimes criticized the formal religious ceremonies and declared that they were out of touch with the needs of the common people and did not meet the righteous requirements of God (see Amos 5:21-24; Micah 6:6-8).

The Psalms are evidence that much of Hebrew worship was carried on where the people lived—in the family, in the village, and later in the synagogue. The Psalms are quoted in the New Testament more frequently than any other Old Testament book except Isaiah. Evidently the Psalms were a vital part of the religious experience of first-century Christians. In Peter's sermon at Pentecost he quotes Psalms 16:8-11 and 110:1.

People in Judeo-Christian traditions through the ages have found that the Psalms accurately and beautifully reflect their own spiritual histories. Some portions of the Psalms are not suitable for Christian worship (for example, 137:8, 9), but most of the collection has been widely and consistently used. Here is how a poet in 1868 adapted Psalm 23 to rhyming verse:

> The King of love my shepherd is,
>   Whose goodness faileth never;
> I nothing lack if I am His
>   And He is mine forever.
> Where streams of living water flow
>   My ransomed soul he leadeth,
> And where the verdant pastures grow,
>   With food celestial feedeth...

Because Psalms have been the outpouring of the worship life of God's people for three thousand years, they have a fundamental accord with worship today. The more one appreciates and appropriates the riches of the Psalter, the better one will be able to express the broad range of devotional life in worship.

FOR FURTHER STUDY AND REFLECTION

Memory Bank

Develop your own appreciation of the Psalms by studying the twenty-four in the Basic References. Select a few verses to memorize.

Research

1. Review the passages that reflect how David became associated with music and song: 1 Samuel 16:14-23; 2 Samuel 6:5; 1 Chronicles 25:1-8; Amos 6:5.

2. Find out what you can about a variety of the musical directions in the ascriptions in a number of Psalms; for example, 4-9, 80, 88. Use a study Bible and a Bible Dictionary.

3. The Hebrew word *Selah* occurs in nearly forty Psalms. It is also in Habakkuk 3:3, 13 in a prayer-psalm. What can you learn about the word?

4. If you can get a translation of the Dead Sea Scrolls (try a public library), read some of the psalms in that literature. They are sometimes referred to by the Hebrew term *hodayoth*.

5. Many metrical translations of the Psalms have been made in English. Examine a hymn-book that includes some of these (check the indexes). Some are still identified by the first word in the Latin version, for example, the *Venite* for Psalm 95.

Reflection

1. How can literature from a pre-Christian age be applicable for Christian worship and devotion today?

2. Why is poetry particularly appropriate for expressing religious feeling?

GOD'S PEOPLE WORSHIP

Worship in the New Testament Setting

PART 3

SUMMARY
Christian worship was influenced strongly by the Jewish Temple, festivals, and synagogue. Events in Jesus' life are one of the ways these influences came into Christian tradition. The early church and Paul were channels by which the traditions developed. Baptism and the LORD's Supper became Christian sacraments. Other worship practices, including observance of the LORD's Day, have backgrounds in the New Testament.

BASIC BIBLE REFERENCES
Matthew 6:9-13
Luke 2:22-42; 4:14-30; 11:2-4
John 4:19-24
Acts 3:1-11; 7:44-50; 20:7-12
1 Corinthians 10:16, 17; 11:17-34; 14:19, 24-33a, 39, 40
2 Corinthians 13:13
Ephesians 3:14-21
Hebrews 9:1-14
Revelation 4:8-11; 5:9-12

WORD LIST
LORD's Day
LORD's Prayer
LORD's Supper
Prophesying
Proselyte
Sacrament
Speaking in tongues

Background of Christian Worship

The early Christian church emphasized worship from the very beginning. *Day by day, as they spent much time together in the temple, they broke bread at home and ate their food with glad and generous hearts, praising God...*(Acts 2:46, 47). They prayed, they sang hymns, and they preached.

When they shared meals, they remembered Jesus. Two disciples from Emmaus declared that the risen Jesus was *made known to them in the breaking of the bread*, which had included a blessing (Luke 24:30, 31, 35). Jesus promised, *where two or three are gathered in my name, I am there among them* (Matthew 18:20). The book of Revelation is full of worship imagery, and John the seer is commanded, *Worship God!* (Revelation 19:10; 22:9).

Influences on Early Christian Worship

Judaism had a profound influence on early Christian worship. Because the Christian mission moved beyond Jerusalem almost at once, the background of the Temple remained only in ideas and vocabulary. This suggests that the synagogue was a greater influence. Emphasis on the reading and expounding of Scripture, together with prayers and hymns, come from this connection.

Paul regularly contacted local synagogues as he went about his missions. At Antioch in Pisidia he used the synagogue as a springboard for preaching that stirred up the whole town (see Acts 13:14, 43, 44, 48, 49). On at least one occasion he found an informal meeting: *On the sabbath day we went outside the gate by the river, where we supposed there was a place of prayer; and we sat down and spoke to the women who had gathered there* (Acts 16:13).

The church did not directly embrace any of the Jewish festivals, but their mark on the New Testament is indelible. Pilgrim festivals are reflected in Jesus' movements in the Gospels (mentioned in Part 1). Pentecost is the setting of what is sometimes called "the birthday of the church" (see Acts 2:1, 44-47). Paul refers several times to festivals. More on that later.

Jesus

From his birth and childhood, Jesus is related to the Temple. Read **Luke 2:22-42**. The families of John the Baptist and Jesus were pious Jewish folk. The offering mentioned in Luke 2:24 is specified in Leviticus 12:6-8. The stories about Simeon and Anna tell us something about Temple activity that is not mentioned elsewhere.

Read **Luke 4:14-30**, a Basic Reference in Theme 1, Part 3. Note the phrase *as was his custom*. In the next passage Jesus goes to Capernaum and is again in the synagogue. Matthew's Gospel also mentions that he was in the synagogue of *his hometown* (Matthew 13:54). Whatever antagonism arose between Jesus and Jewish religious leaders, they could not charge him with abandoning the places of worship of his people.

The synoptic Gospels mention specifically only one festival journey that Jesus made, his last Passover. John, however, tells of several other visits to Jerusalem. Jesus' public ministry must have lasted more than one year, so John's details in this respect are undoubtedly correct. (Even so, a definite outline is hard to set.)

Another difference between the synoptics and John appears in connection with a Passover visit to Jerusalem. The cleansing of the Temple is placed at the beginning of Jesus' last week according to the synoptics, but John locates it in a Passover visit near the beginning of Jesus' ministry (John 2:13-17; compare Matthew 21:12, 13; Mark 11:15-19; Luke 19:45, 46). We are not concerned with the problem of chronology here, but the event certainly illuminates Jesus' attitude toward the Temple.

Jesus' conflict with religious authorities involved the Temple. According to John 2:18-21, he made a statement about destroying *this temple*, but John says he was *speaking of the temple of his body*. On another occasion he told his disciples that *these great buildings* would be leveled some day—a prediction that came true about forty years later (Mark 13:1, 2).

During his ecclesiastical trial he was accused of forecasting the destruction of the Temple (see Matthew 26:60, 61; Mark 14:58).

During Jesus' last week much of his teaching took place within the Temple precincts. In the months that preceded, he often worshiped out-of-doors. He engaged in private prayer on many occasions (see Matthew 14:23; Mark 1:35; Luke 6:12). His most familiar prayer—the LORD's Prayer—is recorded in **Matthew 6:9-13** and the less familiar parallel **Luke 11:2-4**. His longest prayer is during the last meeting in the upper room, John 17. In conversation with a Samaritan woman at Jacob's well he made a memorable statement about worship; read **John 4:19-24**.

Early Church Transition

After Jesus' death and resurrection, the Temple in Jerusalem continued to draw the first Christians (see Luke 24:53). Judaism allowed some flexibility in worship assemblies, and there is no indication of an immediate rift between the Christians and Jewish ways. Peter and John begin their public ministry in the Temple area; read **Acts 3:1-11**. Very early, however, differences arise. Part of Stephen's sermon in his own defense includes an open attack on Temple worship; read **Acts 7:44-50**.

Although the Temple worship lost its direct influence on the Christians, its vocabulary passed into the Christian tradition. Jesus mentions *offering your gift at the altar* (Matthew 5:23, 24), but there is no evidence that the early Christians ever used an altar in their worship. Though there is no mention of altar sacrifices, the vocabulary of sacrifice appears widely. Paul appeals to the Romans *to present your bodies as a living sacrifice* (Romans 12:1). He thanks the Philippians for gifts, *a fragrant offering, a sacrifice acceptable and pleasing to God* (Philippians 4:18). In 1 Peter 2:5 the readers are exhorted, *like living stones, let yourselves be built into a spiritual house, to be a holy priesthood, to offer spiritual sacrifices acceptable to God through Jesus Christ.*

Particularly with reference to the death of Jesus the symbolism of sacrifice is employed. Paul writes of *Jesus Christ, whom God put forward as a sacrifice of atonement by his blood* (Romans 3:24, 25). Read **Hebrews 9:1-14**, where the symbolism is worked out in great detail. The references to blood are to be understood in this connection, for example, *the blood of Jesus [God's] Son cleanses us from all sin* (1 John 1:7).

Occasionally the idea of cleansing implies purification by water. *Christ loved the church and gave himself up for her, in order to make her holy by cleansing her with the washing of water by the word* (Ephesians 5:25, 26). We shall consider baptism below. The book of

Revelation is crammed with worship symbols; for example, *golden bowls full of incense, which are the prayers of the saints* (Revelation 5:8).

Paul

At Antioch in Pisidia during Paul's first mission in Asia Minor, the initial success of his preaching aroused jealousy and opposition among the Jews. Finally, he says plainly, *we are now turning to the Gentiles* (Acts 13:46). Though he moved out of Judaism, Paul never completely severed himself from it. In his defense before the governor Felix, Paul recounts the occasion when the Jewish leaders caused his arrest. *I went up to worship in Jerusalem... I came to bring alms to my nation and to offer sacrifices...they found me in the temple, completing the rite of purification* (see Acts 24:11, 17, 18; the full story is told in 21:17-36).

Much of what we learn about the earliest Christian worship we gather from Paul's letters. He dealt directly with many churches, so he faced considerable diversity in local practice. We shall note some of this material as we take up various aspects of worship.

The LORD's Day

The change of the principal day of worship from the seventh day of the week (the "Sabbath") to the first day (much later called "Sunday") may only be inferred from the New Testament. Paul exhorts the Corinthians, *On the first day of every week, each of you is to put aside and save whatever extra you earn, so that collections need not be taken when I come* (1Corinthians 16:2). In Troas a meeting was held *on the first day of the week* (Acts 20:7; see below). The only explicit reference to *the LORD's day* is in Revelation 1:10. It remained for the "apostolic fathers," who wrote during the years just following the time when the New Testament was produced, to make it plain that the Christian day of worship was set because the resurrection was *on the first day of the week*—as all four Gospels explicitly state.

Baptism

The origin of Christian baptism is not spelled out, but it certainly played an important part in the development of Christian worship. The immediate background is in the baptism of John, but the background of John's practice is not certain. Judaism baptized proselytes as a cleansing rite, and the people of the Dead Sea Scrolls practiced regular ceremonial washings, but the way baptism developed in the Christian church is truly new.

Jesus accepted John's baptism, apparently as a mark of complete identification with the people. Jesus asks James and John, *Are you able to drink the cup that I drink, or be baptized with the baptism that I am baptized with?* (Mark 10:38), symbolizing the sacrificial course that his life is taking. Baptism is mentioned rather frequently in Acts. On Pentecost Peter calls on the people to *repent, and be baptized, and about three thousand persons* responded (Acts 2:38, 41). After Philip's preaching in Samaria, many people were baptized (see 8:12-16). Paul was baptized in the house of Ananias (9:18). Cornelius and *his relatives and close friends* were baptized by Peter (10:24, 47). Paul and Silas baptized the Philippian jailor *and his entire family* (16:33).

Paul compares the theological symbolism of baptism to burial with Christ (see Romans 6:3, 4; Colossians 2:12). He has a practical problem in Corinth, where some people have bragged about who baptized them. He is thankful *no one can say that you were baptized in my name* (1 Corinthians 1:14-16).

The Lord's Supper

Just as the Passover bears great importance in the Old Testament, so the Lord's Supper becomes central in New Testament worship. Common meals were very significant in the early church, a fact that goes back to Jesus' ministry. Accounts of the Lord's Supper are in Matthew 26:17-30; Mark 14:12-26; Luke 22:7-20. Before these were recorded, Paul had written about it to the Corinthians. Read **1 Corinthians 10:16, 17; 11:17-34**.

The Supper came out of a Passover setting but took on a whole new range of meaning. The meaning of *body* in 1 Corinthians 11:24 should be understood in relation to 10:16, 17 and by the discussion of *the body* in 12:12-27. This latter passage is Paul's longest illustration and concludes, *Now you are the body of Christ and individually members of it*. The meaning of *the cup* should be understood in relation to Mark 10:38 (see above under Baptism) and by the phrase *of the new covenant*. What does this phrase suggest?

Baptism and the Lord's Supper are sometimes referred to as "sacraments." The term does not occur in the Bible but came into use early in the second century. The "oath" of allegiance taken by Roman military recruits was called *sacramentum*. It came to mean the rites by which Christians bound themselves to their faith.

Other Details of New Testament Worship

What were worship services like in New Testament times? There are no precise descriptions, so we must read between the lines. Immediately after Pentecost, *they devoted themselves to the apostles' teaching and fellowship, to the breaking of bread and the prayers* (Acts 2:42). The meal setting appears to be usual, but there were other occasions. Most of the meetings were in houses; note Philemon 2, *to the church in your house*. The first recorded instance of someone falling asleep during a sermon is in **Acts 20:7-12**. It was *on the first day of the week*, and the meeting was in a house.

Scripture was regularly read and expounded, as we have already noted. Scriptures also figured in private worship. To the Romans Paul writes, *whatever was written in former days was written for our instruction, so that by steadfastness and by the encouragement of the scriptures we might have hope* (Romans 15:4). Apollos, an Alexandrian Jew, *was an eloquent man, well-versed in the scriptures* (Acts 18:24). Traditional material from and about Jesus must have been used. Apollos showed *by the scriptures that the Messiah is Jesus* (18:28). Occasionally apostolic letters were read; Paul commands *that this letter be read to all of [the brothers and sisters]* (1 Thessalonians 5:27).

Prayers were certainly said on all occasions of worship. When Paul and Silas were in prison in Philippi, *about midnight they were praying* (Acts 16:25). One of the most beautiful prayers outside of Jesus' words is in **Ephesians 3:14-21**. Benedictions were well known from synagogue practice. The best-known is **2 Corinthians 13:13**, often referred to as the "apostolic" benediction.

Paul and Silas in prison were also *singing hymns to God*. Hymns were a regular part of worship. Probably they were chanted, following the precedent of the psalms. The Colossians are exhorted to *sing psalms, hymns, and spiritual songs to God* (3:16). Sometimes it is hard to determine whether a passage is a hymn or a confession; Philippians 2:5-11 and 1 Timothy 3:16 are examples. 1 Corinthians 13 is a hymn, whether or not it was actually sung (see Theme 7, Part 4). Revelation is loaded with fine hymns. Read **Revelation 5:9-12**. (Some of them appear in Handel's *The Messiah*.)

Baptism was usually accompanied by a special manifestation of the Holy Spirit. At Ephesus Paul *found some disciples* who had received *John's baptism* and did not *receive the Holy Spirit*. Paul rebaptized them *in the name of the LORD Jesus* and *the Holy Spirit came upon them, and they spoke in tongues and prophesied* (Acts 19:1-7).

Speaking with tongues was a common occurrence in the early church. At Pentecost this appears to have made the message understandable in various languages of those present there (Acts 2:4-11). At other times it was a kind of ecstatic experience that required someone else to interpret. *Speaking in tongues* was a particular problem at Corinth. Paul approves of "tongues" as a personal, devotional experience, but in public he is wary of the practice. 1 Corinthians 14 has a long critique of worship in that congregation. Read **1 Corinthians 14:19, 24-33a, 39, 40**.

Apparently worship in the Corinthian church could become chaotic. Paul considers prophesying to be an *especially desirable spiritual gift* (1 Corinthians 14:1). This was not foretelling the future but a kind of spontaneous preaching with a serious message. Paul says that it *will build up the church* (14:4). He uses *build up* and the corresponding noun over twenty times in his letters.

Another problem in the early congregations was the role of women. As in Judaism, women did not always enjoy privileges equal with men. The freedom that the gospel was bringing tended to create social disorder, and the church struggled to adjust. Paul specifies details of women's dress in church, but he notes in the context that women were praying and prophesying there (1 Corinthians 11:5). Thus when he writes later (14:33b-36) that *women should be silent in the churches*, he seems to be contradicting himself. Note, however, that he is speaking of *wives* (the Greek word can mean "woman" or "wife"); verse 35 mentions *their husbands*. He is dealing with social decorum, not religious principle.

It is difficult to know how much of the rich symbolism in Revelation reflects practices in the contemporary churches. John the seer is dealing in visions, but his words have certainly colored later language of worship. Read **Revelation 4:8-11**, a marvelous vision of worship in heaven. (What is the source of the song in verse 8?)

FOR FURTHER STUDY AND REFLECTION

Memory Bank

1. 1 Corinthians 11:23-26

2. 2 Corinthians 13:13

3. Ephesians 3:20, 21

4. Revelation 5:12

Research

1. Paul made a collection for the poor of the Jerusalem Christian church; see Romans 15:25, 26; 1 Corinthians 16:1-3; 2 Corinthians 8:3-6; 9:5. How may you relate this to the worship theme? To modern practices?

2. Paul mentions *baptism on behalf of the dead* in 1 Corinthians 15:29. How does he use this in the context? What else can you learn about this practice?

3. *Anointing...with oil* is mentioned in James 5:14. Study the context, 5:13-16. What is the relationship to prayer? What else can you learn about this practice?

4. How did Jesus relate to women? What was the place of women in the community of his followers? What else can you learn about the role of women in the first-century churches?

Reflection

1. What difference might it have made in subsequent history if Judaism had not actively opposed early Christian preaching?

2. To what extent do you think modern Christian worship should be regulated by biblical practices?

3. Sacraments—in this part, baptism and the LORD's Supper—have been a source of conflict in the history of the Christian church. What does your denomination teach about these sacraments? How does it differ from other church bodies?

GOD'S PEOPLE HAVE HOPE

THEME 10

Israel's Hope

PART 1

SUMMARY

Hope has been woven through all our themes, beginning with God's saving actions. Hope is often linked to the nation and focused on David's dynasty. The exile redirected hope. Expectation for the future depended heavily upon God's intervention. Personal living was fixed in the present. Sheol, the abode of the dead, and life after death are discussed very little. The prophecies of Isaiah are particularly filled with hope.

BASIC BIBLE REFERENCES

Genesis 17:1-8
Deuteronomy 11:8, 9, 20, 21
Job 19:23-27
Isaiah 7:10-17; 9:1-7; 11:1-10; 42:1-4; 60:1-3; 65:17-25
Jeremiah 29:10-14
Lamentations 5:19-22
Haggai 1:12-2:9, 23
Zechariah 4

WORD LIST

Apocalyptic
Branch
Eschatology
Messianic hope
Suffering servant
Sheol

Review: The Promised Land

In Theme 1 God's saving action is viewed first of all as a present experience, but it also produces hope that sustains God's people when the present is a bad time. The theme of hope also appears in our other themes even when it is not specifically mentioned. In Theme 10 we are concerned with particular kinds of hope, but it will be useful to begin by reviewing some details from other themes.

God is the creator and sustainer of the world and is finally sovereign over history. This is the basis for firm hope. The Psalms in particular express this faith. Hope, however, has complications. It is somewhat limited because in the Old Testament God's people understand the future mostly in terms of family and nation. That is, their expectation is concerned first of all with this world, and they hope for material things.

God's promise through most of the Old Testament offers hope for land and family descendants (particularly sons to bear the family traditions). Already in the prehistory *God blessed Noah and his sons, and said to them, "Be fruitful and multiply, and fill the earth"* (Genesis 9:1). The covenant with Abraham makes this promise more specific; read **Genesis 17:1-8**. In the story of the exodus, hope for a Promised Land is held before the people. The wilderness generation, you remember, did not reach that land, but the next generation did. The land embodies the hope of the longed-for nation. The families settled there according to their tribes, that is, their family backgrounds.

Hope and the Promise to David

When the people were united under a king, Yahweh's promise to David gave them hope that there would always be a ruler on David's throne. When the exile turned this hope into despair, the people were forced to rethink their hope. God's promise would surely be kept, so they grasped at any evidence that the national monarchy might be revived. The book of Lamentions reflects the despair (for example, 4:18-20; 5:15-18). Read **Lamentations 5:19-22**, a desperate plea as the writer wrestles to understand Yahweh's power.

The people who returned from exile attempted to recover the glory of the kingdom. Besides Ezra and Nehemiah, who are studied in Theme 5, there were four other key figures. The prophets Haggai and Zechariah interpreted Yahweh's will. Zerubbabel, who was a descendant of David, and Joshua, a priest, became the political and religious leaders. Read **Haggai 1:12-2:9, 23**. Unfortunately, this restoration was unsuccessful. Zerubbabel disappears from the scene, and priests become prominent. The Maccabean period (Theme 1, Part 2) revived hope. The Roman occupation dimmed the hope again.

New Images of Hope

As long as David's descendants ruled, hope was bolstered by theology, as in the royal Psalms. When there was no longer a Davidic ruler in Jerusalem, hope had to be rethought. New images of expectation were formed. There is no simple, clearly defined line of development. We use the term "messianic hope" to describe one kind of expectation that arose in the desperate times. Recall that "messiah" comes from a Hebrew word that means "anointed," the term applied to the duly appointed king.

The terms "anoint" and "anointed one" (same root as "messiah") are used in several ways. Elijah is commissioned to anoint not only a king but his own successor (1 Kings 19:15, 16). The patriarchs are called *anointed ones* in Psalm 105:7-15. Very early, priests were anointed (Exodus 30:30). Jeremiah declares that not only will David always have successors, but the *levitical priests will never lack* successors (33:17, 18).

Several other names are given to one who is expected to reestablish the Jewish kingdom. Zechariah refers to Zerubbabel as *Branch* (Zechariah 3:8; 6:12). Jeremiah refers to a *righteous Branch* (Jeremiah 23:5; 33:14-16), and Isaiah uses the term to refer to a descendant of David's father Jesse (Isaiah 11:1). In Isaiah 40-55 a figure called *the servant* appears; we shall return to that later.

Eschatology And Apocalyptic

A special kind of expectation developed that was often cast in the form of visions. Read **Zechariah 4,** where the prophet recounts a vision about Zerubbabel and Joshua. They are both called *anointed ones*. Thus there is both an anointed prince and an anointed priest. In the Dead Sea Scrolls there is reference to "the messiahs of Aaron and Israel," so the idea was also held in that community.

The form of hope expressed in visions brings us to consider two technical terms (neither of which appears in the Bible). "Eschatology" refers to anything having to do with the end time of history, "last things." The term comes from a Greek word that means "last, final." "Apocalypse" is a special variety of eschatology. It comes from a Greek word that means "revelation, revealing something hidden." (The last book of the Bible is sometimes called "The Apocalypse," which is simply the Greek-derived equivalent of "The Revelation.") This literature of revelation is called "apocalyptic."

When trouble or danger threatens a people's existence, they may direct their attention in two different ways. One is to concentrate upon the immediate situation and to look for relief from sources that are in view. The other way is to look to the future and to hope for help from unseen sources. The worse the challenge, the more likely is the second alternative to be chosen.

When the prophets preached in critical situations, they tended to be realists. They never failed to trust the future to God, but they anticipated what might reasonably be expected in the present trouble. The future, however, always involves unseen dimensions. The more complicated and discouraging the future appears, the more difficult it is to anticipate. Visions are therefore appropriate to describe what may take place.

Apocalyptic is a special kind of eschatology that deals with the future in visions and other special ways. Since so much of the future is beyond ordinary perception, the seer casts the message in elaborate imagery. Visions may include supernatural beings, cosmic events, and symbolic language. Contemporary history may be disguised in figurative picture-language. Usually God brings help or renewal "from the outside in," but the concern of the apocalyptic writer is always with the contemporary crisis.

Life after Death

The Old Testament says very little about life after death. The Israelites throughout most of their history associated their survival with the continuation of family on the ancestral land. This made them eager for sons. Recall again the story of Abraham, Ishmael, and Isaac

(Genesis 16:15-17:21). The people believed that their survival and the nation were bound together. The commandment to *honor your father and mother*, states as the purpose *that your days may be long in the land that the LORD your God is giving you* (Exodus 20:12). Read **Deuteronomy 11:8, 9, 20, 21**. The familiar words of Psalm 23:6, *I shall dwell in the house of the LORD forever* (KJV) do not imply life in what we call heaven; compare NRSV: *I shall dwell in the house of the LORD my whole life long*.

In most of the Old Testament the abode of the dead is known as "Sheol." In KJV this is usually translated "hell," "the pit," or "the grave," but Sheol does not mean what we commonly associate with those terms. Sheol was a shadowy place where departed persons might continue to exist in a kind of ghostly state. The references are often difficult to interpret. It was not a place of reward or punishment. It seems rather to have been an alternative to total extinction. Usually it was a final destiny. Among many references, check Genesis 37:35; Psalms 18:4, 5; 55:15; Isaiah 14:11. Yahweh's presence was there (Psalm 139:8), but *Sheol cannot thank* the LORD (Isaiah 38:18). Jonah says of his distress when the fish caught him running away from Yahweh, *out of the belly of Sheol I cried* (Jonah 2:2). In Hannah's song there is a hint that Yahweh could retrieve lives from Sheol: *The LORD brings down to Sheol and raises up* (1 Samuel 2:6).

Job has many references to Sheol; see, for example, 14:13; 17:13-16. Read **Job 19:23-27**, which is often taken as a declaration of faith in life after death. It is not altogether clear what Job expected, but occurrence of the term *Redeemer* and Handel's use of the words in *The Messiah* have fixed this passage in Christian tradition.

Daniel, which is one of the latest books of the Old Testament, contains the clearest mention of survival after death. In one of his visions Daniel is told, *the holy ones of the Most High shall receive the kingdom and possess the kingdom forever—forever and ever* (Daniel 7:18). *Everlasting life* is mentioned in 12:2. The resurrection in 12:1-3 appears to be selective—*many of those who sleep*—but again it promises *forever and ever*.

For the remainder of this part and all of the next, we shall consider books that deal with future hope. Here we study Isaiah and look briefly at Jeremiah. In Part 2 we return to Daniel and Zechariah plus Ezekiel.

Isaiah

The first thirty-nine chapters of Isaiah contain many passages that look to the future. Read **Isaiah 7:10-17**. Verse 14 is quoted by Matthew in reference to the birth of Jesus, *to fulfill what had been spoken by the LORD through the prophet* (1:22, 23). The setting in Isaiah is a message to King Ahaz. Before a child yet unborn grows up, a fearful time will come upon the kingdom. Matthew is probably influenced by three details. One, the Hebrew word for *young woman* is translated in the Septuagint by a word that means "virgin."[1] Two, an expected child is *a sign*. Third, the name *Immanuel* (*Emmanuel* in Matthew) fits the Gospel's message about Jesus.

The ideal king is described in **Isaiah 9:1-7**. It is easy to see why Christians appropriated this passage: it mentions a child, and it has messianic overtones. An ideal messianic rule is described in **Isaiah 11:1-10**. It is really a picture of Eden regained. Another fine passage is 32:1-4. But the prophet can temper hope with severe warning (see 31:1).

Occasionally, there are apocalyptic passages in Isaiah. Heaven and the universe suffer along with the earth in 24:17-23. The promise in 25:8, *the LORD God will wipe away the tears from all faces* is quoted twice in the Revelation (7:17 and 21:4). Several lines hint of future life: *he will swallow up death forever (Isaiah 25:7). Your dead shall live, their corpses shall rise. O dwellers in the dust, awake and sing for joy!* (26:19). The verses are in poetry, however, and the thought is not further developed.

Isaiah 40-66 are unlike anything else in the Old Testament. The sustained beauty of language and the profound hope are unparalleled. Here are the four so-called "servant songs." Read **Isaiah 42:1-4**. The second and third are in 49:1-6 and 50:4-11. The *servant* sometimes seems to be an individual (42:1), sometimes Israel itself (49:3), sometimes a remnant of Israel (49:6). Probably the prophet was content with this ambiguity. 52:13-53:12, which is a Basic Reference in Theme 7, Part 2, so vividly suggests the passion of Jesus that Christian faith has always appropriated it.[2]

The book of Isaiah is really a collection of oracles and other material. The concerns are sweeping. Isaiah 58:6-10 is a ringing call for social justice. **Isaiah 60:1-3** is a particularly beautiful plea for God's people to measure up to their appointed destiny. Yahweh is called *our father* in 63:16 and 64:8, rare examples in the Old Testament of the term of address Jesus taught his followers. God is anxious for the people even though they do not respond (65:1). God promises a wonderful future including a whole new creation. Read **Isaiah 65:17-25**.

Jeremiah

Jeremiah appears prominently in Themes 2, 5, and 7. He expresses hope for the restoration of the fortunes of God's people, and he describes it in this-worldly terms. He writes of the

---

[1] Hebrew has two words for a young woman of marriageable age. Isaiah 7:14 does not use the word that denotes a woman who has not had sexual relations. The Greek word used here in the Septuagint does regularly have that other connotation.

[2] These passages are usually considered to have influenced Jesus' understanding of his mission.

return of a remnant in a context where he mentions the Branch of David (23:3-8). The return of the exiles will be after seventy years; read **Jeremiah 29:10-14**. He elaborates on this promise in several chapters that follow. He buys a field at Anathoth as a witness that God will restore *the good fortune that I now promise them* (Jeremiah 32; note verse 42).

FOR FURTHER STUDY AND REFLECTION

Memory Bank

Isaiah 9:2, 6; 60:1-3

Research

1. What happened when there was no son to maintain the family land in Israel? Read how a family with only daughters kept an inheritance intact: Numbers 27:1-11; 36:10-12. Note that Yahweh assumes a feminine role in Isaiah 66:13.

2. Analyze the passages in Job and Daniel that suggest life after death. What do they say, and what do they not say? For example, what do you make of *many of those who sleep*, Daniel 12:2?

3. In Luke 7:22 Jesus alludes to Isaiah 29:18, 19; 35:5, 6; 61:1. How does he use these texts in replying to an inquiry by John the Baptist?

4. The Wisdom of Solomon was probably written for Alexandrian Jews less than a hundred years before Jesus' time (see Theme 8, Part 1). REB and NJB call Chapters 1-5 *Wisdom and Human Destiny*. Study at least 3:1-11. What change from Old Testament passages about life after death is evident?

Reflection

1. Compare Sheol with popular ideas about heaven and hell today.

2. What hope for the future do family and nation provide today?

3. What do you hope for in your own future? In this life? After death?

GOD'S PEOPLE HAVE HOPE

Apocalyptic Hope

SUMMARY

Ezekiel's prophecies are unusual, partly because of his personality, partly because of their scope. They begin before the fall of Jerusalem and include visions of restoration after exile. Ezekiel's visions anticipate apocalyptic. The book of Zechariah is even closer to apocalyptic. The visions cover diverse subjects. The book of Daniel combines lesson-stories and visions. It is the only true apocalypse in the Old Testament.

BASIC BIBLE REFERENCES

Ezekiel 1:26-28; 3:15-21; 34; 47:22, 23
Daniel 7:13-18, 27, 28; 12:2, 3
Zechariah 1:8-17; 4:1-14; 9:9-17

WORD LIST
Pseudonym
Son of man

Ezekiel

In 597 B.C., King Jehoichin surrendered Jerusalem to King Nebuchadnezzar of Babylon. The Israelite king and a number of prominent people were deported to Babylon, among them the prophet Ezekiel (2 Kings 24:10-14). He came from an aristocratic, priestly family. His call as a prophet is related in Ezekiel 1:1-3. We are not sure what *the thirtieth year* refers to, but the data in verse 2 place Ezekiel's call in July, 593 B.C. He gives more dates than any other prophet.

It is at once apparent that this prophet is a visionary. The book is full of symbolism and drama. Many of the images appear again in the Revelation. Read **Ezekiel 1:26-28**, a vision of *the glory of the LORD*. Because Ezekiel relates his messages so directly to the events around him, he is a prophet. Because so many of his messages are in the form of visions, he is a strong link in the development of apocalyptic.

The LORD addresses Ezekiel over ninety times by a unique phrase, in Hebrew *ben'adam*, which was traditionally translated *son of man* (KJV). Some modern translations have modified this: TEV, *mortal man*; REB, *O man* (see the footnote at Ezekiel 2:1); NRSV, *O mortal* (in deference to inclusive language, but see the footnote at 2:1). Because Jesus used this term to refer to himself, we should keep in mind the original meaning of this term in Ezekiel.

Jerusalem was still standing when Ezekiel began to have his visions, and nearly half of the book pronounces doom against Judah and its capital (Ezekiel 4-24). Some of the accusations are severe. For example, he says that Jerusalem has pagan ancestry and has become God's brazen, unfaithful wife (16). He calls Samaria and Jerusalem shameless whores (23). He employs dramatic actions to catch public interest. He shaves his head and beard with a sword and disperses the hair to symbolize Jerusalem's fate (5). At times his personality seems to be eccentric, but his message is clear enough. Read **Ezekiel 3:15-21**. Ezekiel speaks for Yahweh; he is *a sentinel, a sign* (24:24, 27; 33:7).

Ezekiel 25-32 contains oracles against the nations around Judah. Here he is like Jeremiah, Amos, Obadiah, Nahum, and others. Meanwhile, Jerusalem again rebels against Babylon, and at 33:21 Ezekiel receives word that *the city has fallen*. At once the message of the prophet turns from scolding and doom to hope for the future.

Read **Ezekiel 34**. The false shepherds are the kings and leaders of Israel; the sheep are the people. Now Yahweh will be shepherd! In 20:33 Yahweh says, *I will be king over you*. What connections with Theme 6 do you see?

They will have a Davidic king, and there will be *a covenant of peace*. They will have *a new heart...and a new spirit* (36:26; compare Jeremiah 31:31-34). *Then you shall know that I am the LORD* (Ezekiel 36:11). The restoration will come about, not because of Israel's conduct, but for the sake of Yahweh (36:22-24).

The vision of the valley of dry bones (Ezekiel 37:1-14) is a Basic Reference in Theme 1, Part 2. Review it, and note the new meaning this part has added. The people have despaired, but the prophet declares hope from Yahweh (37:11, 12). Earlier Ezekiel proclaimed doom in the face of false hope; now he announces sure hope in the face of doom.

Ezekiel 38 and 39 are cast in apocalyptic language. They are often used by people who try to plot the end of history. *Gog* and other foes (38:2) are identified only as being *out of the remotest parts of the north* (38:15). Jeremiah warns against *all the tribes of the north* and identifies them with Babylon (Jeremiah 25:9). Ezekiel may have this in mind, or he may mean invaders from Asia Minor. In any case, Ezekiel 39:25-29 forecasts the return of God's people from exile, so connecting these chapters with the end of time is not appropriate.

Ezekiel 40-46 gives a vision of the restored temple. The structure is idealized. The vision includes a physical description of the building and directions for the service in it. *And the glory of the LORD filled the temple* (43:5).

Ezekiel 47 and 48 contain visions of the future of the land. A sacred river will flow from the temple. It will refresh the land and finally turn the Dead Sea into fresh water like the Mediterranean (47:10). The twelve tribes will again share the land. Note **Ezekiel 47:22, 23**; resident aliens will become citizens. The city is to be some five miles in circumference. It will have a new name, *The LORD is There* (48:35).

Zechariah

Zechariah was a contemporary of Haggai and Ezra (Ezra 5:1; 6:14). Their three books, however, are quite different. The date in Zechariah 1:1 places the beginning of his ministry in 520 B.C. For convenience we shall look at the book in outline.

> 1:1-6. The book begins with a brief call for repentance. Then follow eight visions in apocalyptic form with some intervening material.
>
> **1:8-17.** Vision 1—read it. Four horsemen and a message of hope for Jerusalem. An interpreting angel (1:9) is common in apocalyptic visions. The length of the exile is given as 70 years (which agrees with Jeremiah 25:11; 29:10).
>
> 1:18-21. Vision 2. *Four horns* represent nations.
>
> 1:18-21. Vision 2. *Four horns* represent nations.
>
> 2:1-5. Vision 3. *A man with a measuring line* signifies protection for Jerusalem. This is followed by a call for the return from exile, *the land of the north* (not part of the vision). Two phrases have passed into our language: *the apple of my eye* (2:8) and *the holy land* (2:12).
>
> 3:1-10. Vision 4. Yahweh acquits *the high priest Joshua* (identified in Part 1). Satan, the accuser or prosecutor in the court of heaven, is rebuked (3:2; recall Job in Theme 3, Part 3). *The Branch* is mentioned in 3:8.
>
> **4:1-14.** Vision 5—read it. A lampstand and two olive trees; the passage provides interpretation. Note the ringing watchword in verse 6.
>
> 5:1-4. Vision 6. A flying scroll represents God's word. Ezekiel had to eat such a scroll (Ezekiel 2:9—3:3).
>
> 5:5-11. Vision 7. A woman in a basket—*Wickedness*. Shinar is another name for Babylon (as in Daniel 1:2).

6:1-8. Vision 8. *Four chariots* appear to carry heavenly judgment over the earth.

6:9-15. The crowning of *the high priest Joshua*. The details are not clear; it appears to be the inauguration of a messianic time.

7:1-14. A question about fasting.

8:1-23. A series of declarations dealing with the messianic restoration.

9-14. A miscellaneous collection of oracles. They seem to be directed to a later time but are in the spirit of Zechariah.

9:9-17. Expresses joy at the arrival of a triumphant and peaceful king.

11:7. *A shepherd of the flock* appears, but there is no peace.

13:7-9. Yahweh's shepherd is killed, but a remnant of the flock is restored.

14:1-21. Loaded with apocalyptic imagery and action. Yahweh becomes *king over all the earth* (14:9).

Daniel

The book of Daniel is a thoroughgoing apocalypse. The terrible ordeal of God's people is interpreted by lesson-stories and visions set in an earlier time. Apocalypses usually give as their author the name of some historical worthy. This use of a pseudonym is a literary device. It is as though one would write a political piece today under the name of George Washington; there would be no intent to deceive readers.

Daniel is a name known in other biblical books. Ezekiel refers to him along with Noah and Job (Ezekiel 14:14, 20; 28:3). The name is sometimes given as Danel, which is a name also known in North Canaanite literature. Ezra (8:2) and Nehemiah (10:6) both list a Daniel in the time of Nebuchadnezzar, but they give no indication that he was famous or had a position of power.

Apocalyptic writings cover long periods of time that may begin far back in the past, but they regularly project what will happen in the future, and this usually extends to the end of history. Careful study of the visions and their mysterious details may reveal a key to the actual time of composition.

the Maccabean rebellion. The stories and visions are intended to give incentive for loyal, pious Jews (the Hasidim) to withstand Antiochus' violent efforts to Hellenize them. The visions cover the era from the Babylonian empire to Antiochus IV, sometimes in remarkable detail, sometimes less precise. They reach *the time of the end* (Daniel 11:40) and in Chapter 12 include a resurrection.

The book falls into two parts. The first six chapters contain six stories that tell how Daniel and other godly exiles were steadfast in the face of extreme tribulation. The last six chapters have four visions that tell in strange, sometimes bizarre details what is to come after the Babylonian exile. Here is an outline to help your study.

> Chapter 1. Daniel and his friends keep Jewish dietary laws under pagan cultural pressure. They are skilled in wisdom. The setting of the story would be approximately 606-538 B.C.
>
> Chapter 2. By God's wisdom Daniel reveals the meaning of Nebuchadnezzar's dream about coming kingdoms. The symbolism represents Babylon, Media, Persia, Greece (with the Seleucid and Ptolemaic divisions), and God's coming kingdom.
>
> Chapter 3. Shadrach, Meshach, and Abednego survive a fiery furnace and show that apostasy is to be met, if necessary, by martyrdom.
>
> Chapter 4. Daniel reveals the meaning of Nebuchadnezzar's dream about his future. The king goes mad but is restored to *praise and extol and honor the King of heaven.*
>
> Chapter 5. At King Belshazzar's feast a hand writes on the wall, and Daniel interprets the meaning. One of Daniel's rewards is to *rank third in the kingdom.*
>
> Chapter 6. For failing to reverence the king, Daniel is thrown into a *den of lions.* God saves individuals who are faithful.
>
> Chapter 7. Four beasts appear, and their significance parallels Nebuchadnezzar's dream in the second story. Read **Daniel 7:13-18, 27, 28**, a vision within the vision. The *one like a human being* (in older versions, *son of man*) is directly related to the *holy ones* (or *saints*) of the Most High. The "little horn" probably represents Antiochus IV.

Chapter 8. A ram and a male goat are partially interpreted. Since the details reach from the sixth into the second century, naturally Daniel *did not understand it* (8:27).

Chapter 9. Concerning the seventy weeks; related to Jeremiah's prophecy of seventy years. The chronology is very difficult. The *half of the week* (Daniel 9:27—a week = seven years) may forecast three and a half years for the career of Antiochus. The *abomination that desolates* alludes to his desecration of the Temple.[1]

Chapters 10-12. The end time. Details can be paralleled in known events as far as 11:40. Chapter 12 reaches beyond the hidden history. *Michael* (10:21) is Israel's guardian angel; *Gabriel* is mentioned in 9:21.

Read **Daniel 12:2, 3**. Part 1 pointed to Daniel 12:2 as anticipating a resurrection. It speaks of *many*, but good and bad destinies are anticipated. Can this imply a general resurrection? The predictions of so many days have tempted people to try to reckon when the end will be, but they have all been unsuccessful. The future in apocalyptic is not to be toyed with in this manner.

FOR FURTHER STUDY AND REFLECTION

Memory Bank

1. Ezekiel 34:15

2. Zechariah 4:6; 9:9

3. Daniel 12:3

Research

1. Use study resources to interpret the *wheel within a wheel* in Ezekiel 1:15-21.

2. Other apocalyptic writings are known from the period just before the Christian era. They are valuable for study of the Judaism of that time, and several provide some background for the New Testament. One such is the Book of Enoch. What can you discover about this book? What are "pseudepigrapha"?

3. Study the units of measure mentioned in the books in this part, for example, the cubit.

---

[1] Jesus' remark about *the desolating sacrilege* (Mark 13:14) may recall the same event. There are other words here that Jesus quotes.

4. Many images and phrases in these books appear again in the New Testament. Make a list of any that sound familiar. Notes in study Bibles are helpful in such research.

Reflection

1. What kind of prophetic message do you find most fitting for our modern world?

2. How does apocalyptic literature relate to hope?

GOD'S PEOPLE HAVE HOPE

New Hope in Christ

PART 3

SUMMARY

Hope in the New Testament develops out of the Old Testament, but it becomes unique. Jesus relates the future to this life, but he often uses apocalyptic imagery. John's Gospel emphasizes this tension. Jesus' cross and resurrection are central in the message of the early church. The new age is directed by Christ's Spirit and is in direct relationship to the eschatological time. In his letters Paul becomes the theological interpreter of Christian hope. Other letters offer distinct perspectives.

BASIC BIBLE REFERENCES
Matthew 25:31-46
Mark 12:18-27; 13
John 11:1-44; 14:15-26; 15:26-16:16
Romans 5:1-5; 8:11-39
1 Corinthians 15:3-8, 12-28, 50-58
1 Thessalonians 4:13-5:11
Hebrews 9:23-28; 11:1
1 Peter 1:3-21
2 Peter 3:1-13

WORD LIST
Advocate
Paraclete
Parousia
Synoptic Apocalypse

A New Kind of Hope

In a broad sense, hope in the New Testament follows naturally upon hope in the Old Testament, but the situation in the early church differs from pre-Christian times, and the dimensions of hope are changed. Several things contribute to this. Political realities in the world after the exile were far different from the time of the monarchy, and messianic expectation was forced into new patterns. People must hope for more than family tree and tribal land. When God's people viewed their troubles over against God's promises, they became convinced that there must be a future life where accounts would be settled equitably. Meanwhile, evil was very real, and it pressed and shaped thoughts about how the future might come out of the present. In such a theological mix, apocalyptic forms of expression were popular.

Jesus scolds his opponents because they have not really *believed Moses...on whom you have set your hope* (John 5:45, 46). Though Jesus claimed continuity with Moses, that is, with Torah, he maintained that in his own mission and message something new had entered the picture. Mosaic religion centered upon law; Jesus' way centers upon a new life-relationship with God. *The law indeed was given through Moses; grace and truth came through Jesus Christ* (John 1:17). He insisted, however, that he did not *come to destroy the law or the prophets...but to fulfill* (Matthew 5:17). At the heart of this fulfillment are freedom and hope.

Israel's hope always had a nationalistic aspect, but it was hard to feel secure in such a hope. Some of the prophets understood that the problem was theological, and they tried to redirect the people's expectations. Matthew quotes the first servant song, Isaiah 42:1-4, and connects it with Jesus' ministry. *In his name the Gentiles will hope*[1]; such a broadening to include the Gentiles is quite in keeping with Jesus' teaching. Religious officials were not pleased with such interpretation, but *the large crowd was listening to him with delight* (Mark 12:37). We do not know precisely what the crowd hoped for, but Jesus spoke to them and brought them into his circle of hope.

Jesus and the Future

The noun "hope" never occurs in the Gospels, and the verb appears only five times. The idea, however, is everywhere. Read **Mark 12:18-27**. The Pharisees believed in a resurrection and should have been delighted that Jesus met the Sadducees' challenge so cleverly. The conflict arose from the clear insight and the personal power with which Jesus spoke about life. Read **John 11:1-44**. The point of this whole passage is the audacious claim in verse 25. Jesus embodies the hope about which he taught. The words *I am* must have struck the hearers as bold indeed, for they echo the holy name of Yahweh.

Even after Jesus' resurrection there seems to have been some lack of agreement in interpreting sayings and events related to the future. Compare Mark 9:1 and the parallels in Matthew 16:28 and Luke 9:27. How do the variations in these texts reflect the way the future was interpreted by the writer of the Gospel? Mark and Luke include here the phrase *kingdom of God*, and Matthew has *his kingdom*. *Kingdom of God* is studied in Theme 6, Part 3, but it is important here. Review that material.

How other-worldly was Jesus' view of the future? Bible students still debate this matter. Part of the problem is the way Jesus used apocalyptic forms of thought and how his interpreters understand these. Two Synoptic passages claim our attention. Read **Matthew 25:31-46**. This is a kind of allegorical parable. Why are these two terms appropriate? It is a remarkably vivid treatment of the future, but notice how the present specifically affects the future. Do verses 40 and 45 mean that today is the day of judgment?

Read **Mark 13** (parallels are in Matthew 24:1-36 and Luke 21:5-36). This is often called the Synoptic Apocalypse. The setting is quite natural: Jesus' disciples—country fellows—remark about the grandeur of the Temple and its precincts; Jesus predicts their destruction. This forecast is not in itself remarkable, for many Jews were on a collision course with Rome. But the disciples jump quickly in their thinking from the fall of Jerusalem to the end

---

1 Matthew follows the Septuagint text, but the prophet's sense is not altered.

of the age. Simple historical prediction turns to apocalyptic eschatology. Which of the details in Jesus' discourse are truly apocalyptic?

This mixture of mundane and apocalyptic raises important questions. Jesus uses traditional apocalyptic language in other sayings beside this passage. It is plain, however, that Mark 13 is recorded for a succeeding generation; see verse 14 (Matthew 24:15). In place of this verse, Luke 21:20 reads, *When you see Jerusalem surrounded by armies, then know that its desolation has come near.* Signs of the end will be indefinite. The challenge is to *be alert...keep awake.* Mark states flatly that *this generation will not pass away until all these things have taken place.* If this refers to the destruction of Jerusalem, the prediction is fairly accurate. If it refers to an apocalyptic end of history, then Jesus' forecast was wrong. The discourse ends differently in each Gospel, but all emphasize being prepared.

Jesus' farewell message in John is quite different in content and tone (John 14-17). Expectation and hope are strong, but there are no apocalyptic details. Most of the promises seem to relate to a future not very far off. Read **John 14:15-26**. Jesus promises, *I am coming to you*, but this seems to be directly connected with *another Advocate*. This word comes from a Greek term, *Paraclete*, "one called alongside to help."[2] This is immediately identified with *the Holy Spirit*. Read **John 15:26-16:16**. There is no vision of a far-off event. Jesus will be with his followers in the person of the Advocate.

Can we reconcile these two approaches to the future? Probably, if we do not get carried away by the visionary elements of apocalyptic. The early church was convinced that its future hope rested on Jesus' resurrection, but this had to be harmonized with traditional messianic expectation on the one hand and the visions of the future from Old Testament sources. The Gospel writers show candidly that Jesus was not really understood until after his resurrection.

Hope in the Early Church

This alternation between present experience and far-off future hope appears also in many other New Testament writings. The Pentecost story in Acts 2 tells about an immediate experience of the Holy Spirit and the exciting growth of the Christian community that took place. Peter declares that the event *is what was spoken through the prophet Joel* (quoting Joel 2:28-32), a passage that begins with *In the last days* and continues with apocalyptic detail. Peter also says that *the promise is for you, for your children, and for all who are far away* (Acts 2:39).

---

2 KJV translates *Comforter*. In the sixteenth century this word was associated with its Latin roots, *com* = "together, with," and *forte* = "strength" (see English "fort"). The term "Paraclete" is often used in commentaries.

The future life was an element of apostolic preaching from the earliest days. *The priests, the captain of the temple, and the Sadducees* were *much annoyed because* Peter and John *were teaching the people and proclaiming that in Jesus there is the resurrection of the dead* (Acts 4:1, 2). Paul is evidently in accord with this emphasis. In a sermon preached in Athens the resurrection becomes a principal point of discussion; see Acts 17:18, 32.

Twice during the hearings that led to Paul's appeal to Caesar, the resurrection is a crucial matter. As he testified before the council in Jerusalem, he took advantage of the fact that the Pharisees and the Sadducees did not agree about the resurrection. *I am on trial concerning the hope of the resurrection of the dead*, he declared. This caused a *great clamor*, and the hearing broke up (Acts 23:6-10). Later, in his defense before King Agrippa, Paul connects his *hope in the promise made by God to our ancestors* and the hope about which he is accused, *that God raises the dead* (Acts 26:6-8). After recounting his experience on the Damascus road, he says that *the Messiah...by being the first to rise from the dead is the one to proclaim light both to our people and to the Gentiles* (Acts 26:22, 23).

Resurrection and the Future in Paul's Letters

This testimony in Acts reflects what appears in many of Paul's letters. Romans is usually considered to be his most theological letter, probably because he wanted to make his faith plain to a church he had not yet visited. Read **Romans 5:1-5**, and note how hope is important in the development of the apostle's thought. Also read **Romans 8:11-39**. How many ways does Paul express hope? Hope is implied even where the word "hope" is not mentioned; thus *heirs* in verse 17 connotes a definite hope.

Paul's detailed dealings with the Corinthian church are studied in several themes. In his hymn in praise of love[3] he says that love is greater than faith and hope, but *love hopes all things* (1 Corinthians 13:7, 13). 1 Corinthians 15 is the most extended discussion of the resurrection anywhere in the Bible. The chapter is introduced as *the good news that I proclaimed to you* (15:1).

Read **1 Corinthians 15:3-8**. The message about death and resurrection are *of first importance*. The words *received* and *handed on* mark this as part of the accepted Christian tradition. Read verses **12-19**. Paul counters an argument against the resurrection. Hope and resurrection are inseparably connected. Read verses **20-28**. Here is Paul's scenario for the end of all things. The final stage is *that God may be all in all*. There is no apocalyptic development. In verses 29-49 Paul introduces some rather complicated matters about the resurrection. Read verses **50-58**. Here is one of Paul's infrequent references to *the kingdom of*

---

3 A Basic Reference in Theme 7, Part 4.

God. Then there is a magnificent proclamation with just a touch of apocalyptic language and quotation from the prophets. Finally, Paul gives an ethical exhortation; eschatology should affect how Christians live.

Of all the churches Paul writes to, the Thessalonians seem to have been the most concerned with last things. The first three chapters of 1 Thessalonians deal with a variety of church matters, and 4:1-12 enjoins pure living and mutual responsibility. Then Paul takes up Christian hope. Read **1 Thessalonians 4:13-5:11**. The Thessalonians were expecting the LORD to return soon. Apparently they thought that those who were dying before that event would be at a disadvantage—perhaps they would miss it altogether. Paul embellishes his comments about the resurrection with apocalyptic detail. (This is the passage from which some people derive belief about a "rapture.") As in 1 Corinthians 15, the apostle moves on to urge faithful living. Like Jesus, he tells them to *keep awake*. They should *build up each other*.

2 Thessalonians shows further how that church was caught up in apocalyptic thinking. After the customary introduction, Paul quickly assures them that God will avenge their afflictions *when the LORD Jesus is revealed from heaven with his mighty angels in flaming fire* (1:7, 8), an unusual expression for the apostle. It is evident that the Thessalonians have some strange ideas that are not reflected elsewhere in Paul's writing. It is no wonder, then, that we have difficulty understanding them. Apparently some members of the community, expecting the end to come soon, were *living in idleness*, so Paul commands: *Anyone unwilling to work should not eat* (3:10, 11). Again we observe how the apostle connects future hope closely with present responsibility.

Hebrews and General Epistles

The book of Hebrews affirms that future hope depends directly upon what God has already done. The first ten chapters emphasize the superiority of Jesus over other revelation. Read **Hebrews 9:23-28**. Note the finality of what Jesus has done: his *sacrifice* happened *once for all at the end of the age*. His appearance *a second time* is for the future dimension of salvation.[4] Read **Hebrews 11:1**, an often-quoted text about faith and hope.

Read **1 Peter 1:3-21**. This book emphasizes hope. The clause *when Jesus Christ is revealed* (1:7) includes the root of the word "apocalypse." The word in verse 20, *revealed*, is from the root that is in our word "epiphany," which means "appearance." Note that *the end of*

---

4 GOD'S SAVING ACT IN JESUS CHRIST is a past event at a specific moment in history for Gods people, it is a continuing experience of God's people, and it will be consummated in the future with God's people.

the ages here refers to Jesus' life on earth. The death and resurrection of Christ are a tie between the past and the future.

Read **2 Peter 3:1-13**. The writer addresses the matter of timetables for the end of the age. He explains the delay by referring to Psalm 90:4. Paul also warns that *the day of the Lord will come like a thief* (1 Thessalonians 5:2, 4). 2 Peter adds apocalyptic embellishment. The Greek word for *coming* in verse 12 is *parousia*—the word now appears often in English. Its basic reference is to the presence of the one who comes rather than to the event of coming. Again, the writer moves from expectation of the future to an exhortation to *grow in the grace and knowledge of our Lord and Savior Jesus Christ* (2 Peter 3:18).

FOR FURTHER STUDY AND REFLECTION

Memory Bank

1. John 11:25

2. Romans 5:5

3. Hebrews 11:1

Research

1. Mark 12:35-37 and parallels tell of a dispute between Jesus and some religious experts regarding the Davidic Messiah. Summarize and explain the argument.

2. In a concordance compare the frequency of references to death and resurrection in the Pauline letters. Include such words as "cross," "die," "be raised," etc.

3. Some texts in Handel's *The Messiah* come from 1 Corinthians 15. Get a copy of the oratorio, and identify these texts.

4. Do you think 1 Thessalonians 5:1-11 is a "scare tactic"? Give arguments pro and con.

5. A modern Israeli national song is entitled *Hatikvah*. Find out what the title means.

Reflection

1. The Judeo-Christian belief in the resurrection of the body differs from the Greek philosophical belief in the immortality of the soul. In light of this, formulate your own understanding of the meaning of resurrection.

2. What is the relationship between hope and love (a) in your personal life, (b) in Christian faith, (c) in the world today?

GOD'S PEOPLE HAVE HOPE

THEME 10

The Book of Revelation

PART 4

SUMMARY

The book of Revelation is unique in the Bible. It is apocalyptic with a distinctly prophetic emphasis for the first-century churches. John's visions shift between earth, where God's people are in dire jeopardy from a demonic government, and heaven, where Christ's victory over all opposing powers is celebrated. Final victory brings *all things new*. The book—and the Bible—end with an invitation to the world and a prayer to the LORD.

BASIC BIBLE REFERENCES
Revelation 1; 4; 5; 12:1-12; 19:6-16; 20:11-15; 21:1-7; 22:16-21

WORD LIST
Angel
Babylon
Lamb
Saints
White robes

Introduction

One book in the New Testament is thoroughly apocalyptic; indeed it is often called The Apocalypse. It is really unique in the Bible, for it is more completely apocalyptic than Daniel. This means that there is much in the Revelation that is hard to interpret, so it demands careful study. Apocalyptic is meant to be somewhat cryptic, and even after our best efforts we will not explain everything.

Our study up to this point should warn us against some kinds of interpretation. We must begin by trying to understand what the book meant to the churches to which it is addressed. Then, if we find that our contemporary situation is similar in particular respects to the situation of those early Christians, we shall be prepared to say confidently what it means for us today. The book attracts a lot of interest today. Because it is important to interpret it carefully, we devote the last part of our last theme to the book.

The Revelation is different in several respects from other apocalyptic material we have studied. Read **Revelation 1**. The book begins in the form of a letter. The letter-form we have seen at the beginning of all of Paul's letters occurs in Revelation 1:4, 5. We soon meet the individual churches to which the book is addressed. The seer of Revelation has a first-century name, John. For a number of reasons, most scholars agree that he is not the writer of the Gospel or of the three Johannine letters. Other apocalyptic writings claim as author a person revered from antiquity, but we must assume that the addressees knew this John as a contemporary leader. He considers himself a prophet.

Be careful not to call the book "Revelations." The first words state that the whole book is *the revelation of Jesus Christ*; that is, it is not a group of revelations from Jesus Christ but a message that has Jesus Christ as its object. It comes from *him who is*. The Greek phrase is precisely the name that identifies God in Exodus 3:14 (Septuagint). The God revealing to John is the same as the God who revealed to Moses. *Who was* suggests that God is the one who has been with the people throughout history. *Who is to come* is literally "the coming one"; God is characterized by coming. Just as "coming" in English can mean right now or next year, so God comes to the people in the present and will come in the future.

Thus a connection with the Old Testament is established immediately. John seldom makes an extended quotation, but the whole book is heavily loaded with Old Testament allusions. These have been variously counted as some six to eight hundred—in 405 verses! Identify as many as you can as you go along.

Setting on Earth: The Seven Churches

The number seven is important. It represents completeness (as, seven days in a week). It will appear again and again in the book. There are seven blessings or beatitudes throughout the book; try to spot them. The first is in Revelation 1:3. *Blessed is the one who reads aloud...and blessed are those who hear*. This makes it clear immediately that the message is set in the worshiping church. There was no machine to copy handouts for the congregation; the book was read to the assembled people.

The churches addressed in 1:11 are in western Asia Minor. John selects seven, but he could have chosen more (again, seven is a special number). A map shows that the churches are in a kind of circuit, and it is likely that the book circulated in the order named. Ephesus is first. It is the chief city in the area; indeed it was one of the greatest cities of the Roman empire. Recall how important it was in Paul's ministry.

In Chapters 2 and 3 each church receives an individual message. It is carefully crafted for the particular church. For example, Laodicea is scolded for bragging about its wealth, and we know that city was a banking center in the first century. This individual attention is very important, for it indicates that the message of the Revelation meant something specific, applicable, and contemporary for the churches that were addressed. Thus it is unfaithful to the book to interpret it as though it were directed entirely to the future. Its meaning for today and for our future must begin with and be disciplined by the meaning for the churches to which it was first sent.

The little messages are composed with great literary skill. There is much pictorial language and imagery, and they draw upon the details of Chapter 1. Here are crowns, swords, the morning star, white garments, the book of life, doors, new Jerusalem, and so on. There are allusions to Old Testament persons: Balaam, Jezebel, David. Nearly every sentence has some detail that calls for careful study.

John's first vision is in Revelation 1:12-20. The last verse offers a key to the interpretation of the vision. The figure *like the Son of Man* is the exalted Christ. He is in the midst of the churches and holds their safety in his hand. All that follows in the Revelation depends upon this initial affirmation: the end is sure from the beginning. The vision links earth and heaven.

Setting in Heaven: God, the Lamb, and the Scroll

The scene shifts to heaven. We must adjust to texts that move easily and quickly between visions of earth and heaven. Chapters 4 and 5 introduce the next fifteen chapters of the book. If you think of the scenes as drama, perhaps on a cosmic, two-level stage, you will understand them better than if you treat them as narrative. The theater was prominent in Greek cities such as Ephesus. (For Paul's experience there, see Acts 19:23-41.) Things that are hard to describe in ordinary prose may be effectively portrayed in drama. The literary elements of the text are essential to what is being revealed. We are reading the description of John's visions. It is one thing to have a vision; it is quite another to relate it in literary form. If we say, then, that John is an artistic genius, we are not implying that the visions are simply made up. To convey in words what has happened in such visionary experiences requires unique ability.

Read **Revelation 4**. John, *in the spirit, beholds one seated on the throne,* an awestruck way of referring to God. Imagery is abundant, much of it from Ezekiel and Isaiah. There are two hymns of praise (Revelation 4:8 contains words you should already know). The Revelation has more poetic material than any other New Testament book. Here God is praised as creator.

Read **Revelation 5**. God has *a scroll...with seven seals*, and John seems to know that it contains the information about the future that he has been promised. A lion-figure who has messianic titles suddenly becomes a Lamb, and he is the one who can open the scroll of destiny. This is because he was *slaughtered...and ransomed for God saints* and *made them to be a kingdom...and they will reign on earth*. Christ's sacrifice is thus presented as the key to the future. Saints are the people of God (compare Romans 1:7, 1 Corinthians 1:2, etc.). Christ is praised as savior.

The Seven Seals

The seven seals are opened one by one (Chapter 6). The first four seals reveal four horsemen, figures of destruction drawn from Zechariah 6. The fifth seal reveals martyrs who are impatient for the justice of the final judgment. They must wait, but they receive white robes, tokens of the victory already theirs. The sixth seal has terrible, apocalyptic events anticipating the end.

Now there is an interlude; the delay heightens the dramatic expectation of the final scene. John sees a throng of those on earth who are sealed—guaranteed final safety (7:1-8). Their number is 144,000. This is 12 (tribes or apostles) squared and multiplied by 1000 (the largest number used in counting in Greek or Hebrew). The number is symbolic of an immense assembly.

A second interlude vision (7:9-17) presents in heaven *a great multitude that no one could count*. These are (by anticipation) those who survive *the great ordeal* to come (envisioned in Chapters 8-18). The Lamb has saved them. How many words ascribe praise to God in 7:12? The hymn in 7:15-17 is full of Old Testament allusions.

Seven Trumpets and Seven Visions

We expect the seventh seal to reveal the end, but first there is *silence in heaven for about half an hour* (8:1), a kind of short "freeze-frame" to produce suspense. Then instead of the end there comes a series of seven trumpets sounded by angels (8:2-6). These produce a succession of catastrophes reminiscent of the plagues in Egypt. Like the pharaoh, many persons are unmoved by these terrors (8:7-9:21). The seventh trumpet is delayed by another interlude of two visions.

In Chapter 10 a *mighty angel* brings John a scroll, which he eats. This echoes an experience of Ezekiel (2:8-3:3). Now *two witnesses* appear, are martyred, and receive their heavenly reward. They may represent Zerubbabel and Joshua from Zechariah, or they may be identified as Moses and Elijah—in apocalyptic visions more than one identity is quite possible. All of these details are building tension toward the final judgment, but we may pass over them quickly in this survey.

The seventh trumpet announces the fulfillment of God's kingdom, but again the end is delayed, now by more visions. Read **12:1-12**. The first portent (REB, sign) presents a woman, a child, and *a great red dragon*. The details in 12:1 are astrological—*the sun...the moon...a crown of twelve stars*. The woman and child may be identified in more than one way. Can you think of two?

Michael and his angels eject the dragon from heaven, a vision that has been much developed by poets (as in Milton's *Paradise Lost*). Note in 12:9, 10 the multiple identification of the dragon. All evil power is here viewed as one. It may be manifested in particular ways, as immediately becomes plain.

Two beasts act for the dragon in Chapter 13. Apparently the series of kingdoms symbolized in Daniel is revived. The addition would now be Rome. The second beast seems to represent emperor worship. *The number of the beast*, 666, is famous. It probably refers to Nero or Domitian, Roman emperors. Undoubtedly the readers in the seven churches knew who was meant. Modern interpreters who say that the number refers specifically to some wicked leader today are implying that the text did not mean what it said to the seven churches. Evil may appear in many guises, however, and the same kind of dreadful force that beset John's churches may confront God's people today.

Three visions in Chapter 14 are a strange mixture of reassuring glory and scary wrath. The scenes shift rapidly and not necessarily in a time sequence. Verses 14-20 give a frightening picture of what we sometimes call "the grim reaper." For background in the teaching of Jesus, see Matthew 13:24, 30, 36-43; Mark 4:26-29; Luke 10:2; John 4:35. There is also a strong echo of Isaiah 63:1-6. *Outside the city* probably reflects the place of Jesus' death (see Hebrews 13:12). Thus the blood of the martyrs is associated with Christ's sacrifice.

Seven Bowls and Babylon's Fall

A new series of seven (Chapters 15 and 16) sees angels with *golden bowls full of the wrath of God*. Before they pour them on the earth, the scene in heaven shows a throng singing *the song of Moses, the servant of God, and the song of the Lamb*. If you read what each bowl brings, you will readily recognize the plagues in Egypt. The seventh bowl seems to announce the final end, and indeed it is very near.

There is a vivid vision of the fall of Rome, alluded to here as *the great whore* and *Babylon the great, mother of whores and of earth's abominations*. She is seated on a *scarlet beast* with *seven heads and ten horns* (17:1, 3, 5). When John writes, *the seven heads are seven mountains on which the woman is seated* (17:9), the identification with Rome is sure. The heads also represent kings, and unfortunately we cannot be sure which emperors John includes. The one *that was and is not* and *is an eighth* (17:11) probably means Nero, for contemporary legend held that he had not really died and would shortly reappear. The poetry in Chapter 18 is like dirges in Isaiah, Jeremiah, and Ezekiel, where they pronounce woes over Tyre and Babylon.

Final Victory and Judgment

God's final victory is portrayed in Chapters 19 and 20. Read **19:6-16**. By now we should be well aware that we cannot construct a rigid time sequence for the details in the visions. *The marriage supper of the Lamb* is a messianic banquet, an apocalyptic figure that appears elsewhere (for example, Isaiah 62:5; Matthew 25:1-13; Ephesians 5:25-27).

References to a *thousand years* in 20:1-8 have been given a wide variety of interpretations. Ideas about "the millennium" arose early in church history and have caused much regrettable contention. We should be wary of reading more into this passage than a dramatic portrayal of the reward to Christ's martyrs. It leads into the ultimate defeat of all forces arrayed against God. Read **20:11-15**. This sets the stage for the final vision of the new creation.

All Things New

Read **Revelation 21:1-7**. A *new heaven and a new earth* are from an old vision; see Isaiah 65:17, 18; 66:22. Here is the bride figure again (Revelation 21:9), and other Old Testament imagery makes a final appearance. Identify as much as you can. The description of the new Jerusalem is full of figurative details. We are not supposed to make a literal reconstruction. For instance, we need not ask who will live in heaven, and who will live in the new Jerusalem—and how many people will a city of two and a quarter million square miles hold?

John thinks of the new creation as a biblical prophet would: it is a renewal of the old, and it is significant for the hearers. *The leaves of the tree [of life] are for the healing of the nations* (22:2), yet presumably the nations have already been healed when God makes *all things new* (21:5). Here we have come full circle to the setting in the seven churches to which the book is sent.

Read **Revelation 22:16-21**. We are again in the worshiping community. *The bride* is the church and with *the Spirit* invites those outside *to come*. John's message is complete. In response we hear the actual words of the first-century church: *Come, Lord Jesus!* (Paul uses almost the same prayer in 1 Corinthians 16:22.) In the concluding benediction remember that in the New Testament all the people in Christ's church are called *saints*. In placing the Revelation at the end of the canon the church provided a fitting conclusion to the Bible.

FOR FURTHER STUDY AND REFLECTION

Memory Bank

Revelation 5:12; 14:13; 21:3-5a; 22:17

Research

1. What is the meaning of *Alpha* and *Omega* in Revelation 1:8 and 22:13? How would you paraphrase this in English?

2. Locate each of the seven churches with the help of an atlas, and check the information about them in a Bible Dictionary.

3. In Reginald Heber's well-known hymn *Holy, Holy, Holy!* how many references from the Revelation can you find?

4. For unique and surprising perspectives on heaven and hell, read C. S. Lewis, *The Great Divorce*.

Reflection

1. Prepare a short essay on "The Revelation as a fitting conclusion to the Bible."

2. What new symbols would you use today to illumine visions like John's?

3. What signs of hope are there for Christians today?

10:4

CONCLUSION

Last Things

SUMMARY
This is the end of the program, not in a final sense, but because we have reached a goal. Review and assessment are in order. We have learned to hear the Bible and adopt what we hear. Several texts are instructive at this point. We are now prepared to move into a new phase in Bible study.

BASIC BIBLE REFERENCES
Psalm 119:97-105
2 Corinthians 13:13
2 Timothy 3:14-17

The End

The word "end" has two meanings. (1) It's all over. We have studied thirty-three parts of *Kerygma: The Bible in Depth*. Now one more session concludes this program. That's all there is. (2) This is the goal we have worked toward, the end we have had in view from the beginning. We have been studying to upgrade our biblical knowledge and our ability to find our way around in the Scriptures. We have learned much that equips us to study further.

Both of these meanings apply. The work we have done has a kind of completeness and is therefore concluded. But if we have done a good job, this has been a few steps in a long walk. Certainly we have become aware how much more there is to know, and we have a good base upon which to build further knowledge.

A Time For Review

When you take a pleasant trip, one of the joys afterward is to relive the finest moments. You share pictures with friends. You talk it over with others who have shared the trip. You will recommend that others go where you did. You will reflect on how this experience fits in with your plans for the future.

So review the ten themes. Can you put them together in a significant sequence? There is the large and very rewarding task of reflecting on how the various parts fit together now that you are acquainted with them all. How many of your deposits are still in the Memory Bank? The Research section at the end of this part suggests a number of helps for a review. This review should be directed more toward end (2) than end (1).

A Time for Assessment

As you reflect upon the end of this program and review what you have learned, you should become aware of what the study has done for you. Several times we have talked about what a Scripture passage meant as distinct from what it means. Now you may apply that difference to your own experience. As we studied each part, it had a meaning for that session, and often we considered how its meaning was related to what had gone before. Now it is time to ask what the succession of meanings then mean to you now.

There is no Reflection section at the end of this part. The whole part should be an exercise in reflection. The Reflection sections have been aimed at helping you to stretch the application of what you have studied. Let that be one function of these Last Things.

Hearing the Bible

The word "hear" has three shades of meaning. (1) I hear a sound. It may or may not have significance. It may be gently falling rain, or it may be a siren. It may be a thump upstairs, or it may be a distant rumble. Elijah heard *a sound of sheer silence* (KJV, *a still small voice*; 1 Kings 19:12). (2) I hear what you are saying. It is understandable. I may or may not agree, and I make no commitment to act on it. The prophets repeatedly said, *Hear the word of the LORD*. (3) I hear it, that is, I accept and shall act on it. So Paul told the Ephesians about Jesus, and *on hearing this, they were baptized in the name of the LORD Jesus* (Acts 19:5).

The word "listen" works the same way. (1) Listen! What was that? (2) Now listen to this! (3) I listened to what she said, and it saved my life. See Revelation 2:7, *Let anyone who has an ear listen to what the Spirit is saying to the churches* (repeated to all seven churches).

It is important for us to hear, listen to the Bible in the second way above. It is more important to hear, listen to the Bible in the third sense. Throughout our program we have been trying to hear what the Bible says when we have a grasp of it whole. From time to time we have noted how dangerous and misleading it may be to hear only a part of the Bible.

It has often been said that the Bible is its own best interpreter. This does not mean that it is easy to fit together all parts of the Bible; sometimes we cannot do this. It does mean that if we read the parts in light of the whole, we shall find a valid meaning. In this way we hear the Bible—in the third way.

Two Texts

This is a Bible study, so let us take a last look at some Bible texts. We have referred to Psalm 119 a number of times. In review you should recall that it is a huge acrostic. It has twenty-two groups of eight verses, and each verse of each stanza of eight begins with a letter of the Hebrew alphabet in order. Every verse says something about the law of God. *Law* is used in its broad, Old Testament sense, so there are other words that are almost synonyms of *law: commandments, ordinances, precepts, word, decrees, statutes, promise*. This is a summary of how a pious Jew expressed faith in God. Read **Psalm 119:97-105**. This is the thirteenth stanza plus the first verse of the fourteenth. The extra verse should be familiar. The psalmist declares that God's law regulates and blesses every aspect of life. Thus law is not just rules; it is a way to serve God. This is a good passage with which to conclude our study of the Old Testament. It is also an important aspect of how we regard Scripture.

Read **2 Timothy 3:14-17**. *The sacred writings* would be what we know as the Old Testament, but Paul is certain that those scriptures lead to *Christ Jesus*. Verse 16 may be read in two ways. There is no verb "is" in the Greek text, so it may be supplied in more than one place. Check the footnote in NRSV; also KJV and REB. *Inspired* is literally "God-breathed"; Genesis 2:7 is an interesting commentary.

Notice two things. First, the phrase *all scripture* must be understood in light of how the canon took final shape. Paul certainly did not have in mind a Bible as we know it today. Undoubtedly he would have been surprised to learn that some of his letters later would be considered Scripture. One cannot, then, jump from this statement to a doctrine of inspiration. As we study the Bible, we surely experience God breathing through Scripture, and that is the real test of inspiration.

Second, Scripture is the source of equipment for *everyone who belongs to God*. In Paul's judgment, study of Scripture is not an option, it is a necessity. It should be the basis of all that the church undertakes. We have only hints about the end of Paul's life. The last chapter of 2 Timothy appears to deal with this very matter: *I am already being poured out as a libation, and the time of my departure has come*. Then follow the familiar words, *I have fought the good fight, I have finished the race, I have kept the faith* (2 Timothy 4:6,7). Before his death Paul offers advice and instruction to his younger colleague and tells how he, too, can keep *the faith*.

Where Do We Go from Here?

In the Thessalonian letters and in the Revelation we saw how concern with "last things" does not eliminate duties to be done now and in the immediate future. The end is not a shut-off valve but a channel for life yet to be lived. So what do we do with *Kerygma: The Bible in Depth?*

We have studied much of the content of the Bible. We have touched all the books, but you are aware how much more there is to study and learn. Indeed, the judgment of most of the thousands of persons who have studied the program before you is that we have only made a good beginning.

You now have a very stable foundation for further study. If the program has been effective, you are now equipped to move on in three ways. (1) You can go on to the further study we have just mentioned. (2) Your increasing biblical knowledge supplies a foundation and some superstructure for the enrichment of your understanding of your faith. (3) You have the information to inspire and teach others who have not had an opportunity to add this dimension to their Christian learning.

The grace of the Lord *Jesus Christ, the love of God, and the communion of the Holy Spirit be with all of you* (**2 Corinthians 13:13**).

FOR FURTHER STUDY

Memory Bank

1. The titles of each of the ten Themes

2. Psalm 119:105

3. 2 Corinthians 13:13

Research

1. Introduction, Part 1, asked the question, What is the Bible? If you kept notes from that session, review them. How would you answer the question now?

2. Organize all of your notes if you haven't done so. You may find some "unfinished business." Put that in a folder or notebook *for further study*.

3. Study as many of the following review suggestions as you can find time for:

    Theme 1. Explain this statement: the Bible does not deal with "salvation" as an abstract term. Illustrate your answer from the four parts.

Theme 2. How do "promise" and "covenant" in the Bible help people find God is faithful?

Theme 3. Tell several ways in which Jesus Christ clarifies people's questions about God.

Theme 4. Give a brief overview of how God's people's view of the world expands in biblical history.

Theme 5. Show how the story-line of the Bible may be said to proceed in the stories of biblical leaders.

Theme 6. What is the problem of "kingship" in the Bible? How is it resolved in the New Testament?

Theme 7. Explain the relationship between law and righteousness in the Old Testament and in the New Testament.

Theme 8. How is biblical wisdom similar to and how does it differ from the wisdom of the neighbors of God's people?

Theme 9. Discuss elements of worship that are common to both Testaments.

Theme 10. Explain how the range of hope changes through the Bible books. What elements are constant?

4. Consider how you will react to the last group session.

5. What will you plan ahead as a result of this study?

The Books of the Bible
Varieties of the Old Testament Canon

THE PROTESTANT OLD TESTAMENT

Law
- Genesis
- Exodus
- Leviticus
- Numbers
- Deuteronomy

History
- Joshua
- Judges
- Ruth
- 1 & 2 Samuel
- 1 & 2 Kings
- 1 & 2 Chronicles
- Ezra
- Nehemiah
- Esther

Poetry
- Job
- Psalms
- Proverbs
- Ecclesiastes
- Song of Solomon

Major Prophets
- Isaiah
- Jeremiah
- Lamentations
- Ezekiel
- Daniel

Minor Prophets
- Hosea
- Joel
- Amos
- Obadiah
- Jonah
- Micah
- Nahum
- Habakkuk
- Zephaniah
- Haggai
- Zechariah
- Malachi

THE HEBREW BIBLE

Torah
- "In-beginning"
- "These (are) the names"
- "He called"
- "In the wilderness"
- "These (are) the words"

Former Prophets
- Joshua
- Judges
- Samuel
- Kings

Latter Prophets
- Isaiah
- Jeremiah
- Ezekiel
- The Twelve
  - Hosea
  - Joel
  - Amos
  - Obadiah
  - Jonah
  - Micah
  - Nahum
  - Habakkuk
  - Zephaniah
  - Haggai
  - Zechariah
  - Malachi

Writings
- Psalms
- Job
- Proverbs
- Ruth
- Song of Songs
- Qoheleth
- Lamentations
- Esther
- Daniel
- Ezra-Nehemiah
- Chronicles

THE GREEK BIBLE[1] (Septuagint)

Laws
- Genesis
- Exodus
- Leviticus
- Numbers
- Deuteronomy

Histories
- Joshua
- Judges
- Ruth
- 1-4 Kingdoms (Samuel and Kings)
- 1-2 Paralipomena (Chronicles)
- 1 Esdras
- 2 Esdras
- Esther
- Judith
- Tobit
- 1-4 Maccabees

Poetical Books
- Psalms
- Proverbs
- Ecclesiastes
- Song
- Job
- Wisdom of Solomon
- Wisdom of Jesus the Son of Sirach
- Psalms of Solomon

Prophetical Books
- Hosea
- Amos
- Micah
- Joel
- Obadiah
- Jonah
- Nahum
- Habakkuk
- Zephaniah
- Haggai
- Zechariah
- Malachi
- Isaiah
- Jeremiah
- Baruch
- Lamentations
- Letter of Jeremiah
- Ezekiel
- Daniel: (The Prayer of Azariah; The Song of the Three Young Men; Susanna; Bel and the Dragon.)

---

[1] There were several versions of the Greek Old Testament in ancient times, and the lists of included books varied. The books that were not part of the Hebrew canon usually appear in "the Apocrypha" today.

The New Testament Canon

Gospels

Matthew
  sermons, parables, O.T. testimonies

Mark
  shortest; narratives, sayings

Luke
  literary; parables; breadth

John
  "signs" and discourses

History

Acts
  of the apostles
  (volume 2 of Luke)

Pauline Letters

Romans
  most theologically complete letter

1 & 2 Corinthians
  local problems and statements of faith

Galatians
  to a church disaffected from Paul's gospel

Ephesians
  mature consideration of the Church and its people

Philippians
  appreciation and advice for a favorite church

Colossians
  reflects on Christ and the Church

1 & 2 Thessalonians
  churches stirred by the future

1 & 2 Timothy
  pastoral, for developing churches

Titus
  pastoral

Philemon
  to the owner of a converted slave

General Letters

Hebrews
  superiority of new covenant

James
  faith and works

1 Peter
  sermonic

2 Peter
  late church problems

1 John
  reflections on Christian love

2 John
  to a favorite church

3 John
  to "Gaius"

Jude

Apocalypse

Revelation
  assurance for the Church under persecution

CHRONOLOGY OF THE BIBLE

DATE — Time scales represent varied number of years.

B.C. = Before Christ
c. = circa (around)*

PREHISTORY

THE BEGINNINGS: EVENTS IN PREHISTORY

Creation

Adam and Eve in the Garden

Cain and Abel

Noah and the Flood

The Tower of Babylon

2000 B.C.

THE ANCESTORS OF THE ISRAELITES

Abraham comes to Palestine. *c.* 1900

Isaac is born to Abraham.

Jacob is born to Isaac.

1800 B.C.

Jacob has twelve sons, who become the ancestors of the twelve tribes of Israel. The most prominent of these sons is Joseph, who becomes adviser to the King of Egypt.

THE ISRAELITES IN EGYPT

The descendants of Jacob are enslaved in Egypt. *c.* 1700 — *c.* 1290

1600 B.C.

1250 B.C.

Moses leads the Israelites out of Egypt. *c.* 1290

The Israelites wander in the wilderness. During this time Moses receives the Law on Mount Sinai. *c.* 1290 — *c.* 1250

THE CONQUEST AND SETTLEMENT OF CANAAN

Joshua leads the first stage of the invasion of Canaan. *c.* 1250

Israel remains a loose confederation of tribes, and leadership is exercised by heroic figures known as the Judges.

THE UNITED ISRAELITE KINGDOM

Reign of Saul *c.* 1030 — *c.* 1010

1000 B.C.

Reign of David *c.* 1010 — *c.* 970

Reign of Solomon *c.* 970 — 931

---

* A "circa" date is an approximation. Generally speaking, the earlier the time, the less precise is the dating. Changes in calendar reckoning through the years contributed to the difficulty of establishing dates. Archaeology constantly seeks to make chronology more precise. Therefore in the books you consult you may find variations of a year or so from the chronology here.

CHRONOLOGY OF THE BIBLE

DATE		
950 B.C.	\multicolumn{2}{c}{THE TWO ISRAELITE KINGDOMS}	

THE TWO ISRAELITE KINGDOMS

JUDAH (Southern Kingdom)		ISRAEL (Northern Kingdom)
Kings		*Kings*
Rehoboam 931-913		Jeroboam 931-910
Abijah 913-911		Nadab 910-909
Asa 911-870		Baasha 909-886
		Elah 886-885
Jehoshaphat 870-848	*Prophets*	Zimri 7 days in 885
		Omri 885-874
	Elijah	Ahab 874-853
Jehoram 848-841		Ahaziah 853-852
Ahaziah 841		Joram 852-841
Queen Athaliah 841-835	Elisha	Jehu 841-814
Joash 835-796		Jehoahaz 814-798
Amaziah 796-781		Jehoash 798-783
Uzziah 781-740		Jeroboam II 783-743
	Amos ⋮ Jonah	
Jotham 740-736		Zechariah 6 mo. in 743
		Shallum 1 mo. in 743
Ahaz 736-716	Hosea	Menahem 743-738
	Micah ⋮ Isaiah	Pekahiah 738-737
		Pekah 737-732
Hezekiah 716-687		Hoshea 732-723
		Fall of Samaria 722

THE LAST YEARS OF THE KINGDOM OF JUDAH

Manasseh 687-642

Amon 642-640

Prophets

Josiah 640-609   Zephaniah

Joahaz 3 mo. in 609   Nahum

Jehoiakim 609-598   Jeremiah

Jehoiachin 3 mo. in 598   Habakkuk?

Zedekiah 598-587   Ezekiel

Fall of Jerusalem July 587 or 586

CHRONOLOGY OF THE BIBLE

DATE	
550 B.C.	**THE EXILE AND THE RESTORATION**

The Jews taken into exile in Babylonia after the fall of Jerusalem

Persian rule begins. 539
Edict of Cyrus allows Jews to return. 538
Foundations of New Temple laid. 520
Restoration of the walls of Jerusalem
    445-443

Prophets
Haggai   Zechariah
Obadiah   Daniel
Malachi
Joel?

THE TIME BETWEEN THE TESTAMENTS

[400 B.C.]

Alexander the Great establishes Greek rule in Palestine. 333

Palestine is ruled by the Ptolemies, descendants of one of Alexander's generals, who had been given the position of ruler over Egypt. 323 to 198

[200 B.C.]

Palestine is ruled by the Seleucids, descendants of one of Alexander's generals, who had acquired the rule of Syria. 198 to 166

Jewish revolt under Judas Maccabeus reestablishes Jewish independence. Palestine is ruled by Judas' family and descendants, the Hasmoneans. 166 to 63

The Roman general Pompey takes Jerusalem 63 B.C. Palestine is ruled by puppet kings appointed by Rome. One of these is Herod the Great, who rules from 37 B.C. to 4 B.C.

THE TIME OF THE NEW TESTAMENT

[A.D. 1]

Birth of Jesus*

Ministry of John the Baptist; baptism of Jesus and beginning of his public ministry

[A.D. 30]

Death and resurrection of Jesus

Conversion of Paul (Saul of Tarsus) *c.* A.D. 37

Ministry of Paul *c.* A.D. 41 to A.D. 65

Final imprisonment of Paul *c.* A.D. 65

---

*The present era was calculated to begin with the birth of Jesus Christ, that is, in A.D. 1 (A.D. standing for *Anno Domini* 'in the year of the Lord'). However, the original calculation was later found to be wrong by a few years, so that the birth of Christ took place perhaps about 6 B.C.

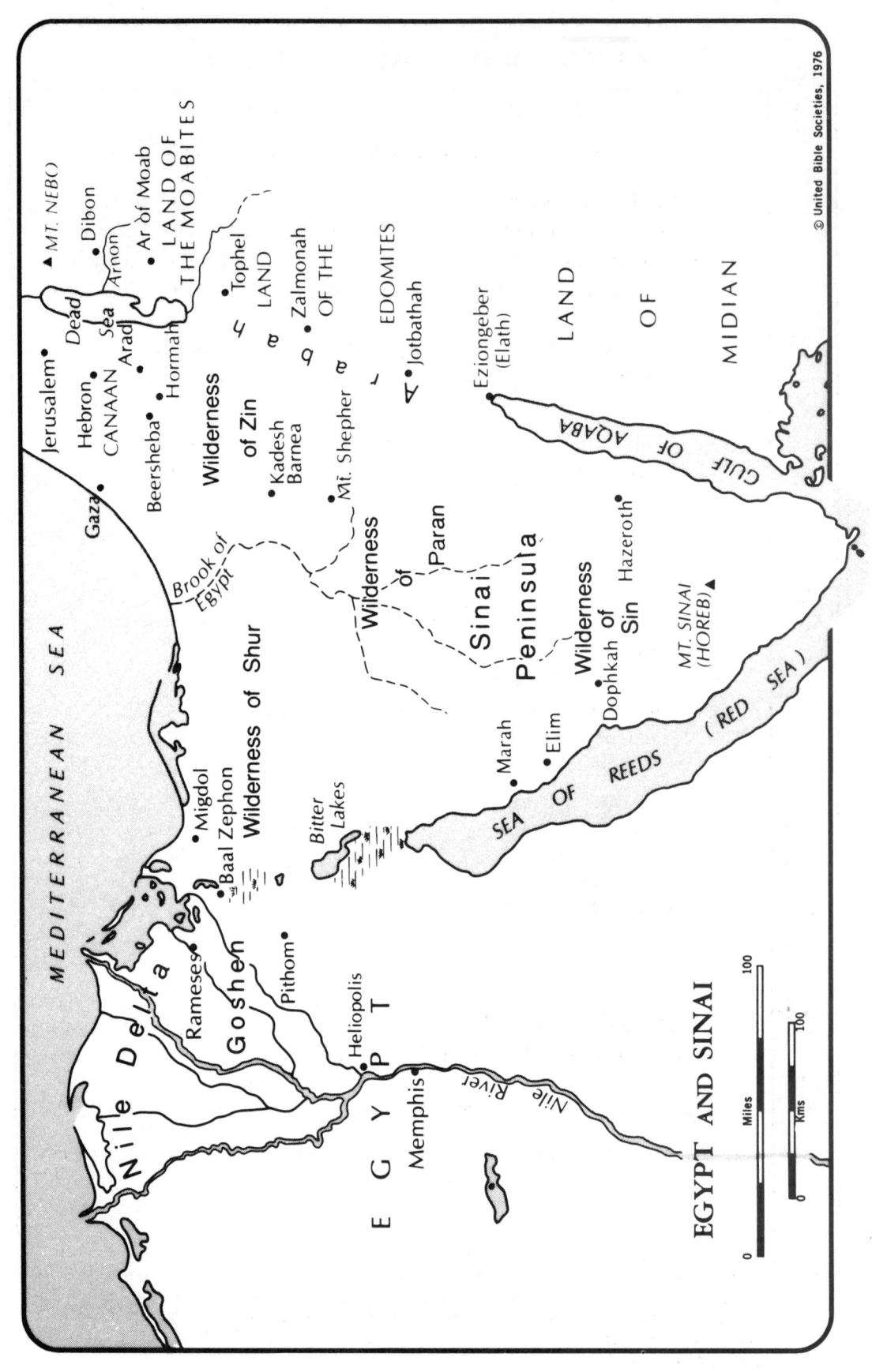

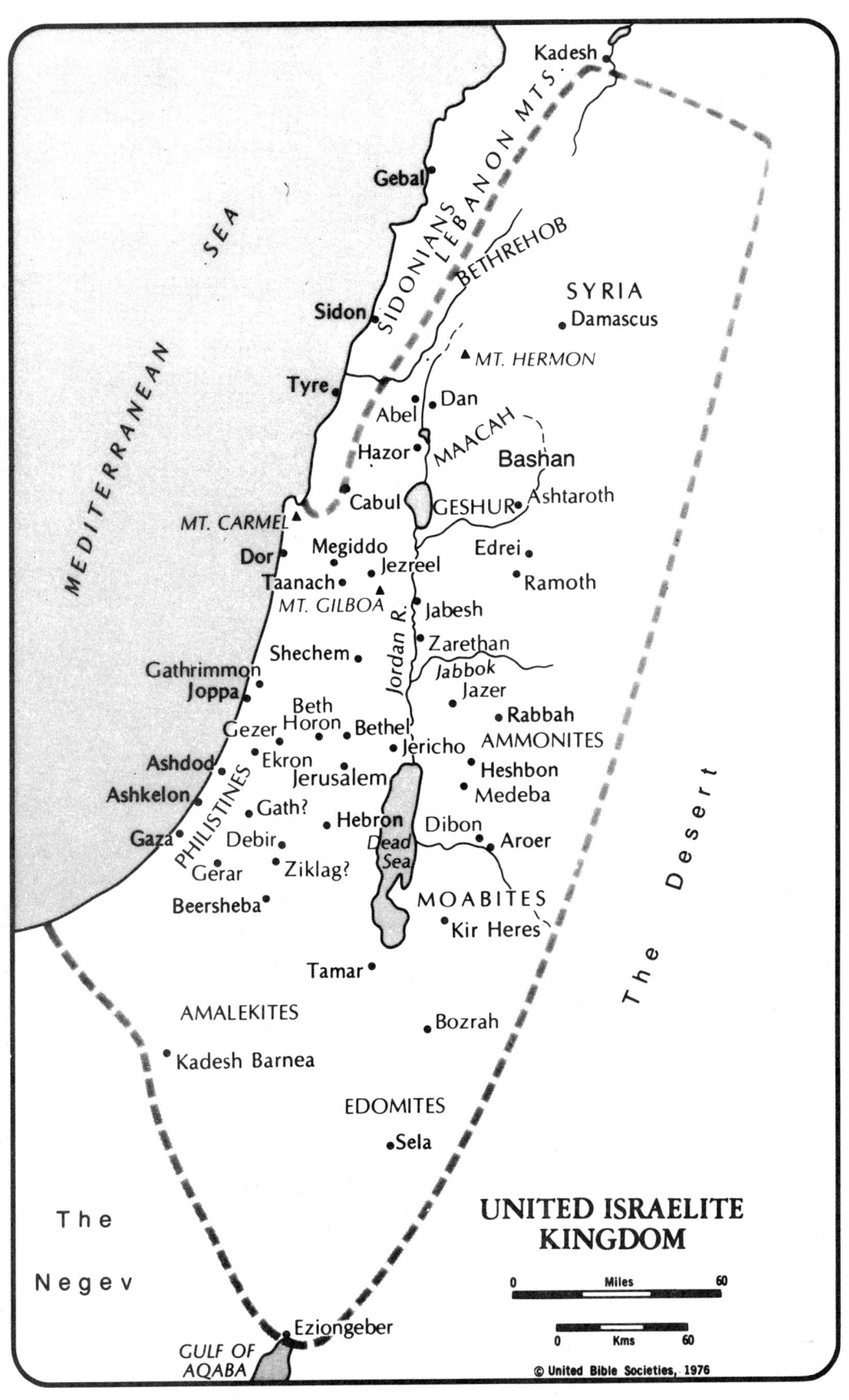

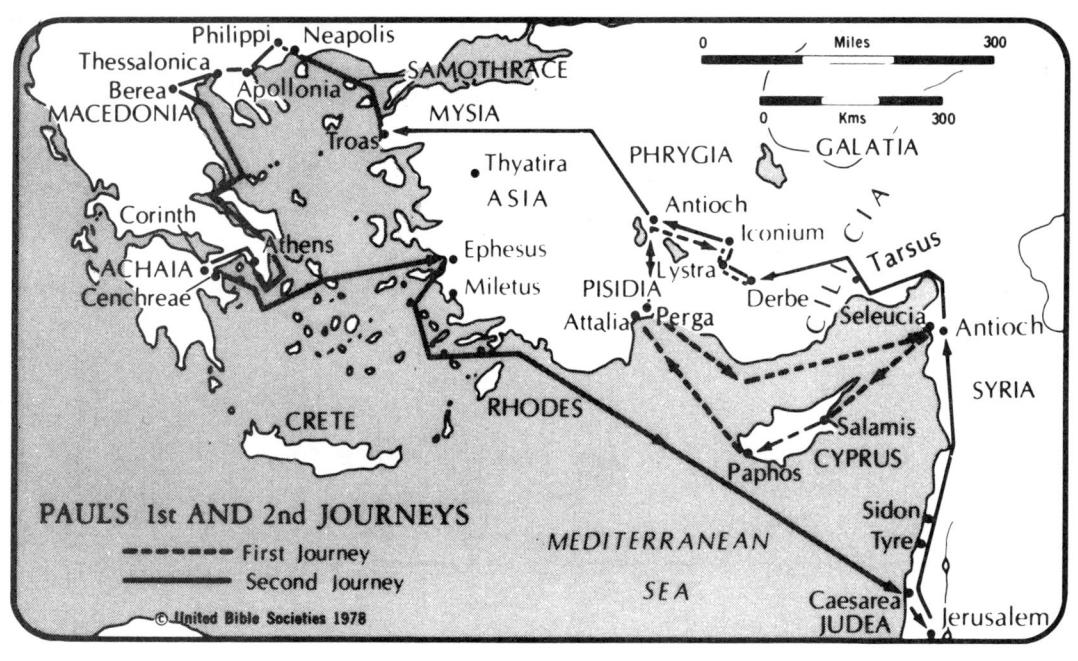

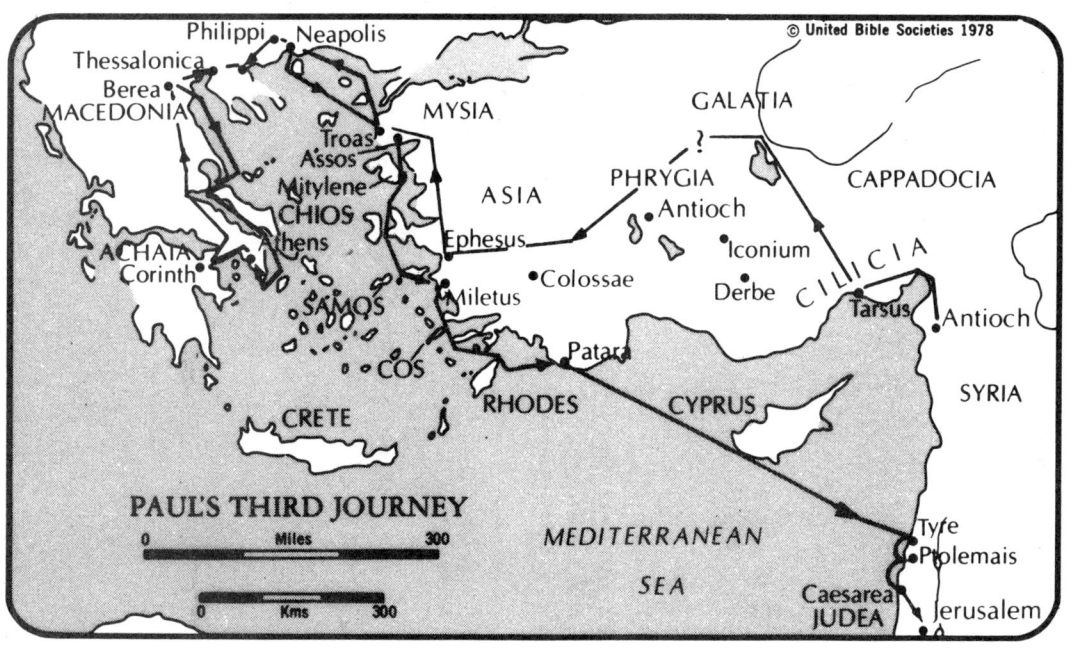

PAUL'S JOURNEY TO ROME
Rome
Three Inns
Market of Appius
Puteoli
ITALY
MACEDONIA
Philippi
THRACE
BLACK SEA
Thessalonica
BITHYNIA
GALATIA
MYSIA
Adramyttium
CAPPADOCIA
PHRYGIA
ACHAIA
Corinth
Athens
Ephesus
SICILY
Rhegium
Syracuse
CILICIA
Tarsus
Antioch
Cnidus
Myra
MALTA
MEDITERRANEAN
RHODES
CYPRUS
SYRIA
CRETE
Phoenix
CAUDA
C. Salmone
Lasea
Safe Harbors
Sidon
SEA
0 Miles 300
0 Kms 300
Caesarea
JUDEA
Jerusalem
LIBYA
© United Bible Societies 1978

JERUSALEM IN OLD TESTAMENT TIMES
0 Yards 400
0 Meters 400
Wall of Zion (Jebusite)
Solomon's Expansion
Later Monarchic Wall
Post-exilic Wall
Hananel Tower
Altar
Temple
NEW
CITY
Palace
Solomon's Wall
Nehemiah's Wall
Post-exilic Tombs
Kidron Valley
To Mount of Olives
UPPER CITY
Manasseh's Wall?
Central Valley
Gate
CITY OF DAVID
OPHEL
Gihon Spring
Hezekiah's Tunnel
Lower Pool
SILOAM
Steps
Old Pool
Hinnom Valley
Royal Garden
Enrogel Spring
© United Bible Societies, 1976

A

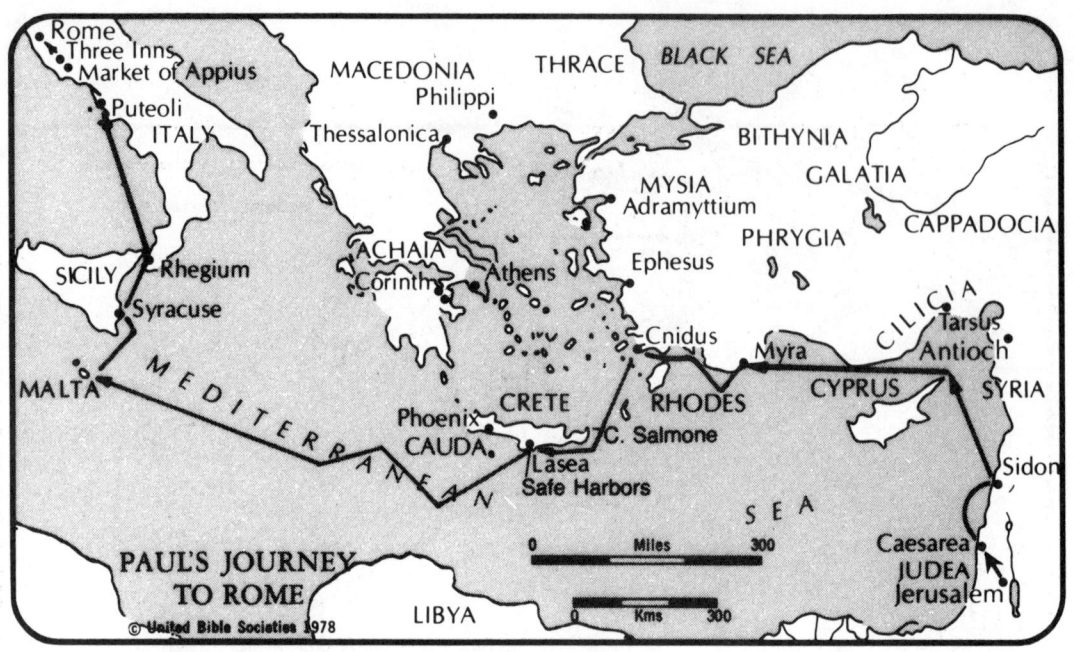

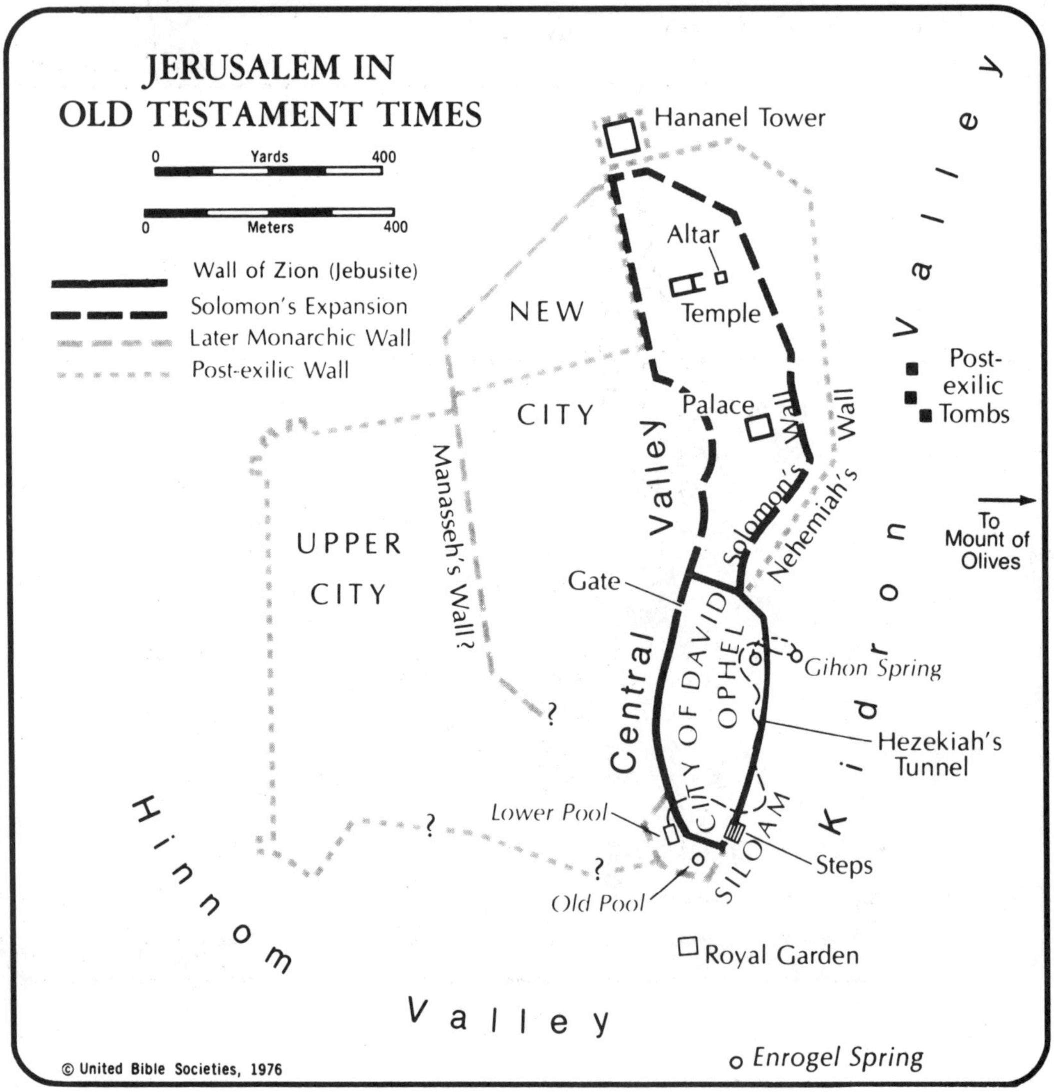

The Twelve Disciples

	Matthew 10:2-4	_Mark 3:16-19_	_Luke 6:14-16_	_Acts 1:13_	_John_
1.	Simon	Simon	Simon	Peter	Simon Peter 1:40
2.	James	Andrew	Andrew	John	
3.	John	James	James	James	
4.	Andrew	John	John	Andrew	Andrew 1:40
5.	Philip	Philip	Philip	Philip	Philip 1:43
6.	Bartholomew	Bartholomew	Bartholomew	Thomas	Thomas 11:16
7.	Matthew	Thomas	Matthew	Bartholomew	Nathanael 1:45
8.	Thomas	Matthew	Thomas	Matthew	
9.	James of Alphaeus	James of Alphaeus	James of Alphaeus	James of Alphaeus	
10.	Thaddaeus	Thaddaeus	Simon the Zealot	Simon the Zealot	
11.	Simon the Cananaean	Simon the Cananaean	Judas of James	Judas of James	Judas 14:22 (not Iscariot)
12.	Judas Iscariot	Judas Iscariot	Judas Iscariot	Judas Iscariot	Judas 6:71 (son of Simon Iscariot)
				Matthias	

BS 605.2 .K48 1992 v.1

Kerygma

GENERAL THEOLOGICAL SEMINARY
NEW YORK

3844 CH 1069
4-4-00 30978